INNOVATIVE INTERVENTIONS IN CHILD AND ADOLESCENT MENTAL HEALTH

Innovative Interventions in Child and Adolescent Mental Health is a unique composite of the literature on various innovative interventions for children and adolescents, and provides a developmental and neurobiological rationale for utilizing innovative interventions with this population. Based on the latest research, this book emphasizes that children and adolescents need more than just talk therapy. These innovative interventions can be applied in a variety of practice settings including schools, juvenile justice, community-based counseling centers, and residential treatment. This book bridges the gap between theory and practice, and provides a historical, theoretical, and research-based rationale, as well as a helpful case study, for each type of intervention being discussed.

Christine Lynn Norton, Ph.D., LCSW, Assistant Professor of Social Work at Texas State University-San Marcos, earned her Ph.D. in Clinical Social Work from Loyola University Chicago in 2007. She has over fifteen years experience working with high-risk youth in a variety of settings including therapeutic wilderness programs, juvenile justice, schools, and mentoring organizations, and she is passionate about researching and utilizing innovative interventions with children and adolescents in order to promote healthy psychosocial and neurological functioning.

TITLES OF RELATED INTEREST FROM ROUTLEDGE

Social Work and Social Welfare: An Invitation Second Edition by Marla Berg-Weger

Human Behavior and the Social Environment Second Edition by Anissa Taun Rogers

Research for Effective Social Work Practice Second Edition by Judy L. Krysik and Jerry Finn

Social Policy for Effective Practice: A Strengths Approach Second Edition by Rosemary K. Chapin

Social Work Practice Second Edition by Julie Birkenmaier, Marla Berg-Weger, and Marty Dewees

INNOVATIVE INTERVENTIONS IN CHILD AND ADOLESCENT MENTAL HEALTH

Edited by

CHRISTINE LYNN NORTON

Texas State University, San Marcos

Routledge
Taylor & Francis Group

NEW YORK AND LONDON

First published 2011
by Routledge
270 Madison Avenue, New York, NY 10016

Simultaneously published in the UK
by Routledge
2 Park Square, Milton Park, Abingdon, Oxon OX14 4RN

Routledge is an imprint of the Taylor & Francis Group, an informa business

Typeset in Minion and Optima by EvS Communication Networx, Inc.
Printed and bound in the United States of America on acid-free paper by Edwards Brothers, Inc.

Library of Congress Cataloging in Publication Data
Innovative interventions in child and adolescent mental health / edited by Christine Lynn Norton.
p. ; cm.
1. Child psychotherapy. 2. Adolescent psychotherapy. I. Norton, Christine Lynn.
[DNLM: 1. Psychotherapy—methods. 2. Adolescent. 3. Child. 4. Infant. WS 350.2 I581 2010]
RJ504.I565 2010
618.92'8914—dc22
2010007396

ISBN 13: 978-0-415-87984-2 (hbk)
ISBN 13: 978-0-415-87985-9 (pbk)
ISBN 13: 978-0-203-84500-4 (ebk)

This book is dedicated to my children Mahalia, Will, and Wendell
who remind me each day of how important it is to create a healthy
and just society for young people.
And to my husband, Billy, for supporting me in this,
and every, endeavor.

CONTENTS

PREFACE

Concept for this Volume

The idea for *Innovative Interventions in Child and Adolescent Mental Health* began with a paper that was presented at the University of Texas School Social Work Conference in February 2009. Dr. Christine Norton (Ed.) and Dr. Betsy Wisner (contributing author), both faculty at the School of Social Work at Texas State University-San Marcos, presented a paper titled "Innovative Interventions for Adolescent Group Work in Schools: A Developmentally Grounded Approach." In this paper, we discussed using adventure-based group work and meditation to reach adolescents in a school setting through more non-traditional mental health interventions. This presentation was well received, and led to the concept of highlighting various innovative interventions for children and youth in one text. Much like the paper that we presented, this book focuses on providing a strong developmental and neurobiological rationale for why innovative interventions are necessary in child and adolescent mental health. While many practitioners have already been using creative approaches to working with youth, the idea for this book was that it would bring together theory, research, and practice through a variety of innovative intervention strategies. I wanted to include interventions that are becoming increasingly more popular in the field of child and adolescent mental health, yet often without the theoretical or empirical grounding needed for clinicians to engage in what the Council on Social Work Education refers to as "research-informed practice." That is why each chapter offers a historical, theoretical, and research background on the intervention strategy that is covered.

Not only did I think it was essential to bring together these innovative intervention strategies in one volume, but it was also important to me to balance advocating for these approaches with a critical lens of taking into account the ethical and cultural considerations of each intervention. This book highlights the need to use critical assessment skills to decide for whom each intervention would be appropriate. It was never the intention of this book to provide a one size fits all approach to treatment with young people—quite the opposite. Instead, this book tries to provide multiple treatment options to help mental health students and practitioners think outside of the box, while still utilizing each intervention as an adjunctive approach to treatment.

While I feel that innovative intervention strategies are an important part of child and adolescent mental health, I also feel that it is important to consider the client and the client system as a whole. Therefore, this book presents these innovative interventions within the system of care, and advocates for enriching the environments of young people so as to promote positive youth development, social justice, and youth empowerment. It is my belief and commitment that these things are just as essential as innovative treatment approaches in child and adolescent mental health.

Finally, the development of this book could not have happened without the scholarship and expertise of the contributing authors. I selected my authors based on their stellar reputations as both academics and practitioners in their various fields of study. I am honored that they have taken the time to collaborate with me on this important project, and I am hopeful that this book will serve as an important learning tool for students, practitioners, and even parents interested in making the lives of young people better.

ACKNOWLEDGMENTS

I would like to acknowledge Routledge Publishing, especially Steve Rutter and Leah Babb-Rosenfeld, for their belief in this project and their support and flexibility. Comments from reviewers were also very important to the development of the book, and I would like to thank Crystal Mills at the University of Hawaii, Christina Risley-Curtiss at Arizona State University, and Nora Smith at Monmouth University for their reviews. I would like to thank the School of Social Work at Texas State University-San Marcos for helping me become a scholar and take new and exciting intellectual risks as an academic. I would especially like to thank all of my contributing authors for their hard work, expertise, and care and concern for children and adolescents.

1.
REINVENTING THE WHEEL
From Talk Therapy to Innovative Interventions
Christine Lynn Norton

Overview of Chapter

> This chapter sets the context for using innovative interventions in child and adolescent mental health and includes the following sections:
> - Introduction
> - Child and Adolescent Mental Health: Background, Prevalence, and Treatment Needs
> - The Need for Innovative Interventions: Creating a Developmental and Neurobiological Rationale
> - Innovative Interventions: Promoting Neural Integration
> - Commonalities of Innovative Interventions: The Six Aptitudes
> - Summary
> - Activities to Extend Your Learning

Introduction

> There is always one moment in childhood when the door opens and lets the future in.
> — Deepak Chopra

As those concerned with child and adolescent mental health, we can only hope that this quote is true for all children, and yet we know that sometimes children's and adolescent's life experiences, particularly traumatic ones, can close the door to the future. The idea for this book came from my work as a clinical social worker with children and adolescents. I have worked in a variety of settings including outpatient community mental health, youth and family counseling, schools, juvenile justice, youth mentoring programs, and wilderness and adventure therapy. The greatest gains I have seen young people make in therapy have come from corrective emotional experiences that have occurred outside of a talk therapy setting.

People are always saying, "you don't have to reinvent the wheel," but if the wheel isn't working so well, then maybe you do. The "wheel," in this case, is traditional talk therapy with children and adolescents. While this book does not have an axe to grind with talk therapy, it seeks to provide a developmental and neurobiological rationale to promote the idea that children and adolescents need *more* than just talk therapy. The goal of this book is to advocate for a more holistic approach to child and adolescent treatment of mental health issues, setting the stage for innovative interventions that may reach young people on a deeper, more integrated level. What is clearly needed most is an *interactive blend of therapies applied across the system of care* that can foster optimum emotional and mental integration in children and adolescents.

If therapy is to meet the developmental needs of children and adolescents, than our work as mental health professionals becomes about providing them with *experiences* that produce new evidence of self—experiences that facilitate empathy, connection, creativity, and wellness. These experiences can help them to create a new narrative about their lives, one that is more cohesive, more hopeful, and allows them to begin to see themselves in a new place and begin to "let the future in." Saari's (1991) work reaffirms this idea. She discusses the concept of *transcontextualization,* which she defines as the ability to imagine oneself in a different situation or emotional place. The interventions presented in this book all have the ability to foster this type of creativity and imagination. For children and adolescents this is critical, and is related to the development of both identity and sense of purpose (Norton, 2010). In fact, transcontextualization is necessary if children and adolescents are going to let the future in and move forward into adulthood in a more confident and robust manner. *Letting the future in* is a beautiful way to reconsider mental health treatment for children and adolescents, and is something the interventions in this book attempt to do through art, music, story, wilderness and adventure, connection with animals, and contemplation.

Child and Adolescent Mental Health: Background, Prevalence, and Treatment Needs

Childhood is a vulnerable time in human development. During the childhood years, children need a supportive care-taking surround in which to grow and develop. Likewise, adolescence is a developmental period that is rife with both pitfalls *and* opportunities for growth. According to Highland (1979), *development is both a cause and a cure of stress for children and adolescents.* Children and adolescents are idealistic, impressionable, and curious about the meaning of life. They take risks, some positive and some detrimental, all with the goal of discovering more about who they are and their place in the world. While many young people weather the storms of childhood and adolescence just fine, others struggle with intense socioenvironmental stressors such as chronic poverty and violence, and others still with debilitating mental health problems.

Background of Child and Adolescent Mental Health

It has not always been widely recognized that children and adolescents can suffer from mental health problems. Childhood was assumed to be a relatively care-free period of development, with the thinking being that children did not have to deal with the stressors that afflict most adults (American Psychiatric Association, 2002). It is now acknowledged that mental disorders in childhood and adolescence are not stage-specific, and are the result of genetic, developmental, psychosocial, and physiologic factors. Research showing that children suffer from mental disorders began in the 1960s, yet it wasn't until the third edition of the *Diagnostic and Statistical Manual of Mental Disorders* (*DSM-III*) of the American Psychiatric Association in 1980 that child and adolescent mental disorders were classified in a separate section (National Institute of Mental Health, 2001).

Mental health problems that appear in children and adolescents can disrupt emotional, neurological, cognitive, and relational functioning. They appear in youth from all different races, ethnicities, social classes, and backgrounds. However, according to the U.S. Department of Health and Human Services (1999), children with the following risk factors are at greater risk of developing mental health problems:

- physical problems
- intellectual disabilities (mental retardation)
- low birth weight
- family history of mental and addictive disorders
- multigenerational poverty
- caregiver separation
- abuse and neglect

There has also been a lot of recent research done on the impact of various types of trauma on child and adolescent mental health (Malchiodi & Perry, 2008). With the increasing effects of immigration, war, natural disaster, and childhood sex trafficking occurring in the United States, the number of children and adolescents who experience some kind of trauma in their lives can be expected to rise, increasing the mental health needs of this population.

As mental health issues in childhood and adolescence have become more prevalent, systems of care for children with serious emotional disorders and their families have been developed in the last two decades (Arbuckle & Herrick, 2006), and early intervention in mental health is emerging as a new focus in the field of early childhood (Woodruff et al., 1999). Mental health practitioners, researchers, and consumers now believe that mental health services are an important and necessary support for children and adolescents who experience mental, emotional, or behavioral challenges, as well as for their families. What is less understood, however, are what particular interventions can be effective for the complex and often co-occurring issues faced in childhood and adolescence. This book seeks to compile important theories and research on innovative interventions that can be applied to a variety of child and adolescent issues.

Prevalence of Mental Disorders in Children and Adolescents

Because of the complexities of childhood and adolescence, the onset of mental disorders is often seen during childhood and adolescence (New Freedom Commission on Mental Health, 2003). Child and adolescent mental health is an important issue facing society, which some have even deemed a "public health crisis" (Stroul, 2006). According to the American Psychiatric Association (2002), 12 million American children suffer

Table 1.1   Children and Adolescents Ages 9-17 with Mental or Addictive Disorders

Disorders	Prevalence
Anxiety Disorders	13.0%
Mood disorders	6.2%
Disruptive disorders	10.3%
Substance use disorders	2.0%
Any disorder	20.9%

Source: InCrisis, 2005.

from mental illness; however, only one in five receives treatment. The National Institute of Mental Health (NIMH) estimates that half of all mental disorders begin by the time people are age 14 (NIMH, 2005). Likewise, nearly half of all individuals with one mental disorder met the criteria for two or more disorders (NIMH, 2005).

When these mental health issues go untreated, the consequences are severe. Not only can these disorders become prevalent over the life span, but in some cases, such as mood disorders, they can result in impairment, disability, or even death. According to The Center for Mental Health Services, 11% of children in the United States have at least one significant mental illness accompanied by impairment in home, school or peer contexts (U.S. Department of Health and Human Services, 2001). Table 1.1 highlights the most common disorders in childhood and adolescence and the prevalence of these disorders.

Child and Adolescent Mental Health Treatment: The Search for Best Practices

If children and adolescents who struggle with mental health problems do not receive appropriate treatment, these problems can escalate and become worse in adulthood. According to InCrisis (2005), 74% of 21-year-olds with a diagnosed mental health disorder were reported to have had prior difficulties. If left untreated, childhood and adolescent mental health disorders can lead to school failure, involvement in the juvenile justice system, and/or placement outside of the home. Other problems can arise such as self-destructive behaviors, family conflict, and substance abuse. The financial and emotional cost of these issues to society is incredibly high; therefore, it is important to identify serious emotional disturbances early in childhood and interrupt the cycle of mental health problems by making sure that the child receives appropriate care (New Freedom Commission on Mental Health, 2003).

The issue at hand is how one defines "appropriate care." Various treatments, services, and methods for preventing mental disorders in children and adolescents have developed over the past several decades. Despite a growing awareness of children's mental health issues, knowledge about treatment is still emerging. In *Mental Health: A Report of the Surgeon General* (1999), the report called for closing the gap between research and practice, ensuring evidence-based treatments for children. The push for evidence-based practice comes from the goal of improving treatment for child and adolescent mental health problems.

The report highlighted the guidelines established by NIMH in order for a treatment to be considered evidence-based, which include:

- at least two control group design studies or a large series of single-case design studies
- minimum of two investigators
- use of a treatment manual
- uniform therapist training and adherence
- true clinical samples of youth
- tests of clinical significance of outcomes applied
- both functioning and symptom outcomes reviewed
- long-term outcomes beyond termination

According to Fonagy (2000), the goal of using evidence-based practice in mental health treatments is to promote the effective use of resources and simultaneously allow for improvements in the clinician's ability to identify, understand and apply the best-evaluated methods of child and adolescent mental health treatment.

While the call for *research-informed practice* is an important and critical step, there is also a need for *practice-informed research* in which mental health practitioners identify creative and effective practices for which new research questions must be applied (CSWE, 2009). Clearly, most mental health professionals can agree on the need for providing empirical support for their interventions; however, some believe that a sole reliance on evidence-based practice may limit the practitioner to administering treatments rigidly without "… variation, creativity, or flexibility and without consideration of the individual differences with which the patients present" (Nock, Goldman, Wang, & Albano, 2004, p. 777).

It is important to mention here that this book introduces innovative interventions in child and adolescent mental health, many of which do not yet qualify as "evidence-based" practices, per the specific NIMH guidelines; however, a growing body of research is provided for each intervention, along with specific ethical and cultural considerations that can help facilitate each intervention towards the use of best practices. Likewise, each intervention in this book is illustrated via a case study so that readers may begin to see how these innovative interventions play out in "real world" treatment setting. Finally, it should be said, that it is the hope of the authors in this book that each of these interventions will continue to undergo rigorous research that will eventually help to elevate them to the level of evidence-based practices, per NIMH guidelines, so that children and adolescents who are struggling can access these interventions in the context of the various systems of care in which services are provided.

Systems of Care

The interventions presented in this book provide mental health professionals with non-traditional methods of meeting the developmental needs of children and adolescents in a variety of interdisciplinary settings. These interventions can be used in schools, hospitals, residential treatment centers, juvenile justice, mental health, family therapy clinics, and can be implemented as a part of wrap-around services for youth, Multi-systemic Therapy, and other forms of systemic interventions for youth. Though the interventions in this book are multi-theoretical in nature, the goal of promoting wellness and creativity in the face of mental health challenges is the goal of the authors. As such, we believe that these interventions can be situated on the continuum of care for children and adolescents known as system of care. According to Sproul (2006) the core values for the systems of care specify that services provided be:

- community-based
- child-centered
- family-focused
- culturally appropriate

It is within this framework that the interventions in this book can be embedded and applied. Most of the innovative interventions presented naturally fit with the systems of care model. Even the interventions such as wilderness therapy, which temporarily remove the youth from his/her environment, must be linked back to the community through follow-up services.

The Need for Innovative Interventions: Creating a Developmental and Neurobiological Rationale

Because children are so obviously different from adults, we have begun to adapt our therapeutic approaches with them to use play and expressive arts in the therapeutic setting. The literature presents a neuroscience framework for these types of interventions with children (Malchiodi & Perry, 2008); however, many traditional therapeutic approaches with children and adolescents have mimicked adult psychotherapy, in large part involving behavioral, cognitive-behavioral, and interpersonal approaches to talk therapy. These approaches have been utilized in individual, group, and family settings, and focus primarily on problem solving, decision making, and cognitive restructuring. In particular, it is often assumed that adolescents are capable of participating in talk therapy; however the literature does make some exceptions for young people with "significant expressive language disorders or mental retardation" (Seligman & Reichenberg, 2007, p. 58). Just because some children and adolescents have the verbal ability to engage in talk therapy, however, doesn't mean that this is the only or best modality for them. According to the Child Development Institute (2009), adults often expect children to think like adults when they are not yet capable of doing so. Based on this, we readily encourage parents to have realistic expectations for their children, yet we must make sure we do the same when addressing child and adolescent mental health. An important consideration in child and adolescent mental health is that interventions are developmentally appropriate (Barber & Crockett, 1993). This requires a consideration of the basic aspects of childhood and adolescent development and neurobiology so that these target needs can be met.

Child and Adolescent Development: The Need for Developmentally Appropriate Interventions

Human development has been studied for centuries. In particular, child and adolescent development has been highlighted due to the sensitive and important developmental shifts that occur during this time. Development in childhood and adolescence is multi-faceted and includes biological, cognitive, psychological, moral, relational, and spiritual domains. Theories of child and adolescent development have centered primarily on the works of four major theorists: Piaget, Freud, Erikson, and Vygotsky. Table 1.2 provides an overview of the stages of development according to these four theorists. While it is beyond the scope of this chapter to examine each of these developmental theories in depth, it is the goal of this section to help readers understand why and how interventions in child and adolescent mental health need to be developmentally appropriate; that is, they should help children and adolescents move through the various stages of development *experientially*, and address the various domains in which development occurs.

Freud's theories illuminate the psychosexual stages of development; while Erikson's theories more closely examine social-emotional growth and development related to the individual's life context. Each of these theories highlights various *developmental tasks that are important for movement to the next stage of development*. While human development is not always so linear, it is widely believed that resolution of these stages of development is needed for healthy psychosocial functioning.

Piaget's theories focus more on the intellectual development of children and adolescents. According to Piaget, "knowledge is acquired (in his words 'constructed') through action" (Cole & Cole, 1996, p. 167). Through early childhood actions and experiences, children develop schemas or mental structures that represent the way that child sees the world. Piaget's theories provide an understanding of how children and adolescents adapt these schemas through the processes of *assimilation and accommodation*. As children and adolescents are exposed to novel situations, they must

Table 1.2   Stages of Development According to Four Theorists (Cole & Cole, 1996, p. 41)

Conventional	Piaget	Freud	Erikson	Vygotsky
Infancy (birth–2½ years	Sensorimotor	Oral Anal	Trust vs. mistrust Autonomy vs. shame	Affiliation
Early childhood (2½–6 years)	Preoperations	Phallic	Initiative vs. guilt	Play
Middle childhood (6–12 years)	Concrete operations	Latency	Industry vs. inferiority	Learning
Adolescence (12–19 years)	Formal operations	Genital	Identity vs. role confusion Intimacy vs. isolation	Peer activity
Adulthood (19–65 years)			Generativity vs. stagnation	Work
Old age (65 years–death)			Ego integrity vs. despair	Theorizing

assimilate these new experiences into their existing schemas. When the situation does not fit into pre-existing schemas, then children and adolescents modify their existing schemas to adapt to these new experiences. This is highly relevant to the innovative interventions highlighted in this book as each provides young people with *opportunities for new experiences* that may alter the way they view themselves and the world.

Vygotsky's theories were also built on action and examined the importance of learning and growth through *play and activity*. He was interested in the gradual development of autonomy and interdependence and believed that the developmental and educational environments of children and adolescents should be based on the zone of proximal development which he defined as the "gap between what children can accomplish independently and what they can accomplish when they are interacting with others who are more competent" (Cole & Cole, 1996, p. 211). In the *zone of proximal development*, adults provide children and adolescents the support they need to be able to accomplish actions they will later be able to accomplish independently, which is similar to the goal of interventions in child and adolescent mental health.

While all of these theories have distinct differences, the commonalities of each developmental model include a focus on epigenetic or stage specific growth in which human beings develop from one stage of life to the next through some kind of *action*. This developmental movement occurs in relationship to one's environment and the *life experiences and relationships* one encounters. This is especially true for adolescence. Deutsch (1960) referred to adolescence as the space between a world that is disappearing and another world that has *yet* to appear. This is clearly a Western view of adolescence in which there is a gap between the genital phase and adulthood. As Cole and Cole (1996) wrote: "The biosocial shift to adulthood is complicated by the fact that sexual maturity does not necessarily coincide with adult status. The resulting conflict between biological and social forces gives this transition its unique psychological characteristics" (p. 663).

Much like other stages of development, adolescents must accomplish certain developmental tasks in order to lead productive, psychologically healthy lives. Some of the important tasks that have been identified include achieving independence from primary caregivers, preparing for a career, adjusting to the emotional and physical changes of puberty, and moving toward a sense of personal identity by developing personal values independent from the values of others (Radkowsky & Siegel, 1997). The development of a sense of identity is perhaps the most salient developmental task of adolescence, and occurs most often in the context of relationships and novel experiences (Sylwester, 2007).

For this reason, many of the innovative interventions in this book are embedded in the context of positive relationships: with adults, with peers, and with animals and nature. They offer opportunities for children and adolescents to discover *new evidence about themselves* through art, music, challenge and adventure, nature, human-animal bonds, literature, and meditation. Each of these innovative interventions focuses on client strengths and assists in the construction of a more positive sense of personal identity and future. These interventions are considered to be developmentally appropriate because they provide young people with *novel experiences in the context of supportive human (and non-human) relationships* that may help move them forward through the various stages of human development.

Brain-Building Interventions

Part of being able to accurately assess the developmental appropriateness of the intervention is to understand child and adolescent neurobiology. We know that child and adolescent mental health problems occur because of genetic, developmental, psychosocial, and physiologic factors. Therefore, it is important that interventions in child and adolescent mental health also address these factors. The innovative interventions in this book not only seek to address these multiple factors, but also seek to be *brain-building experiences that help the brain work together and become more integrated and fully functioning.* Before we explore in depth what that means, it is important to have a basic understanding of human brain development and functioning, as well as an understanding of what makes child and adolescent brains so different.

Basic Brain Development and Functions

As humans, we are each born with an existing pattern and number of neurons (brain cells) that conduct impulses throughout the body and send messages to and from the brain. As we grow and develop, each new experience and layered experiences, cause two things to occur: (a) *myelination*: the axon (nerve cell body) becomes thicker with added coats of myelin, a fatty covering on the nerve known as the myelin sheath, that as it grows, conducts an impulses faster and more effectively; and (b) *dendritic growth*: the dendrites, which are like little branches that connect one neuron to the next, also grow bushier with use. With no or little use, they do not grow and are naturally pruned. Much like a tree, it is harder to prune large branches, so once something is learned or felt for a long time, it is harder to change. These are the two main structures that give way to the development of various neural networks or pathways.

There are many different parts of the brain that are important to understand in the development of children and adolescents. The *brain stem*, which is fully formed at birth, is the inner core of the brain. It regulates temperature, breathing, heart rate, other reflexes such as sucking, and generally aids in survival of the species, by maintaining biological homeostasis. The *limbic system* is composed mainly of the amygdala and the hippocampus. The *amygdala* is responsible for emotional and somatic organization of experience and plays an important role in the fight/flight response to fear. The amygdala also plays a role in attachment and early memory, and interacts with the hippocampus and the cerebral cortex. The *hippocampus* organizes explicit memory with the cerebral cortex, and is responsible for processing emotional memories. Finally, the *cerebral cortex* organizes our experiences and how we interact with the world through the creation of ideas, mental representations, and schemas. The cerebral cortex is made up of four different lobes for processing and is also divided into the right and left hemispheres, which creates a lateral division of labor in the brain. The *corpus callosum* consists of long neural fibers that connect the right/left hemispheres.

The *prefrontal cortex* is the foremost portion of the frontal lobe that is responsible for executing functions such as reasoning, judgment, planning, anticipating consequences, etc. This is the part of the brain that is not fully formed until adulthood, which is critical to understand when working with children and adolescents.

Child and Adolescent Neurobiology

While healthy pre-natal neurological development is hugely important to human development, this chapter focuses on the brain as an organ of adaptation and looks at the interplay between neural development and the environment *after* a child is born. An important part of understanding a child's brain is to know that 75% of brain development occurs after birth (CDI, 2009). As Cozolino (2002) says,

> That so much of the brain is shaped after birth is both good and bad news. The good news is that the individual brain is built to survive in a particular environment. Culture, language, climate, nutrition, and each set of parents shape each of our brains in a unique way. In good times and with good parents, this early brain building may serve the child well and throughout life. The bad news comes when factors are not so favorable, such as in times of war or in the case of parental psychopathology. The brain is then sculpted in ways that can become maladaptive. It is in these instances that a therapist attempts to restructure neural architecture. (p. 12)

From birth to 18 months, neurons (brain cells) that existed at birth become connected in networks, with rapid connections formed in the sensorimotor, visual cortex, and, eventually, the frontal lobes. From 18 months to 3 years, the synaptic growth in a child's brain continues to expand and becomes twice as dense and twice as active as the adult brain. This density continues throughout the first 10 years of life and gradually declines due to the pruning of grey matter that happens during adolescence. According to Frost (1998),

> This discarding of synapses is a lifelong process of refining or pruning to eliminate those that are not used in favor of those that are used through every day experiences. The early experiences of children play a critical role in determining the wiring of the brain, and it is hypothesized, the range and quality of the child's intellectual abilities. As the child grows, a complex system of synapses or neural pathways is formed. The pathways that are repeatedly activated or used are protected and retained into adulthood. (p. 6)

The *need for enriched environments and relationships* during this time cannot be underscored, as the child develops the building blocks for other learning experiences. Cozolino (2002) contends that "for humans, enriched environments can include the kinds of challenging educational and experiential opportunities that encourage us to learn new skills and expand our knowledge" (p. 23). He goes on to say that various forms of psychotherapy, much like the innovative interventions presented in this book, can be considered enriched environments the promote the development of cognitive, emotional, and behavioral abilities (Cozolino, 2002).

Recent research on the adolescent brain has shown that during adolescence, the brain is going through a second phase of rapid neural development and reorganization, which creates opportunities for creativity, but also vulnerability (Koplewicz, 2002). The pre-frontal cortex, the seat of executive functions such as planning, anticipating consequences, and organization is not yet fully formed. Likewise, the limbic systems of adolescents, the part of the brain that is responsible for sending emotional messages, is in hyper-drive, so to speak. The amygdala, the alarm center of the brain, is actually swollen by sex hormones released in adolescence, causing impulsivity, irritability, and aggressiveness to flair. Likewise, teenagers often experience a drop in serotonin levels, a neurotransmitter that is related to mood regulation, which causes even more irritability and aggression in adolescence.

Because of the emotionally charged time period of adolescence, *it is imperative for the limbic system and the pre-frontal cortex to work together, or become integrated, in order to achieve optimal impulse control and health emotional functioning.* As Luna et al (2001) wrote, "Functional integration of widely-distributed circuits lays the groundwork for enhanced voluntary control of behavior during adolescent cognitive development" (p. 786). This type of integration is called top-down integration and allows the cortex to better "process, inhibit, and organize the reflexes, impulses, and emotions generated by the brain stem and limbic system" (Cozolino, 2002, p. 29). Since this integration is not complete in adolescence, what we know most about the adolescent brain is that it is *a work in progress* and also *requires an enriched environment*, complete with novel experiences and positive relationships in which to become integrated and fully functioning. As Healy (2004) said, "At any age, hands-on experience is the first step" in growth and development (p. 74).

Innovative Interventions: Promoting Neural Integration

In Louis Cozolino's book *The Neuroscience of Psychotherapy*, he defines neural integration as the formation of interconnected neurons which form neural networks that in turn become integrated to perform increasingly complex tasks. Cozolino (2002) says, "For example, networks that participated in language, emotion, and memory need to become integrated in order for us to recall and tell an emotionally meaningful story with the proper affect, correct details and appropriate words" (p. 21). Healy (2004) refers to this as "stretching out the brain." (p. 113). She also advocates for "building bridges between the hemispheres" (p. 160) so that humans can become more balanced between right and left-brained thinking. Left-right integration "allows us to put feelings into words, consider feelings in conscious awareness, and balance the positive and negative affective biases of the left and right hemispheres" (Cozolino, 2002, p. 29).

Neural integration is an important concept in child and adolescent mental health because it can lead to the healthy functioning of neural networks (complex interaction of individual neurons) *which positively affects memory, attachment, emotion, and conscious awareness.* Furthermore, the converse is true. When there are non-linkages between neural networks or when networks become "unlinked," as can occur in trauma, this affects memory, attachment, emotion, and conscious awareness negatively. Cozolino (2002) believes that neural integration and growth in psychotherapy are enhanced by six important components.

1. *The establishment of a safe and trusting relationship.*
   A safe and trusting relationship most often occurs in the context of a client-centered therapeutic relationship that involves unconditional positive regard, genuineness, attunement, and concreteness with the client (Rogers, 1942). This type of relationship role models healthy attachment and bonding and promotes growth through approachable interaction, while still maintaining appropriate boundaries, and physical and emotional safety. In a meta-analysis of hundreds of studies measuring the outcomes of psychotherapy, Orlinsky and Howard (1986) found that the emotional connection established between the client and the therapist was one of the most important therapeutic factors in establishing positive outcomes.

2. *Gaining new information and experiences across the domains of cognition, emotion, sensation, and behavior.*
   The involvement of cognition, affect, sensation, and behavior means engaging clients on multiple levels, which fosters the integration of dissociated neural circuits (Cozolino, 2002). According to Cozolino, it is not enough in therapy to have insight without change or catharsis without cognition or understanding. Therefore, when intense emotional states are evoked via therapy, they should be combined with appropriate opportunities for reflection and processing. This can help assist the client in developing emotional regulation skills which are critical to child and adolescent development.

3. *The simultaneous or alternating activation of neural networks that are inadequately integrated or dissociated.*
   In order to promote neural integration, various neural networks need to be activated or used at the same time or in an alternating pattern. As in Cozolino's earlier example of the various parts of the brain responsible for language, memory and speech working together, the idea is that *neurons that fire together, wire together.* In innovative interventions, not only are cognitive and affective neural networks being activated at the same time, but often so are networks related to movement. Physical involvement in the learning situation deepens the impact of the learning experience (Schmidt, 1997) and can bring together experience *and* emotion to create strong neural connections.

4. *Moderate levels of stress or emotional arousal alternating with periods of calm and safety.*
   In any type of therapeutic intervention, there must be a balance between nurturance, achieved through physical and emotional safety, and optimal stress, which involves the client in some way being outside of his/her comfort zone. Fritz Perls (Perls, Hefferline, & Goodman, 1951) referred to this process in therapy as being a *safe emergency.* Cozolino (2002) says that a "safe emergency is a challenge for growth and integration in the context of guidance and support" (p. 32). He goes on to say:

   > All forms of successful therapy strive to create these safe emergencies in one form or another. As in development, the repeated exposure to stress in supportive interpersonal context of psychotherapy results in the ability to tolerate increasing levels of arousal. (pp. 32–33)

In other words, the process must involve novel experiences that involve some level of risk (cognitive, emotional, physical, etc.) in the context of supportive relationships, as was mentioned earlier.

5. *The integration of conceptual knowledge with emotional and bodily experience through narratives that are co-constructed with the therapist.*

As mentioned earlier, novel experiences often give young people new evidence about themselves. As they engage in positive growth experiences, they widen their sense of identity and competence in the world, and this becomes part of a new story that is created in part by processing these novel experiences in the context of the therapeutic relationship or through some other means of self-expression. As Cozolino says, "Stories serve to bridge and integrate neural networks both in the present moment and through time" (p. 64).

6. *Developing a method of processing and organizing new experiences so as to continue ongoing growth and integration outside of therapy.*

This final component of therapy necessary in the promotion of neural integration is probably the most important in terms of child and adolescent mental health treatment for it involves the *transfer of learning* from the therapeutic setting back to the real world, so to speak. Innovative interventions for children and adolescents must not only provide novel experiences in the context of supportive relationships, but they must also help to secure lasting coping skills that will help young people face future challenges and be open to accessing support and other healing experiences as adults. For Cozolino (2002), this method of processing and organizing new experiences that allows for ongoing growth and integration outside of therapy has to do with (a) providing the child with *the capacity for self-soothing* and (b) increasing their *ability to form positive relationships*. He believes these are some of the primary goals of both therapy and parenting, two processes which often mirror one another in work with children and adolescents.

While these six components can certainly occur in various approaches to talk therapy, they are more clearly and deliberately evident in the interventions highlighted in this book. Through art, music, literature, connection with the natural and animal worlds, and in meditation the innovative interventions presented in this book seek to spark the imagination of young people and build upon Daniel Pink's (2006) *six aptitudes:* design, story, symphony, empathy, play, and meaning.

Commonalities of Innovative Interventions: The Six Aptitudes

In his book, *The Adolescent Brain*, Robert Sylwester (2007) continues to discuss the importance of *novel experiences* in neurological development. Novel experiences can be defined as new experiences that promote learning and growth, and engage a young person on a multi-sensory level. They are often active and involve a balance of nurture and positive stress (Cozolino, 2002). All of the interventions highlighted in this book provide children and adolescents with novel experiences through art, music, literature, the natural world, the human-animal bond, and meditation. These types of experiences are processed by the right hemisphere of the brain, which "is organized to process novel challenges and creative solutions" (p. 29). Whereas, the left hemisphere is meant to process "familiar challenges and established routines" (p. 29). For this reason, Sylwester goes on to say, "learning thus typically begins with the *right hemisphere exploration*" (p. 30).

Recently, the importance of right-brain directed thinking was highlighted in Daniel Pink's (2006) book *A Whole New Mind*. While this book is not geared towards mental health, it has profound application towards learning and development, and has some applicability in providing a rationale for utilizing innovative interventions in child and adolescent mental health. Pink identified six right-brain directed aptitudes that he believes are essential cognitive and affective skills for living in a modern world. These six aptitudes are reflected in many of the innovative interventions in this book, and provide new opportunities for positive growth and development in child and adolescent mental health.

- *Design*: Pink (2006) states that "design, stripped to its essence, can be defined as the human nature to shape and make our environment in ways without precedent in nature, to serve our needs and give meaning to our lives" (p. 69). This idea is very similar to *self-efficacy* which Bandura (1997) described as belief in one's agentive capabilities, in other words, that one can have an impact on his/her environment or situation and produce given levels of attainment. In traditional therapy, verbal persuasion is the technique most often employed to increase self-efficacy, but as Bandura (1977) suggests, verbal persuasion has the greatest impact on people who already have some reason to believe that they can produce effects through their actions. This approach for increasing self-efficacy is backwards, beginning with the therapist's insight and the client's preconceived beliefs about him/herself. *Active means of increasing self-efficacy* must begin with a primary experience that provides new evidence about a person's capabilities, followed by the development of a new or reaffirmed belief system about the self. Through participation in innovative interventions, children and adolescents engage in novel experiences and begin to see what they are capable of, thus experientially building their own perceptions of self-efficacy. Research shows that perceived self-efficacy in young people can positively impact cognitive, motivational and affective processes (Bandura, 1993). By increasing self-efficacy, innovative interventions help children and adolescents become designers of their own lives. Pink (2006, p. 72) quotes a former architect who says that *designers learn to bring disparate things together to a solution*, which can be thought of as a treatment goal for children and adolescents who are struggling to solve problems in their lives that keep them from moving forward developmentally.
- *Story:* Cozolino (2002) previously highlighted the positive impact of story on neural integration, and Pink (2006) reaffirms this idea. Cozolino refers to story as being at the heart of imagination. For children and adolescents, the ability to imagine may be directly related to the ability to transcontextualize, or envision their lives to be different someday (Saari, 1991). Healy (2004) highlights the importance of the power of pretending that occurs when young people combine storytelling and play. According to Healy, story helps children "enlarge their own mental frameworks, get outside their own minds, practice using language, and gain information about others values and points of view" (p. 67). This intentional use of narratives also helps children and adolescents to tell a cohesive and meaningful story about their own lives.

- *Symphony:* Pink refers to symphony as "the ability to put together the pieces" (p. 130). It is integrated thinking, feeling and being at its best. This holism is similar to the idea of congruence in which the child or adolescent client begins to establish connections between his/her life experiences which helps to create the "rhythmic movement from events of doubt and conflict to events of integrity and harmony" (Crosby, 1995, p. 10). In support of this need for congruence, Dewey (1965) stated:

  > A divided world, a world whose parts and aspects do not hang together, is at once a sign and a cause of a divided personality. When the splitting-up reaches a certain point, we call the person insane. A fully integrated personality, on the other hand, exists only when successive experiences are integrated with one another. It can be built up only as a world of related objects is constructed. (p. 520)

  This world of related objects is one in which the client is able to actualize the potential meaning of his/her life due to the connections that he/she makes (Frankl, 1959, p. 175).

  Healy (2004) refers to this as seeing relationships and patterning information. "Patterning information really means organizing and associating new information with previously developed mental hooks" (p. 61). Healy goes on to say that "Children who can 'see' relationships and organize input at a sensory level seem to have an easier time organizing thoughts and ideas" (p. 62). This is certainly an important skill to help children develop in the course of mental health treatment and is exactly what Pink is talking about when he refers to symphonic thinking.
- *Empathy:* Empathy is, of course, related to one's ability to form connections with others; thus, it is a critical trait for young people to develop. However, many children and adolescents have not developed empathy for others because they themselves have never experienced empathy on the part of a caregiver or other meaningful relationship. Pink (2006) refers to empathy as the "ability to imagine yourself in someone else's position and to intuit what that person is feeling" (p. 159). According to Pink, this right-brain directed skill is related to attuning oneself to another and often involves an element of mimicry. In other words, empathy is often developed experientially by being in situations in which we have the opportunity to experience and try to understand what another person (or in the case of animal-assisted therapy, an animal) is going through. The development of empathy is hugely important in child and adolescent mental health because empathy is a well-known protective factor that can help reduce the likelihood of adverse outcomes for youth (Resnick, 2000).
- *Play:* Not only is play an important part of childhood development, it is a key factor in many of the innovative interventions presented in this book. Play needs to be an essential component of child and adolescent mental health treatment because it is developmentally appropriate and promotes neural integration. According to the Child Development Institute (2009):

  > Play activities are essential to healthy development for children and adolescents. The activities engaged in by children both stimulate and influence the pattern of the connections made between the nerve cells. This process influences the development of fine and gross motor skills, language, socialization, personal awareness, emotional well-being, creativity, problem solving and learning ability. The most important role that play can have is to help children to be active, make choices and practice actions to mastery. They should have experience with a wide variety

of content (art, music, language, science, math, social relations) because each is important for the development of a *complex and integrated brain*. Play that links sensorimotor, cognitive, and social-emotional experiences provides *an ideal setting from brain development.*

Not only is play important for individual development, it can also be used to rebuild families and communities. A group known as Play for Peace travels to various war-torn areas around the world to use play as a way of helping children heal from the trauma of war and poverty, and rebuild and heal the community cross-culturally as well (Play for Peace, 2009). Play creates a context of hope, and play also opens up new possibilities as it becomes the "gateway to metaphor...insight and to invention" (Healy, 2004, p. 67).

• *Meaning:* Finally, Pink addresses meaning, the creation of which seems to distinguish humans from other species. According to Healy (2004), meaning allows us to organize our life experiences in such a way that helps us make sense of them. In this sense, organizing our life experiences serves to counteract the "detrimental influence of that feeling of which so many patients complain today, namely, the feeling of total and ultimate meaninglessness" (Frankl, 1959, p. 167). This happens as the client is confronted with and reoriented to meaning in his or her life. The possibility of this occurring in the innovative interventions presented in this book is astounding because meaning is not simply talked about; it is experienced, created, and risked. The client(s) can be "piloted through the existential crises of growth and development" not merely through talking about these crises, but through corrective emotional experiences involving action and metaphor (Frankl, 1959, p 163). Meaning is a necessary component of child and adolescent mental health because it creates a bridge "between what one has already achieved and what one still ought to accomplish, or the gap between what one is and what one should become" (Frankl, 1959, p. 166).

Pink's six right-brained directed aptitudes will be evident in many of the innovative interventions presented in this book. They serve as important reminders about what children and adolescents need in mental health treatment, and create a framework for thinking developmentally and experientially about child and adolescent mental health. It is important to note, however, that as young people engage in right-brained exploration that involves design, story, symphony, empathy, play and meaning, they will also need time for contemplation and reflection. According to Healy (2004), it is important to remember that "the brain needs downtime to firm up all this work and to make space for quiet reflection and pondering" (p. 63). This certainly supports the inclusion of meditation as the final chapter on innovative interventions in child and adolescent mental health.

Summary

Child and adolescent mental health is a very real concern in our society. By focusing on child and adolescent development and neurobiology, we are guided to apply innovative interventions with this population that go beyond traditional talk therapy. By providing youth with novel experiences in the context of supportive relationships, the innovative interventions presented in this book represent an opportunity infuse the system of care for young people with enriched therapeutic environments and experiences.

The interventions presented in this book include Cozolino's (2002) six components that promote neural integration, which can facilitate learning and growth. They provide experiential opportunities for moving youth forward developmentally and re-shaping the brain via art, music, bibliotherapy, animal-assisted therapy, wilderness therapy, and meditation. These interventions have in common Pink's (2006) six right-brained directed aptitudes and help facilitate *emotional tolerance, regulation and integration*. The possibilities for healing that can come from utilizing innovative interventions with children and adolescents are vast and applicable across a variety of treatment settings. It is the hope that by learning about each of the different interventions in this book, the reader can think critically about the function of the intervention in moving the client forward developmentally, as well as the possibilities for neural integration.

Lastly, it is important to note the commitment to positive child and adolescent development that is present in each chapter of this book. While each chapter highlights important mental health issues that can be addressed by the specific form of treatment, each chapter also focuses on the importance of harnessing human strengths and the forward momentum of child and adolescent development through novel experiences and supportive relationships.

Activities to Extend Your Learning

- Discuss what is needed for children and adolescents to develop and maintain positive mental health.
- Dyad activity: pick a partner and discuss why you think people develop mental health problems. Is it for psychosocial reasons? Neurological reasons? Spiritual or cultural reasons? A combination?
- What does it mean for an intervention to be developmentally appropriate?
- Based on the information presented in this chapter, why do you think children and adolescents may need more than talk therapy?
- Visit http://systemsofcare.samhsa.gov/ and read more on systems of care for children and adolescents.
- Visit the Society for Neuroscience website to view adolescent brain scans. http://www.sfn.org/index.cfm?pagename=brainBriefings_Adolescent_brain
- Read Daniel Pink's book *A Whole New Mind* and select several of the portfolio activities he assigns in each of the six aptitudes.

Recommended Resources

American Academy of Child & Adolescent Psychiatry (AACAP): http://www.aacap.org/clinical
Child Development Institute: http://www.childdevelopmentinfo.com
National Alliance for the Mentally Ill (NAMI) National: http://www.nami.org/helpline
National Institute for Mental Health: http://www.nimh.nih.gov/publicat/violence.cfm
Technical Assistance Partnership for Child and Family Mental Health: http://www.tapartnership.org

2.
ART THERAPY WITH CHILDREN AND ADOLESCENTS
Inspiring Creativity and Growth

Barbara Parker-Bell

Overview of Chapter

- Introduction
- A Very Brief History
- Advantages of Art Therapy
- Neuroscience and Art Therapy
- Creating a Safe Setting for Work with Children
- Understanding Artistic Development in Children
- Individual, Groups, Families, and Communities
- Adolescents
- Case Study
- Ethical Issues and Culture
- Summary
- Activities to Extend Your Learning

Introduction

Art therapy is a relatively new discipline in the field of psychotherapy. To put this in perspective, in 2009 the American Art Therapy Association celebrated its 40th year in existence as a professional organization. It is therefore understandable that many helping professionals are unaware of the discipline or have limited information on the effectiveness of art-based treatment. Yet, more recently, clinicians have become aware of art therapy and the potential for healing in the aftermath of manmade and natural disasters such as September 11th, the 2004 tsunami, and Hurricane Katrina. Following these events artworks of survivors and their stories were made visible. Many art therapists (Appleton, 2001; Chilcote, 2007; Goodman, Chapman, & Gantt, 2008; Kalmanowitz & Lloyd, 2005; Wise, 2005) have engaged in post-traumatic therapy work with children. They have discovered that when children could not speak or verbally express what occurred, art became a voice for the pain and a container for the experience. Art engagement can reach children in ways that other therapies cannot because it is appealing and familiar. Art is embedded in cultural activity, school, and family life and is seen normative and reassuring. Positive associations with art and art making help children and adolescents accept an art-based healing approach (Goodman et al., 2008).

A Very Brief History

It is important to note that artists and art therapists have a long history of working with children and adolescents in emotional pain using an art-based approach. Friedl Dicker-Brandeis, an artist/educator interned at Terezin concentration camp between 1942 and 1944, provided art classes to children who were also interned (Wix, 2009). According to Wix, Dicker-Brandeis's supportive and unobtrusive approach to encouraging artmaking in this most traumatic of settings created a space for children to engage in processes of imaginatively exploring, seeing, and creating. These processes allowed children to claim their own experiences and expressions. Dicker-Brandeis hoped in some way that these experiences would protect the children psychological from the devastation of their environment. The beautiful artifacts that remain are a testimony to the children's ability to hold on to hope and beauty.

Similarly, in the late 1930s Edith Kramer, an artist and a future founding mother of art therapy, worked with many refugee children who had escaped occupied Europe under the tutelage of Dicker-Brandeis. She asserted that she could see "different responses to stress as they manifested in children's art" (Kramer, 1971 p. xiv). In addition she saw that the creative capacity of children could survive and resurface with the support of the creative art classes.

When Kramer immigrated to the United States and began working with emotionally disturbed boys, she formed a concept of art therapy based on her experiences as an artist, her own psychoanalysis, and her knowledge of psychoanalytic theory (Kramer, 1958, 1971). Kramer understood the functioning of her patients in terms of ego function, drive material and successful sublimation of drive material. In terms of the art, sublimation occurred when the children were able to achieve the expressive goal in artistic form which in turn would support ego strength. She ascertained that the healing potentialities of art therapy depended on the psychological processes that were activated in creative work. In this case the art therapist appeared to function as a teacher of art skills. However, Kramer would define her role as an auxiliary ego. Art therapists offered benign artistic support and non-intrusive themes for artistic work that were necessary to help the child contain and honor emotional expression. Finding pleasure and success with the materials was seen as a means to neutralizing negative affect. Discussion of the work's expressive content was not emphasized.

Margaret Naumburg and her form of art psychotherapy may be better known to non-art therapists (Naumburg, 1973). Naumburg, another founding mother of art therapy, began her work with children in the United States in the 1930s and 40s. Naumburg was also inspired by psychodynamic theories and psychoanalysis. However, Naumburg attributed less importance to developing the form of the expression itself. Instead, she emphasized free expression in which fantasy and imagination revealed the child's expression of personality and allowed for catharsis. Unconscious materials represented in symbols were seen as clues to understanding functioning or maladjustment. These themes could be addressed within the framework of a thera-peutic relationship that more closely resembled psychotherapy. Art engagement was more similar to play that allowed for verbal free association and reflection. Naum-burg felt that the use of art could be even more important with children than adults "because children are less able to express their thoughts and feelings in words and are closer to the more primitive expression of themselves through the language of images and play" (p. 51). Particular approaches such as scribble drawings were used to help free expression and to promote spontaneous imagery.

Naumburg and Kramer created very different approaches to art therapy. The art therapists who followed were said to be theoretically polarized between Kramer's art as therapy approach and Naumburg's art psychotherapy approach (Wadeson, 2002). However, Wadeson asserted that many art therapists have found a place somewhere in the middle of the spectrum. Alternatively, art therapists have also found themselves shifting their approach to art and discussion based on the interests, characteristics, needs, and goals of the patient.

Art therapists' styles have been informed by their interactions with diverse patients and theory that influences a broad range of psychotherapeutic disciplines. For example, art therapists use Jungian approaches, humanistic approaches, transper-sonal approaches, cognitive behavioral approaches, group therapy approaches, family systems approaches and more (Rubin, 2001). Currently, the profession of art therapy is not dominated by one theoretical approach.

As a whole, art therapists share the broad vision of the American Art Therapy Association (2009), which defines art therapy as:

> a mental health profession that uses the creative process of art making to improve and enhance the physical, mental and emotional well-being of individuals of all ages. It is based on the belief that the creative process involved in artistic self-expression helps people to resolve conflicts and problems, develop interpersonal skills, manage behavior, reduce stress, increase self-esteem and self-awareness, and achieve insight.

Art therapists often believe that the use of the creative process holds advantages over traditional verbal therapy work.

Advantages of Art Therapy

Wadeson (1980) describes several advantages of art therapy. These advantages include: imagery, decreased defenses, objectification, permanence, spatial matrix, and creative and physical energy. While verbal skill has been highly valued in contemporary cul-tures, individual's conceptions of the world are often based on visual perception and imagery. Experienced imagery shapes our core experiences, therefore using imagery can help access those experiences. Yet, when imagery is used in the context of therapy, defenses are often decreased. This reduction occurs because people are frequently less adept at controlling or disguising their visual expressions. Consequently, images may tell people's secrets without them being aware.

The advantages of objectification and permanence relate to the physical nature of the art product (Wadeson, 1980). Expression is externalized in the art form and allows the maker to achieve some separation from that expression. The emotional space created allows a person to distance, view, acknowledge, and integrate the symbolic communication. Fortunately, this symbolic communication does not evaporate into the air like conversation, but remains a visual testimony to the experience. Therefore the artifact is witnessed and experienced by both patient and therapist. Like a cherished art work in a museum, it can be revisited time and again for appreciation or further exploration of meaning.

People are intrigued by artifacts and images in museums because they tell a story about a specific culture, person, place or time in history that cannot be communicated in other ways. This advantage and appeal also applies to art therapy. Wadeson (1980) called the spatial matrix or visual/spatial nature of art an advantage because it can bring numerous fantasy or reality based elements into the same composition. In addition, relationships between the elements can be seen and experienced not just explained. Compare an artwork to a dream image. A dream image provides a snapshot of a story that has personal meaning. Yet it is hard to verbally communicate all that it may represent. The linear nature of verbal communication demands a different type of expression and it is at best a translation of what has been seen and experienced. Moon (1994) calls art therapy metaverbal because the imagery created goes beyond words.

For some people the most rewarding aspect of art therapy is the opportunity to work with creative materials. Visually and kinesthetically stimulating materials can enliven emotional and imaginative energy. Similarly, the action of art play can create physical energy (Wadeson, 1980). Ultimately, creative engagement generates energy that can be channeled into the constructive process of growth and healing.

Neuroscience and Art Therapy

More recently, art therapists have looked to the developments in neuroscience to understand and explain the mechanisms of change in art therapy particularly related to Post Traumatic Stress Disorder (Goodman et al., 2008; Spring, 2004; Tripp, 2007). Goodman et al. consider theory when they assert that creative art interventions address traumatic material that is stored in the right hemisphere of the brain. The authors refer to the work of Perry, Pollard, Blakely, Baker, and Vigilante (1995) who explain that in times of trauma or post trauma the left frontal pre-cortex, the area associated with language and cognitive problem solving, is shut down. This shut down condition impacts the individual's ability to store verbal information and to later recall the traumatic experience via a linguistic approach. Since the right side of the brain is associated with visual-motor functioning and emotions, imagery can be used to access this material. Traumatic events can be approached symbolically or metaphorically at a level matching the ability to tolerate the exposure to the content. Finally, words and meanings can be attached to the imagery allowing for some integration of right and left hemisphere activity, which promotes integration of the two hemispheres. Non-verbal narratives paired with words can help build a coherent linguistic narrative that may allow for some resolution of the trauma (Chapman, Morabito, Ladakakos, Schrier, & Knudson, 2001).

Spring (2004), an art therapist with years of experience with sexual trauma survivors, incorporated this knowledge into her own explanation of the artmaking, person, and healing interaction. She formed the acronym KISS which stands for Kinesthetic-optical, Imaginal-emotional, and Sensory perceptual elements to Speech, a process description of how the coherent linguistic narrative is achieved. She states, "Artmaking is a conversion of image through sensory components leading to the interpretation of symbolic form through verbal narrative; it fills in or rearranges autobiographical memory as a means to make sense out of experience" (p. 207)

To investigate brain changes scientifically, Belkofer and Konopka (2008) conducted a single case design study to compare a person's brain activity before and after an hour long drawing and painting activity. They hypothesized, "… if art therapy affects our emotions, it alters the circuitry and activity in the brain. Conversely, if art therapy alters our brain, one can expect it to affect our emotions" (p. 57). The subject of their research, a 29-year-old male Caucasian graduate art therapy student, engaged in two 22-minute Electroencephatograph (EEG) recordings, the first establishing the baseline brain activity and the second to assess the impact of art engagement. The authors noted increases in higher frequency bilateral, parietal, and temporal lobe activity. Additionally, the authors noted a decrease in higher frequency pre-frontal activity. Belkofer and Konopa explain that the increases in the occipital and parietal lobes relate to the visual spatial processing associated with artmaking. Temporal lobe activity may be associated with "the strong emotional and spiritual connection and the transcendental consciousness that are frequently associated with making art" (p. 61). Or, that activity in the temporal lobe area may relate to memories that are stimulated. Replication of this study and the creation of others like it must be conducted so that art therapists and other clinicians can better understand the complex interactions between art activity, brain responses, and human healing.

In the light of these findings, art therapists have been asking, "What methods and specific art activities are likely to stimulate such processes of healing?" Orr (2007) conducted a content analysis on available communications (refereed journal articles, news articles, television interviews, and books) that reported on art therapy methods used with children after a variety of natural and manmade disasters. Based on this content analysis, Orr concluded that semi-structured approaches to art tasks were seen as most effective in work with the traumatized children. Semi-structured activities were characterized by some instructions, not many or none, and some material and activity choice, not too many materials or activity choices, or no choices. It appeared that less structure was utilized in short-term responses to victims of disaster and more structure was utilized in later or long-term art therapy responses.

Eaton, Doherty, and Widrick (2007) suggest that future research related to art therapy work with traumatized children should not focus on technique, but on how the common factors of therapy impact healing in art therapy practice. Research on common factors in therapy would assess client factors, client–therapist relationship factors, and placebo effects. Eaton et al. hypothesize that the healing value of art therapy comes from the relationship building that occurs when children engage in creative work with a caring adult who provides a safe setting.

Creating a Safe Setting for Work with Children

It is important for non-art therapy practitioners to note that art tasks must be presented in a sensitive manner in order to be effective. Rubin (1978), a second generation art therapist, described the specific conditions that promote creative growth in children. These conditions include: materials, space, time, order, safety, and respect. These concepts are explained as follows.

According to Rubin (1978), children should be provided with a variety of quality materials *appropriate to age, developmental, and physical functioning.* Drawing, painting, and clay modeling provide a starting point of options. Rubin advocated for an unstructured approach to art media so that children could intuitively choose materials that would match their interests and need for expression. In terms of space, children need to be provided with room, appropriate work surfaces, and means to clean up. As is true in other therapeutic settings, it is also important to have a space that is well-lit, organized and private. Clinicians must also be aware of the time frame they are providing for creative work. Sufficient time should be provided to allow for the creative process to unfold, to be worked through and to be closed once more. Children should be made aware of the time that they will have for creating and clean-up so they learn to manage their engagement. In addition, the provision of time cues later in the session help both the child and the therapist attend to session closure.

When a therapist provides a sense of order and predictability in the setting, this can help establish a sense of safety for children who feel less orderly inside (Rubin, 1978). Physical safety and psychological safety are essential therapeutic factors that precede therapeutic engagement. Therapists can *promote psychological safety through the authentic acceptance of art products and the ideas and expressions* they contain. *Limit setting and gentle containment* offered by the therapist also helps a child feel safe when destructive impulses arise. Finally, when a child and his interests, motivation, and unique artistic contributions are lovingly respected, the conditions are ripe for creative growth and healing.

Understanding Artistic Development in Children

When a therapist chooses to add art to the therapeutic relationship it is important for the therapist *to consider what the child is capable of developmentally.* Specific to art, therapists should know and what art making processes or outcomes may be expected at different developmental levels. Rubin (1978) suggests that children generally move through stages of artistic development that include manipulating, forming, naming, representing, containing, experimenting, consolidating, naturalizing, and personalizing and aestheticizing.

Very young children, infants, or toddlers, will be engaged in their first encounters with materials and will test them in very kinesthetic or sensory ways. Manipulation of the materials may include smearing, putting materials in their mouths or marking walls. As the child matures, a more controlled approach to materials evolves. Actions are more deliberate. Children in the forming stage are seen to scribble, make dots, roll and flatten their clay with the possible result of a shape or form. Next, children tend to add a name to what they create. The scribble becomes "dog" and the clay piece becomes a tool, even if it does not resemble the item named. Following the naming process, children begin to consciously attempt to represent items that they know or care about, based on what they know, but not necessarily what they see (Rubin, 1978).

Further on in artistic development, children achieve more motor and impulse control. In this containing phase, children start to "fill in" their drawings and may attempt to stay inside the lines. Learning and practicing boundaries personally and artistically becomes an important theme. Later, when they have even more fine motor and self-control, children begin to experiment and make more effort to create accurate representations of things in their environment. At this stage, around age 5, children are growing cognitively and are excited to explore new ways of creating and elaborating on their productions. In a human figure drawing for example, more details such clothing or hair styles may be included. As the child goes to school the child's ability to consolidate information is seen in the artwork. The child begins to place created elements in relationship to one another in the form of a scene. For example, a human figure may be depicted standing on a ground line, or a bird may be drawn in a tree (Rubin, 1978).

Children continue to add detail and more naturalistic qualities to their artmaking as they mature (Rubin, 1978). They may strive for realism and be disappointed that when their skills do not provide them with a means to draw or create what they see in the natural world. Their growing awareness may contribute to the child becoming self-critical and frustrated, and therefore they may be vulnerable to giving up on their work or on artmaking in general without support and guidance. Those who continue to create art after elementary school have likely had some level of success with their work. At this time, budding adolescents may expand their ability to draw naturalistically and may enjoy media exploration, including crafts. Exploration of different styles and achievement of a personal style or way of working may become more important.

Admittedly, these descriptions are extremely general and require some qualifying comments. Artistic stages are not necessarily achieved or retained in a linear manner. It is also important to note that social and cultural differences including cultural values and preferences related to creative activities and access to creative materials impact development and creative preferences (Malchiodi, 2005). Yet, an extensive description of developmental artistic processes is beyond the scope of this chapter. For more detailed information about artistic development as it relates to cognitive and emotional development it is recommended that individuals review resources such as Klorer's (2000) *Expressive Therapy with Troubled Children*, or Levick's (1998) *See what I'm Saying: What Children Tell Us through their Art*. In addition, clinicians may benefit from using some of the established art-based assessments that help clinicians place children's artistic output, particularly drawings, into a developmental framework. One such assessment is the Levick Emotional and Cognitive Art Therapy Assessment

(Levick, 2009). Another well-established assessment with well established validity is the *Silver Drawing Test* (Silver, 2007). Other more process oriented assessments such as *Horovitz's Cognitive Art Therapy Assessment* as described in Horovitz and Eksten (2009). This assessment incorporates drawing, painting, and clay activities. However, evaluation and categorization processes are somewhat ambiguous particularly for those without prior knowledge of developmental art processes.

Individual, Groups, Families, and Communities

Children are brought to therapy to address a variety of needs and concerns. Therefore, the variety of art-based methods and overarching therapy structures are utilized. As much of a child's life is embedded in family, art therapists may choose to use art-based methods with children and their families. For example, Stein (2001) a pediatrician, incorporated the Kinetic Family Drawing (KFD) into his patients' annual health visits. Children were asked to draw their family doing something. The physician then used the drawing to review development, family relationships, and stressors. He also found "… it remarkably helpful on many occasions as a way to open a dialogue with parents and children concerning important behavioral and family issues. Typically, the KFD reveals a behavioral issue that has not been brought to the clinician's attention previously" (p. 855). The KFD highlights the child's perceptions of the family dynamics, but this is not the same as looking at the dynamics themselves.

Creating an opportunity to look at child and family dynamics in action is a good reason to utilize art therapy in family sessions. Hoshino (2008) suggests that family art therapy sessions are where "family stories, dynamics, and structural characteristics" come to life (p. 40). Kerr, Hoshino, Sutherland, Parashak, and McCarley (2008) have provided an excellent resource for those who want to learn more about the history, theory, and practices of art therapy in the family context.

Sometimes children are brought to therapy because they are having difficulty that in their social milieus. In these situations, art work can be an excellent mediator and focus of attention as children learn to interact with others in a group setting. For example, in her work with children with autism, Noble (2001) used art to ease the children into interaction and reciprocity. She directed a very small group of children to draw a story together. Each child chose a color and took turns adding to the drawing and the story. Noble supported them through the process with structures including time prompts, themes that would help them express themselves, and collaborative naming of the completed artworks. Similarly, Safran (2002) utilized an art centered social skills group to help children diagnosed with Attention Deficit Hyperactivity Disorder (ADHD). Art themes related to the challenge of being diagnosed with ADHD and the acknowledgement of existing strengths and the building of new skills. Acceptable ways of interacting and listening to others are modeled and shaped during the group process.

In the extreme, entire communities may be involved with the creative process to provide a broad blanket of support for children and those who care about them. Rode (1995) describes the function of a creative arts therapy team working in a pediatric medical setting for children with life-threatening and chronic illness. She details that in addition to individual and family work the creative arts staff "focuses on interventions which attempt to create a sense of community and relationship to the environment" (p. 106). Visual arts are joined with other creative modalities, and hospitalized children, their families, physicians, nurses, and other health care professionals are invited to participate in art tasks, puppet show performances, and video productions related to silly or serious issues. As a result, entire communities engage in expressive activities that foster personal and meaningful support in difficult circumstances.

Adolescents

As expected, children grow up into adolescents and sometimes these adolescents require therapy. Riley (2001) asserts that art therapy can both address the developmental needs and support developmental strengths of adolescents. Adolescent traits such as "intellectualization as a defense, a narcissistic focus, resistance to adult rules, a spurt of high creativity, and the ability to think both concretely and abstractly … can be used to reach the patient" (p. 142). Riley (1999) explains how art therapy responds to these developmental factors:

> The adolescent youth is at the peak of his or her creativity; art expressions are creative. They are searching for support for individuation while still retaining controlled connection; the art is an individualized statement over which they have control. They are sensitive about criticism and suspicious of interpretation; *the art product is accepted by the therapist without interpretation.* They are often unable to clearly state their feelings or opinions because these sensations are so newly experienced they have an inadequate vocabulary. Adolescents can represent their conflicts more readily than they can verbalize them. The art can speak the unrest and confusion that is pervasive and simultaneously give focus to the session through an art product. (p. 85)

Finally, Riley believes that the concrete roles depicted in the artwork can help the adolescent address the ideal that he or she may be missing in his or her life. The images provide an avenue for dialogue and exploration of identity concerns can be considered.

In contrast, Moon (1999) describes an art therapy model where the dialogue that occurs between the therapist and adolescent is primarily visual. The role of the art therapist in his studio setting is to respond artistically to the adolescent's artwork in the presence of the adolescent. According to Moon, *responsive artmaking* is a therapeutic intervention that helps establish empathic relationships with adolescents, helps the therapist by providing an outlet for his feelings that occur in response to the adolescent and his image, and provides a starting place for imaginative interpretive dialogues. Moon's reliance on imagery and the creative process may circumvent adolescents' difficulty with and resistance to verbal interpretation and disclosure. Communicating through artwork builds a different type of trust, because both artists are taking risks in creating and sharing images to explore meaning. It is important to note, that the art therapists who work this way do not create art to address their own personal issues. The therapist's artwork evolves from careful observation of the adolescent's work process, behaviors, and comments. Figuratively, the therapist's art product is a mirror of the adolescent's emotional expression. It asks the adolescent in a visual way, "Am I seeing you accurately?" The art-based authentic manner of the therapist invites a genuine, less defensive response from the adolescent.

Not surprisingly, a studio approach to therapy, where groups of adolescents may work independently in a loosely structured but safe studio setting appeals to adolescents. Block, Harris, and Laing (2005) created such an environment for at-risk middle school youth. They collaborated with several social service agencies and their police department's youth services division to create an "Art & Action" outreach program which included the Open Studio Project (OSP) as well as other services. Block et al. explain, "The OSP process which includes intention, artmaking, witness-writing, and sharing, as well as no commenting and no forced participation, is versatile enough to nurture people within their own respective circumstances" (p. 33).

For 9 to 12 weeks, selected youth were given the opportunity to express themselves in this non-judgmental environment. An art therapist/facilitator accompanied the youth in this environment, provided some instruction, and made art alongside the youth as a fellow artists. At the beginning of each studio session each young person created and wrote an "intention" identifying their own personal focus for their day's artmaking. They were offered several artmaking techniques and provided access to a broad range of attractive materials in a spacious storefront studio where getting paint on the walls or floor was not a problem. After creating their work, they would engage in "witness-writing" where they would sit with their artwork in an attentive, respectful way, then record their thoughts or create a story or dialogue with their image in a journal. Finally, at the end of the sessions, the individual artists would come together to share. Participants choose their level of disclosure with no pressure. This process of witnessing and listening to others builds empathy and appreciation of one another. Art & Action has helped over 100 youth, "use the creative arts to uncover their own creative inner resources" (Block et al., 2005, p. 36) in a place that promotes "healthy decision making and healthy management of the turbulent emotional world of adolescence" (p. 36).

When working with adolescents, it is important to be mindful of art processes that may appeal to them and honor that appeal. Klingman, Shalev, and Pearlman (2000) spent time reviewing and analyzing spontaneous and elaborate community graffiti that Israeli youth generated after the tragic assassination of the Prime Minister of Israel, Yitzhak Rabin, a much beloved national figure and leader in Middle East peace processes. Although some may have seen the graffiti marks as destructive acts, the authors viewed the processes as efforts to process a traumatic stimulus and take back some control. The authors' extensive review of the graffiti art inspired them to support planned graffiti processes in other traumatic situations. When a 13-year-old girl was murdered by a peer, mental health professionals suggested that her school provide a graffiti wall to create a safe structure for other students to respond to the tragedy. Almost all of the students made use of the "Wall Composition" task which later became a permanent memorial wall. The public marks, symbols, and comments provided social support and a healing process promoted through creativity.

As one can see, *there are numerous ways that art can reach into the hearts and minds of children and youth and join them with a broader community of people who care about them.* Through providing a safe accepting space to create and express, artists, art therapists, and helping professionals can support healthy development, communication, and healing transformation. Future research will reveal more about operational and neurological processes that make art processes healing. These ongoing discoveries will only verify what artists and art therapist have known on a personal level for quite some time.

Case Study

An exciting element of art therapy practice with children and adolescents is the creative process of integrating art therapy and more traditional treatment approaches. Where art therapy protocols do not exist, art therapists write them. In many instances, groups can be considered works in progress, where the synthesis between creative and theoretical elements are attempted and refined. The "Coping Captain" group, a group for children designed to reduce anxiety symptoms and to increase socialization, is an excellent example of how art therapists work and rework strategies to address client needs.

The Coping Captain group was initially conceived as a means *to combine art therapy methods with cognitive behavioral treatment strategies for anxiety treatment.* Specific ideas for the group were derived from March and Mulle's (1998) treatment protocols for children with Obsessive Compulsive Disorder. Cognitive behavioral treatment techniques such as psychoeducational activities, cognitive training to increase a sense of personal efficacy, techniques for preventing anxious or avoidant responses to feared objects and situations (response prevention), imaginal exposure to feared objects, and exposure to graded social situations were incorporated into the group design. Other resources on children and anxiety were also helping formulate specific activities for the group (Frank, 2003; Friedberg & McClure. 2002; Huebner, 2006).

The art portion of the group was designed to engage the children creatively and to give them a pleasurable way to socialize and work on their coping skills. The artistic methods added to the treatment design ranged from traditional art media to digital photography, to use of a computer and computer software called Comic-Life (Plasq Inc., 2009). The artistic goal for the group was to create a complete comic book for each child. Using digital photography each child would be the featured superhero of his or her own comic book. Each week, the children would creatively represent a coping skill. The final comic book would include all the coping methods utilized and would be presented to family members during the last group session.

Children and parents involved in the Coping Captain group were referred to the group by two psychologists in private practice. Originally, the aim of the group was to include children aged 8–12. However, parents and children interested and able to commit to the bi-weekly group for a 16-week period were younger than anticipated. The final group of 4 children included 3 boys aged 6.5 and 1 boy aged 10. Consequently, the referring therapists and the group leader discussed the appropriateness of the age disparity between group members. After careful consideration of the children and their presenting problems, the group proceeded with the four children. At the first meeting, the group leader presented the group goals and procedures to the parents. Parents were informed that they could consider the first meeting a trial run to better establish the goodness of fit between members.

It is important to note that each member of the Coping Captain group brought unique characteristics and concerns to the group. Peter, the 10-year-old member, had suffered from a stroke while in the womb. Throughout his childhood, Peter had received a diverse set of physical, speech, occupational therapy, and learning interventions. Peter had made significant gains in all areas, but was hesitant to engage socially. He was afraid of potential criticism or bullying from peers and tended to avoid them by seeking adult attention. Peter also had some stroke related vision limitations not fully corrected by glasses. Vision issues need to be considered when art tasks were designed. Chris, aged 6.5, had fears of sleeping alone in his room due to concerns of falling, as well as anxiety about bugs and snakes. Additionally, Chris was diagnosed and treated for Attention Deficit Disorder, and did have some learning disabilities that appeared to impact his reading, writing, and processing skills. Tod, another group member also 6.5, had general fears about new situations, and about socializing away from his family. Tod required occupational therapy services and speech therapy to address expressive language and coordination concerns. Kyle, the last member of the group, had specific phobias about toilets and sinks overflowing. He also had fears of thunderstorms, fears of going to new places, and struggles with obsessive thinking, sometimes of a violent nature. Kyle was also extremely fearful of social situations and had only recently been willing to talk to others on a limited basis.

During the first group, the children were introduced to each other, the group leaders, and to the idea of the Coping Captain. Together, the group looked at pictures of popular superheroes and talked about how superheroes use their super powers to fight off bad things. Each child shared a story of their own favorite superhero and talked about the special powers the hero used. While some children drew about a superhero, one child at a time worked on the cover of their comic book. Using the computer's web-cam, digital pictures were taken of each child. The photo was then imported into the Comic Life software program. With the help of the group leader, comic balloons were added to the child's photograph, and introductions were placed in the balloon, "Hi, I'm Kyle, and I'm a Coping Captain." Since each child had social anxiety symptoms, leaders did not demand interaction between group members. The goal was to ease them into social interaction and much of the work was done separately that day.

Upon review of the first group activity, the group leader realized that adjustments needed to be made to the originally planned activities. Due to the varying concerns the children faced and the developmental levels of the children, it was determined that less emphasis would be placed on drawing activities. Since the children appeared to struggle with fine motor control, and appeared self-conscious about drawing skills, the group leader felt that at least initially, drawing would hurt versus help build feelings of self-efficacy. For example, instead of the children drawing self-images as superheroes, the leaders hung paper on the wall and with the child's permission each child's form was loosely traced on a life-sized paper. Then, the group members added facial features to the tracing, colored in a costume, and added any superhero equipment needed. Children were also provided several pieces of 8.5 × 11 paper with pre-printed child figures so they could create superhero pictures in a more manageable way.

The goal of having group members create self-images as superheroes was to help bolster the children's self-efficacy in fearful situations. To add a cognitive dimension, children were asked to come up with "Super Thoughts" that would help them feel brave. These thoughts were written on pre-made cartoon balloons and added to both the larger and smaller images. Digital photos were taken of the results and imported to the software program to be added to their comic book. In addition, children were provided pre-cut foam faces in "multicultural" colors, and the added "brave face" features to the form. Any time they were afraid they could decide to use their brave face to help them face their fear.

As the group members became more familiar with each other the group leader took more risks with group content. In one session, art therapy was combined with play therapy and some exposure elements. Each group member wore a very simple superhero costume that included a simple cape, and the first letter of their name incorporated into a superman type symbol that was taped on to their shirt.

After "Super Thoughts" were rehearsed, digital pictures were taken of the children fighting one of their specific fears. After fighting the fear, a similar image of the fear in a very small size replaced the larger image. A second digital photograph was taken showing them as the master of the very small fear. As photographs were taken with one child, other group members would support them by giving some ideas of Super Thoughts or ways to fight their fears. While children appeared to have fun with the process at the time, the activity had an unexpected negative side effect.

Each group member was exposed to and mastered their own fear, but the group leader did not realize that she was also exposing other children to new fears. One member, Tod, began to have problems at home with fears he had never had before, such as fear of bugs, snakes, and sleeping alone. The new fears Tod mentioned were the very same fears that Chris had worked on in session. As a result, Tod's parents decided to remove Tod from the group, and the additional fears remitted. Individual therapy for Tod was offered as an alternative to group treatment. It is important to note that at the young age of 6.5 children may be more vulnerable and suggestible to others' images. Therefore, *exposure exercises should be restricted to individual sessions.*

For the group leader, this was an unfortunate but important part of learning, and a reminder that *elements of therapy must be delicately synthesized, and refined as needed.* Consequently, further exposure exercises were eliminated from the group and more emphasis was placed on *the learning of coping techniques, the development of self-efficacy, and increasing peer interaction to decrease social anxiety symptoms.*

In the later sessions, Peter, Kyle, and Chris learned how to use Super Thoughts, Super Breath, and Super Actions. Super Breath involved practicing techniques for slowing down of breathing to stay calm. Children were introduced to Super Actions that included using their own magic button (Frank, 2003). In an anxious situation, a child could touch their magic button (a freckle or other selected spot on their hand or arm) and think of a favorite place or activity that would help them feel better. Group members drew pictures of their favorite places or activity to help them visualize the good situation. Children were also asked to engage other senses such as recalling the smells and the sounds of the place if that was helpful to them. Images of favorite places were scanned in to the computer and imported into the comic book pages.

Final activities of the group related to painting a locking box where they could safely put away their worries, followed by the writing and locking away of their fear. Exercises on how to release tension from their body like a sponge releases water as well as interactive games were experienced. During portions of the sessions, children continued to work on their Coping Captain Comic Books.

On the last night of group, the group leader presented the children with the final printout of their Coping Captain Comic book. These books included images of themselves, their artworks, and various reminders of the activities that made them Coping Captains. The children also presented some of their coping exercises to parents and siblings and they practiced along with them. Each family received handouts that included a summary of activities that occurred during the sessions, and a survey to evaluate group outcomes.

The most significant outcomes for group members, based on feedback from the parents, was that children did learn a wide variety of coping skills, and that the social interaction had been valuable in reducing some fears about socializing. The children and families enjoyed the Coping Comic Book and felt it was a nice reminder of skills learned. However, feedback also indicated that additions to the program would make treatment more comprehensive and effective. Parents felt that adjunctive interventions and services needed to be included to help children apply the new skills in the home setting. Therefore, it would be beneficial to add individual and family sessions to fine tune strategies specific to each child, as well as family education sessions to help family members reinforce the skills learned. Unfortunately, since the Coping Captain pilot group ended this author has not had the opportunity to conduct another new and improved Coping Captain Group. On the other hand, this author is pleased to report that similar creative methods have shown positive impact in more individually structured treatment.

Ethical Issues and Culture

Those who commit to a career in art therapy commit to a study of art materials and processes, the art of relationship, and specific methods that help individuals and groups meet their expressive goals. In addition, art therapists study human developmental processes, family, social and cultural dynamics, theoretical frameworks, and the dynamic processes of health and disease. Art therapists agree to a code of ethical practice and pursue the goal of cultural competency. Many of these subjects are content areas shared across the disciplines of helping professions. However, ethical and cultural issues unique to art-based approaches are not.

Understanding Materials and Material Safety

Depending on personal levels of experience with art materials and art engagement health professionals may or may not understand media properties or their expressive potential. Unfortunately, a lack of experience in this area may lead to a poor selection of art tasks which could lead to client frustration and interference with therapeutic goals. As in other areas of therapeutic engagement, it is important to work within your scope of competency and to expand knowledge through research, training, and supervised practice. Collaboration or consultation with an art therapy professional is often indicated. The Southern California Art Therapy Association, for example, responded to its community's need during a particularly difficult time of violence in 1992 and provided art-based services to those in need. When regional artists also wanted to help children process their traumatic experiences, the association created and distributed a guide that helped the artists work positively within their competency levels (Virshup, 1993).

Fortunately, resources that explain materials and processes are available to clinicians. For example, Seiden (2001) has provided an accessible guide to materials used in art education and art therapy. His overview of material properties and their expressive potential also includes thoughtful questions and exercises that encourage exploration of art media such as drawing, painting, sculpting, and clay modeling materials. Lusebrink (1995) provides a deeper analysis of the properties of media and how people interact with those media. Her Expressive Therapies Continuum (ETC) explains kinesthetic, sensory, perceptual/affective and cognitive/symbolic responses to diverse media. No matter which professional ethics document a professional is bound by, a professional who uses art in therapy is required to use materials responsibly. Knowing health hazards and measures required for material safety is also essential (McCann, 2003).

Confidentiality, Ownership, and Care of Art Works

In many ways, the art work created in therapy is part of the treatment documentation. As such, it should be handled with the same rules of confidentiality that other documents are handled. If you wish to share your client's artwork as a part of a professional presentation, or display the person's work in an exhibit about a treatment strategy or population, formal consent should be obtained from the guardian, as well as formal assent from the child or adolescent (American Art Therapy Association, 2009).

Yet, images are more than documentation or data sources for assessment. Artworks created by clients to express and contain their feelings and concerns must be treated as an extension of the person themselves. Moon (2000) states, "The way we treat the artwork can be likened to the way we treat other people, and vice versa. When images are regarded as living, independent, personages, we are obliged to treat them with care and respect" (p. 58). In both practical and metaphoric terms, when therapists care for the artwork, they show care for the individual who created it. If a therapist is careless in handling or storing an artwork and damage is caused, a rupture in the therapeutic relationship may occur. This lack of care can be perceived as a breach of trust even when the client cannot or does not put their disappointment into words.

Curiosity: Questioning versus Interpretation

Interpretation of imagery is a controversial topic in art therapy and can also be an area of misunderstanding between therapist and client. Moon (2000) calls the mislabeling or assumptive interpretation of "ensouled" artwork as "imagicide." He states, "It is possible to harm therapeutic relationships by affixing pathological labels and negatively interpreting clients' artworks" (p. 62). Any interpretation of artwork, if attempted, should be done with care based on a solid understanding of the client, the client's family, and the culture which the client is embedded.

In many cases, interpretative errors and harmful effects can be avoided if artists and artworks are approached with curiosity and care. When a patient creates an artwork, it will be better to ask the patient to tell a story about the artwork, or elements in the artwork, than to guess at content or meaning and name it incorrectly. When working with an adolescent, for example, one might ask the adolescent to write a poem or choose a piece of music to be played in response to his or her artwork. In this case, additional creative communications may help to amplify the emotional content or meaning and will inform subsequent discussion. Treating the artist like the expert and guide to his own artwork is empowering to the patient and supports a positive therapeutic alliance.

Culture

Positive relationships with clients also depend on the multicultural competency of the clinician. The Ethical Principals of the American Art Therapy Association (2009) require that:

> Art therapists are aware of and respect cultural, individual, and role differences, including those based on age, gender identity race, ethnicity, culture, national origin, religion, sexual orientation, disability, language, and socioeconomic status and consider these factors when working with members of such groups. Art Therapists strive to eliminate the effect on their work of biases based on those factors, and they do not knowingly participate in or condone activities of others influenced by such prejudices. (p. 5)

For an art therapist, cultural competency includes an understanding of art traditions and how cultural, regional, and economic conditions impact art experiences, preferences or aversions to particular art tasks, use of media, symbols, and colors. Furthermore, as associations with symbols and colors relate to culture and world views, *therapists should be even more cautious about attempting interpretation without collaboration of the client.* When sensitivity to one's own potential for bias and competency regarding the cultural components cannot be achieved, clients should be referred to a provider who is prepared to deliver culturally attuned services.

Summary

As demonstrated in a variety of art-based therapy examples, utilizing art in therapy can be an effective and rewarding experience for both client and therapist. The creative process attracts and sustains children and adolescents' involvement in therapy because it is a normative and expressive activity embedded in diverse cultures. Groups and individuals may have different media preferences, yet, any art process selected if properly supported, can serve to express and contain feelings that may not be readily verbalized. What makes art-based therapy different than casual artmaking is that it is created, supported, and witnessed in the context of a trusting therapeutic relationship. First, client and therapist build trust through respectful and supportive art engagement. When the art product is completed, client and therapist benefit from having an art product, separate, but powerfully present, to reflect on together. Together, client and therapist may dialogue and generate a linguistic narrative that helps them makes sense of feelings and memories that have only been stored in visual and sensory modes. Through art, children and adolescents can master their stories, and perhaps change their future life scripts. However, if the therapist does not provide a physically and emotionally safe environment the therapeutic value of artmaking will not be achieved.

Therapists can prepare themselves for creative work in therapy by learning and understanding these important factors; the developmental needs of children and adolescents; the developmental stages of artistic engagement; properties and expressive potential of art media; tasks and structures for group and individual sessions; and awareness of clients' culture, values, therapeutic needs, and goals. With good preparation and imagination, therapists can provide rich opportunities to foster creativity and growth.

Activities to Extend Your Learning

- Make an artist out of yourself. If you want to others to make art with you, you need to experience it first. Pick up a copy of *The Visual Chronicles: The No-Fear Guide to Creating Art Journals, Creative Manifestos & Altered Books,* by Linda Woods and Karen Dining available via North Light Books. Have fun!
- Can't do it alone? Take an adult education art class at a local community center. Be mindful about how it feels to learn new skills and create art in the company of others. Take a risk!
- Already do art and/or crafts? Take some time to think about what makes that activity relaxing, enjoying, satisfying, and meaningful to you. Experiment with teaching that skill to someone else. Share your passion with others!
- Look up a book, magazine, or website about *Outsider Art* and find out why people who are not formally trained in art make artmaking a central part of their life. Learn more!
- Deepen your knowledge of art therapy practices. Subscribe to *Art Therapy: Journal of the American Art Therapy Association*, available at www.arttherapyjournal.org Read more!

Recommended Resources

- For more information about the art therapy profession, its professional organization, art therapy educational standards, ethical principles for practice, art therapy events, and related resources please see The American Art Therapy Association website, http://www.arttherapy.org
- For more information about Art Therapists' Code of Professional Practice and the Art Therapy Credentialing Requirements please see: The Art Therapy Credentials Board website, http://www.atcb.org
- For more information about the role of the arts in health care please see: The Society for Arts in Health Care website, http://www.thesah.org
- For an excellent example of art therapy programming for children please see: Tracy's Kids: A Pediatric Art Therapy Program, http://tracyskids.org
- For an excellent example of community-based art therapy program for youth at risk, please see: Raw Art Works, http://www.rawart.org
- For an excellent example of how making art has helped children after a disaster, please see Katrina through the Eyes of Children, http://www.katrinaexhibit.org

3.

WILDERNESS THERAPY
Creating a Context of Hope

Christine Lynn Norton

Overview of Chapter

This chapter presents wilderness therapy as an innovative intervention for struggling teens and includes the following sections:
- Introduction
- Wilderness Therapy: History and Definition
- Examples of Wilderness Therapy Programs
- Wilderness Therapy: Theoretical Perspectives
- Wilderness Therapy: Research on Treatment Efficacy
- Therapeutic Components of Wilderness Therapy
- Ethical and Cultural Considerations
- Case Study
- Summary
- Activities to Extend Your Learning

Introduction

> In wilderness is the preservation of the world.
> —Henry David Thoreau

Thoreau spoke of wilderness as an entity necessary for the survival of our world. People speak of youth in the very same way. How often we hear that the youth of today will be the future of tomorrow. Perhaps, however, it is the relationship between the two that is most important. In his book *Last Child in the Woods: Saving our Children from Nature Deficit Disorder,* Richard Louv (2005) wrote that "healing the broken bond between our young and nature is in our self-interest … because our mental, physical and spiritual health depends on it" (p. 3). Louv's book is not about therapy, but he emphasizes some of the fundamental beliefs inherent in wilderness therapy, primarily that a major "cause of emotional and behavioral disturbances in youth is the lack of significant relationship with the social and natural worlds" (Gass, 1993, p. 24).

While people have long been aware of the increase in general well-being that being outdoors can have on a person (Miles, 1987), the field of wilderness therapy seeks to harness the power of the outdoors in combination with structured therapeutic interventions in a way that promotes healing and personal growth. This holistic approach seeks to create a context of hope that may positively affect a client's emotional state by challenging previously established negative self-concepts. Kimball and Bacon (1993) provided a rationale for the application of wilderness therapy to the treatment of child and adolescent mental health in their explanation of wilderness therapy as a "frontal assault on learned helplessness, dependency and feelings of low self-worth" (p. 20).

Wilderness Therapy: History and Definition

History

Wilderness therapy is not talk therapy; it is experiential therapy with an outdoor component, and it has its deepest historical roots in the tent therapy programs for mental health patients in the early 1900s (Berman & Davis-Berman, 1995). Likewise, the early history of group work in the social work profession contributed to the development of wilderness therapy in its use of camping for therapeutic purposes (Schwartz, 1960). In the United States, therapeutic camping was pioneered by Campbell Loughmiller, whose seminal book *Wilderness Road* (1965) helped start an entire movement of residential, therapeutic wilderness programs for boys and girls with emotional and behavioral problems.[1]

The experiential education movement pioneered by Kurt Hahn, founder of Outward Bound, was also a precursor to the modern-day field of wilderness therapy (Allen & Edwards, 2003). The character-based aspects of Outward Bound provided a structured and challenging milieu for at-risk youth. Since then, other programs have replicated the Outward Bound model, and have developed all around the country (Berman & Davis-Berman, 1994). The concept of wilderness therapy developed from Hahn's character-based model of outdoor education. This educational model began being used for therapeutic purposes. Today, many in the mental health profession have realized that the outdoor wilderness environment, as well as adventure-based activities, provided unique therapeutic opportunities. Alvarez and Welsh (1990) wrote a seminal article about adventure as a model of experiential learning and its role in therapeutic change. The focus on challenge and adventure is still present in wilderness therapy today; however, new approaches also focus on the importance of simply "being in nature" (Norton, in press), reflecting ecopsychology's influence in the field (Roszak, Gomes, & Kanner, 1995).[2]

Defining Wilderness Therapy

Before providing a definition of wilderness therapy from the literature, it is important to note that wilderness therapy is practiced all over the world in a variety of different ways. This chapter presents a very American view of wilderness therapy, yet does not seek to invalidate other perspectives. To examine a global perspective of wilderness therapy is beyond the scope of this chapter.

Berman and Davis-Berman (1994) defined wilderness therapy as involving "the careful selection of potential candidates based on a clinical assessment and the creation of an individual treatment plan for each participant, where outdoor activities are aimed at creating changes in targeted behaviors and group psychotherapy is practiced by qualified professionals" (p. 140). This definition is highly clinical in nature and reflects the shift in thought towards a more intentional therapeutic approach; however, it is acknowledged that many different approaches to wilderness therapy exist. A continuum model can help to define the various types of wilderness therapy opportunities that exist for youth (see Figure 3.1). This continuum is similar to Gass' (1993, p. 74) Depth of Intervention Continuum; the difference being that *all* of the types of wilderness programs included in the Wilderness Therapy Continuum use *therapeutic* interventions as well as adventure activities in a wilderness setting.

While a broad definition of wilderness therapy may be controversial for some, Carson and Gillis' (1994) meta-analysis supports the therapeutic benefit of both clinical and non-clinical wilderness programs for delinquent adolescents, which may support a continuum model definition of wilderness therapy. Norton's (in press) research, which was done in the context of Outward Bound's Intercept program, a wilderness experience program, showed clinically and statistically significant decreases in adolescent depression and improvements in psychosocial health. Weisz, Donenberg, Han, and Kauneckis' (1995) child psychotherapy study in which paraprofessionals (those without graduate mental health degrees, but trained in therapeutic methods) yielded larger therapeutic effect sizes with children than professionals did may also support the validity of the continuum definition of wilderness therapy.

On one side of the continuum are programs like Outward Bound's Intercept program that provides "struggling teens" therapeutic wilderness experiences for personal growth and development. These programs are known as *wilderness experience programs* and are defined as "outdoor programs in wilderness or comparable lands for purposes of personal growth, therapy, rehabilitation, education or leadership /organizational development" (Friese, Hendee, & Kinziger, 1998, p. 40). In the middle of the continuum is *Outdoor Behavioral Health Care*, a modality of mental health treatment in which licensed mental health professionals provide more long term therapy in a wilderness context (Russell, 2003). Many of these programs are used for assessment and treatment of adolescents, and utilize non-clinical field staff who lead trips and work with the clinical staff to implement participants' individual treatment plans. On the other side of the continuum are programs that are known as *adjunctive wilderness*

Figure 3.1   Wilderness Therapy Continuum

therapy that provide therapy in a wilderness context as an adjunctive component of community-based mental health services. These programs are run solely by staff who "possess training and certifications in counseling, wilderness travel and activities, first responder medicine and the use of experiential counseling within a wilderness setting" (OMNI, 2009). From this wide continuum of programs, it is evident that "the history of the use of wilderness as therapy encompasses a diverse range of program responses and critical issues" (Berman & Davis-Berman, 1994, pp. 57–58).

What Is Wilderness Therapy?

Kimball and Bacon's (1993) foundational definition provides a starting point to begin to understand the actual process of wilderness therapy. According to Kimball and Bacon (1993), wilderness therapy contains: (a) a group process; (b) a series of challenges [in the outdoors]; (c) employs therapeutic techniques such as reflection and journal writing, self-disclosure, individual and group counseling; and (d) varies in length. While the definition of wilderness therapy has evolved since this definition to specify more clinical approaches, this definition highlights what most wilderness therapy programs have in common. Wilderness therapy programs usually involve some kind of wilderness expedition that may include hiking, backpacking, canoeing, canyoneering, rock climbing or mountaineering. In this expeditionary setting, youth are responsible for camp craft and wilderness travel and have to develop technical skills for mastery of outdoor activities, but must also develop interpersonal skills to live as a functioning group. The process of wilderness therapy is always sequential and seeks to gradual transfer responsibility to the participant without overwhelming him or compromising his physical or emotional safety.[3]

What Wilderness Therapy Is Not

> Wilderness therapy is not boot camp, brat camp, or survival camp. It is an intentional therapeutic intervention that does not involve punitive or withholding measures. Connor (2007) said it best: A wilderness therapy program is NOT a wilderness boot camp. These two approaches are incompatible and based on entirely different models. Boot camp programs trace their origins to the juvenile justice system and were created as alternatives to jail. Boot camp programs are designed and operate with a high degree of interpersonal confrontation as well as physical and psychological aggression toward students. Boot camps use psychological punishment including intimidation, threats, aggressive gesturing and challenges. Punishment might include being deprived of food, extra work, loss of privileges, isolation, strenuous exercise and corporal punishment. By contrast the standards of care in wilderness therapy programs allow children to experience nature, use experiential action methods that create group bonds, involve licensed mental health professionals and avoid staff use of aggression, punishment and force. (¶ 1)

This distinction is important to make because there have been several incidents reported by the media that have caused mental health professionals to second guess wilderness therapy as a viable intervention for troubled youth.

Examples of Wilderness Therapy Programs

Intercept at Outward Bound Wilderness: A Wilderness Experience Program

Intercept is a special program administered by Outward Bound Wilderness that works with at-risk teens and young adults who are beginning to demonstrate destructive behaviors. According to Outward Bound (2009),

> Intercept expeditions are designed to help students and parents discover the basis of hope for a happier and more productive future—recognizing strengths, good intent, understanding, and potential. (¶ 1)

Intercept is designed to help struggling teens ages 12 to 17 and young adults 18 to 20 years old from all over the United States wanting to transition their lives in more meaningful and positive directions. Common issues that clients on Intercept courses are referred for are:

• poor school performance
• anger management
• defiance
• low motivation
• risky behaviors such as experimenting with drugs or alcohol, sneaking out, or truancy

The Intercept program is a 21-day wilderness expedition, usually consisting of canoeing and rock climbing in Northern Minnesota, Maine, Texas, Alabama, and Florida. This expedition is broken into four stages: training, main, solo, and final. Through these stages, responsibility is gradually transferred over to the participants. During training, instructors provide participants with the wilderness skills they needed to be competent in a new, unfamiliar environment. During main expedition, the group practices these skills, while still having access to guidance from the instructors. During this phase, the group also learns communication and problem-solving skills.

During solo, each individual spends 3 days and 2 nights at a private wilderness site apart from other participants. Instructors check in with students several times a day, doing one-on-one interviews, and providing them with journaling exercises and other reflective assignments to foster self-awareness. After solo, the group participates in a final expedition where they are responsible for all aspects of their experience (i.e., cooking their own food, navigating, setting up camp, etc.). The role of the wilderness instructor at this point is to help the group maintain physical and emotional safety, while still letting the group work toward solving their own problems. Throughout the entire expedition, instructors meet with students one-on-one to work on personal goals, to help them take responsibility for why they are in the program, and to help them think about what positive changes they can make upon returning home.

This expedition is followed by a gradual transition back into society. This transition includes a visit to base camp, where participants challenge themselves through adventure activities such as white water kayaking and a high ropes course. Participants also celebrate the accomplishments of their wilderness phase with a banquet and then travel to a nearby city for their Urban Expedition. During the Urban Expedition, participants work in various community settings, performing community service projects. The Urban Expedition culminates with a parent/guardian seminar, where goals for home are articulated through a therapeutic conversation between the adolescents and their parents, facilitated by the wilderness instructor.

Experienced wilderness instructors, who are well trained in group facilitation and basic counseling skills, lead these trips. Many possess prior experience with at-risk youth, and some hold advanced mental health degrees. These trip leaders also facilitate the transitional phases of the course, both at base camp and in the urban setting. They work with parents/guardians and their children to articulate the learning that occurred during the program, and assist in setting goals for when the adolescent returns home. A Course Director, who also possesses extensive experience working with youth in the field, supervises them.

After the course, the field instructors provide follow-up for the students, their families, and any third parties involved in the referral process by creating a written narrative about each participant's progress during the program. By passing on this information, it is hoped that positive changes on the course could serve as an anchor and catalyst for future change.

Though Intercept is a wilderness experience program that is therapeutic in nature though not considered therapy, the goals of the program are very similar to more clinical wilderness therapy programs. Likewise, Intercept's quality programming and work with youth and families has earned the program the Society for Adolescent Medicine's 2009 Hillary E.C. Millar for Innovative Approaches to Adolescent Health Care, cited for working with challenging teens in such a positive manner that ultimately affects their health as it is directed at positive developmental milestones and well-being.

Catherine Freer Wilderness Therapy Expeditions: Outdoor Behavioral Health Care

(Reprinted from www.cfreer.com with permission)

Catherine Freer Wilderness Therapy Expeditions is a licensed and accredited provider of outdoor behavioral healthcare services for adolescents in need of mental health and substance abuse services. The program provides young people an alternative to traditional psychotherapy by providing them with a wilderness expedition that individual and group psychotherapy, therapeutic behavior management, and substance abuse assessment and treatment, all within a naturally healing wilderness setting.

Adolescent clients join a group of no more than eight other participants. At the beginning of the program, families and their child spend the first day participating in a family meeting. Here families and their child share their personal stories and allow our staff to observe family dynamics. At the conclusion of the meeting the participants say goodbye to their families and leave with staff members to get outfitted for the expedition. Clients are provided with all the seasonally appropriate outdoor gear they will need for their journey including hiking boots and well-fitted backpacks. The group then departs on their expedition.

Each expedition is made up of three staff members. One of these staff members is either a master's level therapist or a certified alcohol and drug counselor. Together the therapist and clients share all of the challenges that an outdoor journey and an intense therapeutic process provide. A seasoned wilderness guide, with advanced wilderness medical training and certification, directs the outdoor portion of the expedition. The other staff member is a support guide.

Counseling focuses on current issues: resolving conflicts, discussing strong feelings, processing solutions (as issues come up), seeing behavior objectively, gaining a sense of control over their behavior, and finding sources of self-confidence. Catherine Freer Wilderness Therapy Expeditions also works to resolve the frustrations, fears, angers, and felt inadequacies that have led to client's problems. These issues are further explored through individual and group therapy sessions, daily journal writing, and in psychoeducation sessions.

The first phase of the expedition (3 weeks) emphasizes self-reflection time. The client will hike quietly, except during trail breaks when staff is present to monitor the conversation and encourage it to remain productive and positive. This individual approach requires the client to spend many hours a day in thought and serious reflection about their problems, their lives, and the therapeutic feedback they are receiving from staff.

By the end of Phase I, most participants have developed insight into their past behaviors and are starting to take responsibility for their actions. In Phase II the focus moves from the individual to the group. The group-oriented focus requires the client to address how they cope with their issues in an environment of increased peer interaction. The client is supported as they begin to internalize, extend, and practice what they have learned in a supportive, therapeutic environment. They are assisted in creating a healthy peer culture that requires them to master new skills and participate in the work necessary to achieve group goals. They are granted leadership opportunities and a greater degree of decision-making power. They are given more responsibility for making choices. In this phase, the client must work their way through a level system, which motivates them to work toward specific goals, meet a clear set of expectations, and master certain tasks in order to earn more privileges, responsibilities and leadership opportunities.

In Phase II, the group moves away from daily backpacking and they spend 3 weeks mastering a different adventure activity such as climbing or horseback riding that often includes a healthy service-based project. One week is dedicated to focus on a service learning project. In addition, Catherine Freer staff work with clients on detailed planning to help create a plan for their future. They also employ some of the following techniques to aid in the transition from the program: cognitive therapy aimed at realism and self-responsibility, role-playing and the practice of difficult situations adolescents expect to encounter, and emotional preparation for the inevitably painful challenges, failures, and successes that will occur.

Catherine Freer Wilderness Therapy Expeditions are designed to help clients work through treatment resistance and denial and to foster emotional awareness and the management of feelings and relationships. Clients begin to recognize their personal strengths and weaknesses and how to make the best of both. They develop new skills, self-confidence, and a strong desire to make the changes that are crucial for their future success.

OMNI Youth Services Journey Program: Adjunctive Wilderness Therapy

OMNI Youth Services provides comprehensive youth and family counseling services to clients in the greater Chicago area. One of the services provided to youth and families as a part of their larger treatment plan is outdoor wilderness and adventure therapy. OMNI's program is called Journey: Skills For Life, and has been internationally recognized as an innovative provider of wilderness and adventure-based programming within an outpatient setting. Journey is also a part of the Outdoor Behavioral Healthcare Industry Council; however, Journey's model is unique to most wilderness therapy programs because it is a community-based program, situated within the larger context of an outpatient youth and family counseling setting. This adjunctive approach is unique and allows youth to experience ongoing treatment in a community-based setting while still being able to participate in shorter wilderness expeditions. Under the guidance of licensed professional clinicians, adolescents and/or families are challenged in outdoor settings. According to OMNI (2009):

> During a Journey experience, the wilderness confronts youth and families with the natural consequences of their good and bad decisions. Outdoor wilderness therapy trips vary from a day-long rock climbing experience to a ten day whitewater rafting trip. Journey trip locations occur throughout North America and feature activities such as ice climbing, backpacking, rock climbing, coastal kayaking, and whitewater rafting. On Journey trips, adolescents learn to work with others, improve team leadership skills, develop trust, take appropriate risks, increase self-esteem, and have appropriate fun. These intense experiences allow youth to test his or her limits as well as encourage him/her to set new personal goals. By the end of the trip, the adolescent will experience a sense of accomplishment and achievement and learn to solve problems and apply these skills to their life situations. (¶ 1)

OMNI applies cognitive-behavioral and family-systems approaches to the wilderness therapy setting and uses the client's continuing individual, group and family counseling session in the outpatient setting as follow-up services to the outdoor wilderness therapy trips. This creates a powerful opportunity for the transfer of learning and systemic change in the client's life.

Summary

Wilderness therapy has a rich historical tradition, and can be defined on a continuum from therapeutic wilderness experiences to outdoor behavioral healthcare to adjunctive wilderness therapy. Each type of wilderness therapy program combines challenge and adventure in a wilderness setting with therapeutic intent. Wilderness therapy programs are not boot camp programs, nor are they designed to be punitive or harsh with clients. Instead, wilderness therapy programs are theoretically informed interventions for working with high-risk youth.

Wilderness Therapy: Theoretical Perspectives

Experiential Learning Theories

Wilderness therapy has always drawn upon a variety of theories; however, it has been built on the philosophical foundation of experiential education, which has its roots in the experiential learning theories and philosophies of John Dewey (1938), educator, psychologist, and pragmatist philosopher. The Association for Experiential Education defines experiential education as "a process through which a learner constructs knowledge, skill, and value from direct experiences" (AEE, 2002, p. 5). Three core principles that are most related to wilderness therapy are:

- Experiential learning occurs when carefully chosen experiences are supported by reflection, critical analysis, and synthesis.
- The results of the learning are personal and form the basis for future experience and learning.
- Opportunities are nurtured for learners and educators to explore and examine their own values. (AEE, 2002, p. 5)

Itin (1999) added that experiential education requires "the learner to take initiative, make decisions, and be accountable for the results" (p. 93). Taken together these definitions create a theoretical foundation for wilderness therapy as a type of intervention that involves direct experiences that can foster personal and psychological growth through the transfer of learning.

How that personal and psychological growth and change happens is explained through a variety of different clinical theories. Just as adolescent treatment has been explained through various models, there are also many theoretical lenses that support and explain wilderness therapy.[4]

Psychodynamic Theories

While many theories have been used to explain wilderness therapy (Berman & Davis-Berman, 1994), psychodynamic theory attends to the psychosocial, developmental and relational aspects of the intervention. According to Crisp and O'Donnell (1998), wilderness therapy may involve an experiential reconstruction of developmental foundations as the individual corrects fundamental assumptions about him/herself and others. Put another way, delayed, incomplete, or unmastered developmental tasks can be addressed by tangible corrective experiences (Crisp & O'Donnell, 1998). Wilderness therapy also combats the polarization and isolation that Blos spoke of by helping the adolescent build relationships with the self, others, and the natural world. As Saari (1991) pointed out, there is a universal need for participation in the human community.

Several authors have framed wilderness therapy from an *object relations perspective*. For example, Gass (1993) believes that the metaphorical role of the wilderness trip leader as the good rapprochement mother can help adolescents deal with unresolved developmental issues as they take on developmentally appropriate tasks and challenges. In Gass' experience, both the trip leader and the group act as a safe base for the adolescent to come back to in between active phases of self and other exploration, similar to the rapprochement mother in Mahler's (1968) developmental theories. The role of the therapeutic relationship in the context of wilderness therapy cannot be underemphasized for it is this adult that provides the adolescent with an extra familial object with whom to work through past conflicts (Gass, 1993).

Much like the trip leader and the group help to create a safe space, it is also important to note that the wilderness itself may act as a *holding environment* for the adolescent, one that involves both illusion and disillusion, and helps the adolescent balance her internal mood with the external reality (Winnicott, 1965). Adolescent participants in wilderness therapy programs have reported that simply being in nature was one of the most important components of the wilderness therapy experience, validating the unique therapeutic context of the wilderness setting (Norton, 2009).

Lastly, wilderness therapy creates a context of hope as it provides depressed adolescents with what Erikson (1968 referred to as *real accomplishments*. As adolescents confront opportunities in the face of uncertain outcomes, they build a sense of mastery which helps them create an identity through the reconstruction of the story or dominant narrative they hold about themselves (Stoltz, 1998). In essence, the challenges they overcome provide them with *new evidence about themselves*. The creation of a new narrative may increase the depressed adolescent's ability to envision themselves in a new place emotionally, creating a deeper sense of future. This process of transcontextualization (Saari, 1991) is a critical factor in the treatment of child and adolescent mental health issues. For the adolescent client who is trying to resolve earlier developmental crises, this new narrative may be part of what impels them forward in their psychosocial development.

Cognitive-Behavioral Theories

Cognitive behavioral theory addresses faulty thoughts, feelings and behaviors through a systematic, goal-oriented approach. Cognitive behavioral therapies can be used in either individual or group therapy settings and have been shown to be highly effective with children and adolescents (Kendall, 2005). Applying cognitive-behavioral approaches to wilderness therapy allows for clients to experience their cognitive distortions in a group setting in which they are exposed to a variety of therapeutic techniques and challenge and adventure activities that help them address these dysfunctional cognitive, emotional and behavioral patterns. As Peterson (2009) writes about applying CBT to wilderness therapy settings:

> The particular therapeutic techniques vary according to the particular kind of client or issue, but commonly include keeping a diary of significant events and associated feelings, thoughts and behaviors; questioning and testing cognitions, assumptions, evaluations and beliefs that might be unhelpful and unrealistic; gradually facing activities which may have been avoided; and trying out new ways of behaving and reacting. Relaxation and distraction techniques are also commonly included. We hike, have team experiential activities and exercises for relaxation.

An example will illustrate the process: Having made a mistake, a person believes, I am useless and can't do anything right. This, in turn, worsens the mood, leading to feelings of depression; the problem may be worsened if the individual reacts by avoiding activities and then behaviorally confirming his negative belief to himself. As a result, a successful experience becomes more unlikely, which reinforces the original thought of being useless. In wilderness therapy programs, the latter example could be identified as a self-fulfilling prophecy or problem cycle, and the efforts of the therapist and student would be directed at working together to change this. This is done by addressing the way the student thinks and behaves in response to similar situations and by developing more flexible ways to think and respond, including reducing the avoidance of activities. If, as a result, the student escapes the negative thought patterns and destructive behaviors, the feelings of depression may, over time, be relieved. The student may then become more active, succeed more often, and further reduce feelings of depression. (¶. 1)

In this way, the application of cognitive-behavioral theories to wilderness therapy provides real life opportunities to identify and correct negative thought patterns and destructive behaviors in the context of a peer group setting, which is critical for adolescents, in particular.

Family Systems Theory

Wilderness therapy has traditionally intervened with the adolescent as the identified client. Usually families or other referral sources identify problem behaviors in youth and refer them to a wilderness therapy program so they can be away from the distractions and dangers in their lives and hopefully learn and grow. While family system theory adheres to the belief that change in one part of the system can effect change in other parts of the system, wilderness therapy programs have realized the importance of *treating the entire family system* in order to anchor the positive changes made by the young person (Berman & Davis-Berman, 1994; Harper & Russell, 2008). Applying a systemic approach to wilderness therapy recognizes that "while the participant may be present in the wilderness therapy intervention, he or she might not be the cause of the program. The clinician intervenes with the participant to effect change in the family system and other social systems in which he or she participates" (Hoyer, 2004, p. 60). For this reason, wilderness therapy programs work with families before, during and after the wilderness therapy program in order to prevent relapse or recidivism, as well as to foster protective factors in the young person's life.

In the beginning phase of the referral, families and guardians are engaged in the goal-setting process, and are an important part of the client's treatment plan. The family has to commit to working on altering negative patterns in the family system and also commit to firmly supporting the youth's participation in the program. While the youth is away at the program, the family must complete homework assignments and maintain contact with the program to support the work their child is doing. Harper and Russell (2008) refer to this time as a *meaningful separation* in which both the adolescent and the family has time and space away from each other temporarily to think about how to make their relationships at home better. At the end of the wilderness therapy process, families work together to decide next steps for the adolescent client.

In many cases, clients return home to their families and are able to use the communication and life skills they learned during the wilderness therapy program in their home environment. Sometimes, however, wilderness therapy is the first step in a young person's treatment plan, and leads to further substance abuse treatment or enrollment in some kind of residential treatment or alternative therapeutic boarding school. Regardless, of the next steps, however, applying family systems theory to wilderness therapy means having a commitment to engaging the entire family in the treatment process, and realizing that just as families create problems together, they must come together to solve problems as well.

Group Development Theory

Adventure-based group work is a core component of most wilderness therapy programs. As such, group development theory has been specifically applied to wilderness therapy. While it is commonly known that groups develop in a series of stages, McPhee and Gass' (1987) adaptation of Garland, Jones, and Kolodny's (1973) framework is very helpful in understanding interpersonal dynamics that occur in wilderness therapy groups. This framework identifies the five stages of group development as: pre-affiliation, power and control, intimacy, differentiation, and separation.

Pre-affiliation is seen as the time when group members are getting to know each other and trying to establish early on what they want their role in the group to be. There is a lot of anxiety in this stage, and with adolescents, often a lot of fronting, in that they are mainly comfortable highlighting certain aspects of their past experiences to identify with others. For many, this may start off with the sharing of negative experiences and war stories.

Power and control are dynamics that run throughout all of the stages, but logically follow pre-affiliation as the group develops their hierarchy. Issues of status, communication styles and values emerge, and the tension between group and individual needs increases. Throughout this stage and others, group members are building intimate connections with one another. The need to develop close affiliations is a normal part of adolescent development, and this can be channeled into a sense of greater group identity. At the same time, factions or cliques may occur, and the role of the trip leader begins to be challenged.

In the phase of differentiation, group members become able to identify the importance of both individual and group needs. Once participants reach this awareness, it allows them more autonomy from the trip leader. The group is also able to compare itself with other groups, again fostering a sense of group identity.

Lastly, separation represents the final stage in which group members must leave one another and find new ways of getting their needs met. The experience can either be positive or negative, or both, as group members try and transfer the learning from the group experience into their own home environment.

What makes this theory of group development pertinent to wilderness therapy is its ability to guide the therapist's interventions based on the stage of the group. In this vein, McPhee and Gass (1987) adapted each stage to applications in wilderness therapy. They identified group indicators for each stage of development that can guide the trip leader's role in each particular situation. See Table 3.1 (McPhee & Gass, 1987, p. 175) to further illustrate the authors' concepts.

The framework presented in Table 3.1 is useful for understanding group development, as well as the response of the therapist mirrors the phases of child and adolescent development and provides a clinical structure for helping a client move forward developmentally and interpersonally.

While this model of group development has gained wide acceptance and can be a useful clinical tool, it is important to consider several feminist variations that account for issues of gender, especially related to the idea of power and control. The

Table 3.1   Adapted Outline of a Wilderness Therapy Group Development Model

Stage	*Group Indicators*	*Instructor's Role*
Preaffiliation	Anxiety	Clearly define program goals and expectations and teach appropriate skills for living and traveling in a wilderness environment; develop rapport with participants
	Fear of expectations	Solicit individual's fears and hopes
Power and Control	Individuals see boundaries and affirmation for their behavior	Relate issues of power and control to the purpose of the group
	Ambivalence about being in the group: "What will I get out of it?"	Help to clarify what is appropriate and acceptable behavior and provide students with positive means of gaining power, i.e., competence in some aspect of wilderness living
		Enforce limits when needed
Intimacy	Individuals have formed a group and have established norms and values	Support positive achievements
	Group members begin to question the role of the group leader	Suggest areas where growth is needed
		Help to clarify the function of the group and the role of the group leader
Differentiation	Individuals understand the different roles that each plays	Leader begins to relate new behaviors to situations outside the group
	Individuals understand how the group is different from other groups (i.e., family, friends, at home, etc.)	Leader encourages individual group members to be flexible in their roles
		Leader is supportive yet begins to represent more societal views (i.e., views of parents, teachers, potential employers, etc.)
Separation	Individuals may feel lost without the group	Leader helps to clarify gains that have been made
	Individuals may regress or flee in attempts to deny the emotional impact	Helps to prepare individuals on how to meet their need without the group
	Members often review their experiences in a comparative way	Encourages individuals to continue the gains they've already made

relational model of group development (Schiller, 1997) mirrors the first and last stages of Garland et al.'s (1973) model; however, differs in the areas of conflict and affiliation. Schiller (1997) believes that conflict occurs much later in women's groups, and that "affiliative strivings come sooner and that safe connections are necessary prerequisites for later emergence of productive conflict" (p. 5).

Integrated Generalist Model

There is an obvious eclecticism in explaining such a dynamic modality of treatment like wilderness therapy; however, it is important to be intentional about how clinical theories work together. One of the best examples of theoretical integration in wilderness therapy is Hoyer's (2004) integrated generalist model. In this model, Hoyer links together various models of psychological and moral development (Maslow, 1962; Kohlberg, 1974; Gilligan, 1982), the stages of change model (Prochaska & Norcross, 2006, stages of group development, strategies of intervention, and an expeditionary program model based on Outward Bound. This model "identifies the concurrent processes present between individual and group systems" by considering the developmental stage of the client, the developmental stage of the group, and the client's motivation to change (Hoyer, 2004, p. 62). The integrated generalist model also assesses what is the best process for which to gradually and sequentially move the client forward developmentally.

The integrated generalist model is grounded in systems theory and a strong constructivist perspective and is influenced by the integrated generalist model of social work practice. This model has seven components which can also be applied to wilderness therapy (Hoyer, 2004, pp. 59–60):

- The behaviors of the individual are a normal and purposeful response to stress given the individual and the stressor.
- Effective interventions must target the problem, not the individual.
- Problems are interactional between the individual and the environment. A "problem" is the dissonance between the individual and the system. Either can be changed to resolve the problem.
- A clinician may intervene with a system, and individual, or the intersection of system and individual, confident that change will occur in each area.
- The clinician is an educator and mobilizer of resources including skills, motivation, and environmental supports to aid the process of change.
- The clinician's role is to promote competency and empowerment because the individual may not recognize that his or her experience can be different.
- Differential role taking, teaching problem-solving models, networking, team building, mutual aid, and self-help are the basic tasks of the clinician. It is the aim of the clinician to transfer the knowledge, skill and motivation to perform these tasks to the participant or system.

Summary

This chapter has only highlighted a few of the theories that are commonly applied to wilderness therapy. However, as Hoyer (2004) wrote, "As the field of wilderness therapy defines itself through the development of theories to explain the process of therapeutic change, it will discover that its strength lies in the complexity of that process" (p. 70). What is more important than simply selecting a theoretical orientation from which to operate is the ability to assess what theoretical framework meets the needs of the client system. After all, "the skilled clinician utilizes his or her awareness of the multiple processes at work to construct and apply intentional interventions" (p. 70).

Wilderness Therapy: Research on Treatment Efficacy

Along with these various theoretical and explanatory foundations of wilderness therapy, research has demonstrated the treatment efficacy of wilderness therapy, as well as its application for specific types of adolescent mental health issues. Wilderness therapy has been implemented for over 30 years, and empirical research has been conducted to measure the treatment efficacy of wilderness therapy and its impact on personal growth and development; however, there have been some limitations to the research due to methodological flaws in research design, inadequate sample sizes, etc. For this reason, this chapter will briefly review several meta-analyses that have been conducted on wilderness and adventure therapy, as well as several specific treatment issues on which current research has been conducted through the Outdoor Behavioral Healthcare Industry Council.

Meta-Analyses

According to Neil (2006), a "meta-analysis is a statistical technique for amalgamating, summarizing, and reviewing previous quantitative research" (¶ 1). Several important meta-analyses of wilderness and adventure programs have been conducted since the early 1990s. Carson and Gillis (1994) conducted the first meta-analysis which examined adventure-based programming with adolescents. Carson and Gillis reviewed 79 published studies, but excluded 36 of those studies for a lack of adequate statistical information or because of flawed methodology and/or research design. In the end, they reviewed 43 published studies, including 11,238 participants and also reviewed the effect sizes for each study based on 19 different outcome measures ranging from clinically-based evaluation measures to measures of locus of control and self-esteem. They found a summary effect size of .314 which indicates a moderate level of improvement for adolescent participants who participated in wilderness and adventure programs. While there were some flaws in this meta-analysis, it was the first of its kind to begin to review the widely divergent research on the impact of wilderness and adventure therapy on adolescents.

In 1997, Han conducted a meta-analysis; however, the scope of her meta-analysis was much smaller in that she focused solely on studies measuring the impact of wilderness and adventure therapy on locus of control. Han examined 24 studies that included 1,632 participants with locus of control as the primary outcome measure. This is an important concept to measure in child and adolescent mental health because of the stress-moderating effects of locus of control on psychopathology (Liu, Kurita, Uchiyama, Okawa, Liu, & Ma, 2000). Han found an overall mean effect size of .36 for locus of control, which indicates a medium shift in clients' locus of control resulting from participation in wilderness and adventure therapy programming.

Hattie, Marsh, Neill, and Richards' (1997) meta-analysis examined effect sizes in a variety of Outward Bound programs for youth and adults and measured outcomes in the six areas of: leadership, self-concept, academic achievement, personality, adventuresomeness, and interpersonal skills. Hattie et al. reported a summary effect size of .34, reflective of moderate gains in these areas. They also found an overall improvement effect size of .51, which they believe indicated that clients were maintaining change upon their return home from the Outward Bound program.

Probably the most significant meta-analysis to date is Wilson and Lipsey's (2000) meta-analysis of wilderness challenge programs for delinquent youth. Evaluations of wilderness challenge programs were meta-analyzed to assess the impact on delinquent behavior. Wilson and Lipsey found an overall mean effect size for delinquency outcomes of 0.18 ($N = 22$), equivalent to a recidivism rate of 29% for program participants in comparison to 37% for control group subjects. Interestingly, program length was not related to outcome among short-term programs (up to 6 weeks) but extended programs (over 10 weeks) showed smaller effects overall, which is the opposite of Hattie et al. (1997) who claimed that longer programs (those greater than 20 days in duration) had higher effect sizes. Aside from program length, however, the most influential program characteristics were the *intensity of the physical activities* and whether the program included a *distinct therapeutic component.* According to Wilson and Lipsey (2000), programs involving relatively intense physical activities or those with therapeutic enhancements produced the greatest reductions in delinquent behavior.

It should be noted that each of these meta-analyses included a variety of wilderness and adventure program models, as well as a wide variety of adolescent and adult clients. Some of the programs analyzed were clinical in nature, and others were considered non-clinical; however, Wilson and Lipsey's conclusions seem to support the need for a blend of challenge and adventure in combination with intentional therapeutic programming at the very least. What is clear, however, is that more rigorous and specific meta-analyses are needed in wilderness therapy in order to begin to validate the effects of wilderness program on specific clinical issues in child and adolescent mental health.

Adolescent Depression

Adolescent depression is a common mental health issue seen in wilderness therapy participants. Russell's (2002) longitudinal study found that 22.4% of adolescents participating in wilderness therapy programs were diagnosed with mood disorders. While very few studies have examined the effectiveness of wilderness therapy in dealing with adolescent depression, several outcome studies have been done on the efficacy of wilderness therapy and mood disorders.

Wall (1992) was one of the first to examine the efficacy of wilderness therapy in this area. In his study, he compared the intervention of psychopharmacology with wilderness therapy and found that wilderness therapy was as effective as the use of pharmaceutical anti-depressant medication. Wall used the Beck Depression Inventory to measure change before and after participating in a wilderness therapy program and reported that meaningful gains were made in the area of decreasing depression. Limitations of Wall's study, however, include a lack of accountability for moderating variables on participants' moods at the beginning and end of the course. Also, follow-up research was not conducted, so the long-term effects on participants' moods were not measured. However, another wilderness therapy study using the Millon Adolescent Clinical Inventory also noted pre- to post-intervention decreases in the area of depressive feelings and symptoms (Clark, Marmol, Cooley, & Gathercoal, 2004).

Russell (2003) examined the pre- to post-test outcomes of wilderness therapy participants' scores on the Youth Outcome Questionnaire (Y-OQ). In this study, participants with mood disorders showed the greatest decrease in their pre- to post-test Y-OQ scores. Yet conclusive findings cannot be derived from this study alone due to the lack of a comparison group.

Nortrom's (2004) study on the efficacy of wilderness therapy on adolescent depression found 70% of adolescent clients reporting decreased depressive symptomology after treatment. Using the Reynolds' Adolescent Depression Scale-2, Nortrom found the combined data from her total sample did not show statistically significant results in the use of wilderness therapy to help lower depressive symptoms. However, when the scores for participants that had moderate to severe depression were analyzed separately, their scores dropped significantly ($p < .02$ level). Through case study narrative data, Nortrom (2004) also found that time spent alone in the wilderness was one of the components of the wilderness therapy program that made the largest impact on depressed adolescents.

Finally, Norton (in press) examined the impact of wilderness therapy on adolescent depression and psychosocial development. The sample for this study consisted of adolescent participants in Outward Bound's Intercept program, a 28-day wilderness canoeing and camping program ($N = 21$). By using a mixed methods research design, this study collected data via pre- and post-tests using the Reynolds Adolescent Depression Scale-2 and the Measures of Psychosocial Development. These measurements were administered one week prior to the wilderness program and one week following the program. Qualitative data was also collected via pre-course paperwork and 3 month, post-course phone interviews. Additionally, this study included survey research to assess the importance of various components of the wilderness therapy intervention.

Through an analysis of pre- and post-test scores on the RADS-2 and the MPD, this study found decreases in rates of depression and increases in rates of psychosocial development. This study showed an average decrease in depression of 4.3 points on the RADS-2, which, based on other RADS-2 pre-to-post studies, was seen as a clinically meaningful level of change (Reynolds, 2002). T-tests revealed statistically significant decrease in depression scores pre/post intervention ($p < .001$) with a medium effect size of .394 (Cohen, 1988). There was also was an increase of 6.1 points on the MPD, reflecting a large shift from low levels of psychosocial development to normal levels (Hawley, 2005). T-tests revealed statistically significant increases in psychosocial health via MPD scores pre/post intervention ($p < .001$) with a large effect size of .848 (Cohen, 1988). Analysis of qualitative data revealed that related to depression, participants experienced a decrease in learned helplessness, an increase in self-worth, and an increased sense of future. While on course, youth reported no symptoms of depression. Upon completing the course, participants reported an actual elevation in mood, and 3 months post-course, 76% of youth still reported experiencing more stability in their moods.

Adolescent Substance Abuse

Adolescent substance abuse is a growing and persistent problem in the United States. According to the U.S. Health and Human Service's 2008 National Survey on Drug Use and Health: National Findings, 9.3% of youths aged 12 to 17 were current illicit drug users. For clients of wilderness therapy programs, this number tends to be much higher than the average community sample, with some programs reporting as many as 70% of clients having substance abuse problems (Catherine Freer Wilderness Therapy Programs, 2009). In many programs, substance abuse treatment has become a standard part of many client's treatment plans in order to meet the increased demand for services (Russell, 2008). This has proved to be an important contribution that is making a significant impact on young people participating in these programs. Russell (2004) conducted a follow-up study that included structured interviews with 71 clients who had substance abuse problems when they started treatment and found that 27% of them had abstained entirely from any form of substance use. Seventy-three percent had used or were still using at the time of the follow-up interviews; however, among this group, only 15% (12 families) reported substance abuse as a "significant problem" still. The other teenagers and their parents said that their use was not a significant problem.

In 2006, Russell, in partnership with the Outdoor Behavioral Healthcare Research Cooperative (OBHRC),[5] administered a long and well-constructed questionnaire, the Personal Experience Inventory (PEI), which measures substance use frequency and related personal, social and family issues. This study found that 6 months after completion of treatment, on the five scales dealing with basic substance use issues, the OBHRC clients' scores improved significantly on 8 of 10 measures, and their scores were about the same as those of the community sample, which showed a dramatic reduction of almost 60%.

Not only does wilderness therapy seem to be an emerging alternative treatment for the reduction of adolescent substance abuse, it seems to do so by improving client motivation for change. In the same OBHRC study, Russell (2006) administered the URICA scale of readiness to change, which measures what stage of change a client is in. He found that upon entering wilderness treatment, 73% of WT clients either had no interest in changing their behavior, or, though they might be thinking about it, were reluctant to take any action. The rest had stopped trying to ignore the problem and were beginning to participate in efforts to change. By the end of their wilderness treatment, none of the clients in the study were still in the first phase (uninvolved) and just 9% were in the second phase (reluctant). The other 90% were either in the active anticipation phase or, having worked through the issues and decided to quit or seriously reduce their use, had gone on to the final phase, maintenance of their decisions). Despite some regression in the follow-up phase of the study, of the 229 clients who filled out this questionnaire at 6 months, 182 fit the participation/maintenance profiles (79%) while only 21% fit the reluctant profile, and none were uninvolved (Catherine Freer Wilderness Therapy Programs, 2009).

Norton (in press) also found a high level of substance abuse among wilderness therapy participants upon referral to the program. In her mixed-methods study examining the impact of wilderness therapy on various aspects of adolescent mental health, she collected qualitative data via pre-course paperwork and structured follow-up interviews with adolescents. Though based solely on adolescent self-report, Norton found a 28.6% decrease in substance abuse 3 months post-intervention.

Family Functioning after Wilderness Therapy

Several outcome studies have been conducted on the impact of wilderness therapy on family functioning. Harper and Russell (2008) conducted mixed-methods research in order to qualitatively and quantitatively evaluate change in family functioning due to a wilderness treatment intervention. To accomplish this, they utilized (a) a qualitative examination of family involvement processes and outcomes, and (b) a quantitative evaluation of family outcomes.

Two wilderness treatment programs were evaluated in this study and were purposefully selected as member programs of OBHRC that clearly identified family involvement as an important part of their treatment philosophy.

In the qualitative phase of the study, Harper and Russell (2008) identified several core themes that emerged when examining family functioning: (a) Family crisis abated, (b) Meaningful separation, (c) Mixed emotions, and (d) New beginnings/Not fixed. These qualitative findings showed that families felt that through their adolescent's participation in wilderness therapy, they avoided a family crisis and were able to have meaningful time away from one another in which to rethink family relationships. At the same time, this separation and reunion caused mixed emotions for families, and they realized that the completion of the program was a new beginning for the family, but that neither the adolescent client nor the family system was "fixed."

Harper and Russell (2008) also administered the Brief Family Assessment Measure which looks at multiple aspects of family functioning from time spent together, to conflict, to communication. Results of the quantitative phase of the study examining family functioning showed a trend toward improvement. Self-perception scores of family functioning upon entering the program showed that 54%–75% of "normal" families have fewer family function problems than perceived by participating parents at pre-treatment. Adolescent scores show even higher problem perception than reported by parents. Parent pre-treatment to post-treatment differences showed some improvement indicated by the parent BFAM general scale showed scores moving from the 75th to 66th percentile, and adolescent pre-treatment to post-treatment BFAM general scale scores showed statistically significant change ($t(49) = 2.79, p < .01$) with a medium effect size of $d = 0.4$. While these results are promising, the study still shows that family functioning perceived by these clients is still far more problematic than the normative group, which highlights the need for increased services to families through wilderness therapy interventions.

In a study with 252 adolescent clients enrolled in a 21-day wilderness therapy program, Harper, Russell, Cooley, and Cupples (2007) developed a 60-item questionnaire that was administered to the parents/guardians of these clients at admission, 2 months post-intervention, and again 12 months following. This questionnaire was developed through practitioner-academic collaboration and measured various aspects of family functioning. At 2 months post-program, they found that clients improved on all measures, but with statistical significance on only one of the "Family Function" questions, while improving on about six of the "Adolescent Behavior" questions and two of the "Mental Health" ones. For the most part, these results were well maintained at 12 months, though family time together was statistically down some, but suicidal thoughts and ideation and school performance measures increased. Interestingly, Harper et al. also found that on one family question, family arguments actually increased upon the young person's return home. Harper et al. speculated that this may be due to an increased awareness on the part of the young person of the negative dynamics in the family that still need work. Through their findings, they make the recommendation for wilderness therapy programs to find even better ways of engaging families in the treatment process along with youth.

Norton's (2009) study, which examined the impact of wilderness therapy on adolescent depression and psychosocial development, also briefly examined changes in levels of family conflict pre-to-post intervention by comparing qualitative data gained via pre-course paperwork with structured follow-up interviews with youth. Norton's results actually differ somewhat from Harper et al.'s (2007) in that she found a 47.5% decrease in family conflict 3 months post-intervention. According to the adolescents interviewed, things were better at home and the quality of their relationships with their families had improved.

Lasting Change

The Outdoor Behavioral Healthcare Research Cooperative's (OBHRC) completed the first big outcome study on wilderness therapy using the Youth Outcome Questionnaire (YOQ) with a sample of 858 kids and their families from nine programs over a full year (Catherine Freer Wilderness Therapy Programs, 2009). The YOQ is a simple but well-researched and solid therapeutic outcome test on which higher scores indicate greater behavioral/mental health disorder. Average scores for adolescents admitted to a psychiatric hospital are about 100; average score for teens in outpatient treatment are 78; the average community adolescent score is 23. The upper limit of the normal community range is 46 (Catherine Freer Wilderness Therapy Programs, 2009). The results of the OBHRC study showed that parents rated adolescent clients with scores of about 100 upon admission.

At discharge, ranging from 3 to 8 weeks later depending on the program, the parents scored their kids at about 49, just outside the normal community range. At 3 and 6 months after discharge, the scores rose slightly, to 56 and 57, but not statistically significantly, before trending back down to 49 again at 12 months. According to OBHRC, the therapeutic and behavioral improvements that clients made were sustained over 12 months (Russell, 2002).

Russell (2004) published a follow-up study to the initial OBHRC study with the same clients. After these clients were 2 to 3 years out of the wilderness therapy program, 88 of them were called to ask how they were doing, using a structured telephone interview. These structured interviews found that 83% were doing better, and 58% were doing well or very well, while 17% were still struggling.

Limitations of Prior Research

While these two sections seem to point to the efficacy of wilderness therapy with a variety of clinical issues and therapeutic populations, it is important to understand the limitations of wilderness therapy research. Much of the existing literature on wilderness therapy includes studies that are unpublished and non-peer reviewed; some are technical reports or program evaluations, as well as internal research studies. Many wilderness therapy studies also lack a true empirical methodology and are lacking in scientific rigor. Therefore, it is essential that quality research and continued meta-analyses be conducted in the field of wilderness therapy.

Summary

While the studies included in this chapter begin to provide the reader with a broad overview of some of the research that has been conducted, this chapter is by no means a comprehensive compilation of all wilderness therapy findings. Instead, this chapter has reviewed the primary meta-analyses of wilderness and adventure therapy that have been conducted by Carson and Gillis (1994); Han (1997); Hattie et al. (1997); and Wilson and Lipsey (2000). Each of these meta-analyses points to potential effectiveness of wilderness programs that utilize challenge and adventure, along with therapeutic enhancements at the very least. Though not a formal meta-analysis, Russell's (2004) review of current research directions in wilderness therapy is the most current overview of the literature on the efficacy of wilderness therapy. This chapter also highlights the new research initiatives of the Outdoor Behavioral Healthcare Research Cooperative, and focuses on the issues of adolescent depression, substance abuse, family functioning and lasting change. It is the hope that this research will pave the way for more rigorous research in these and other important areas of adolescent mental health.

Therapeutic Components of Wilderness Therapy

Along with the research that has been conducted on treatment outcomes and efficacy of wilderness therapy with specific populations, several components have emerged as key factors in the change process of wilderness therapy.

Challenge and Adventure

According to the literature, wilderness therapy provides adolescents with real accomplishments every day (Russell, 2001), and in doing so may create a context of hope for adolescents. As adolescents confront opportunities in the face of uncertain outcomes they build a sense of mastery that helps them create an identity not only through resolution of earlier developmental fixations, but through the reconstruction of the dominant narrative or story the participant holds about themselves (Stoltz, 1998).

Crisp and O'Donnell (1998) believed that in wilderness therapy, "there occurs an experiential reconstruction of developmental foundations as the individual corrects fundamental assumptions about him/herself and others. Put another way, delayed, incomplete or unmastered developmental tasks can be learnt and or rectified by tangible corrective experiences" (p. 353). The corrective experiences an adolescent participates in are experiential. For example, in attempting to combat adolescent depression, feelings of hopelessness oppose the need and will to survive as the adolescent faces the realities associated with wilderness expedition and adventure-based activities (Handley, 1998). Furthermore, Kimball and Bacon (1993, p. 20) stated that "wilderness therapy, by design, is a frontal assault on learned helplessness, dependency, and feelings of low self-worth" by helping build problem-solving and coping skills in the face of adversity.

Professionals who utilize wilderness therapy often speak of adventure experiences as peak experiences, borrowing the term from Maslow (1962), but expanding on it to include "a series of well-designed ... activities which focus on success experiences ... to help a person break the cycles of failure and bring about an increase in that person's ability to feel good about himself" (Schoel, Prouty, & Radcliffe, 1988, p. 14). In this sense, the new success experiences gained in therapy seem to help the client reconstruct his past experiences in a meaningful, yet not wholly determinate manner. According to the literature, the peak experience itself becomes the "primary stimulus" to growth in this process (Goldenberg & Goldenberg, 1985, p. 148).

Through success experiences, adolescents may further their sense of mastery and competence by realizing and building on existing skills, talents, and personality traits that may have been "hidden" in the context of the client's past life experiences (Tippet, 1993, pp. 90–91). Because of the participatory nature of wilderness therapy, behaviors are challenged, but so are attitudes and belief systems, especially about the self. As Berman and Davis-Berman (1994) pointed out, "One of the most often discussed changes participants experience is an increased feeling of responsibility for the events in their lives" (p. 118). The literature speaks to this as an increased sense of self-efficacy, which Bandura (1971) described as the belief that one can perform a given behavior; or competence and self-mastery (as cited in Berman & Davis-Berman, 1994, p. 120). Again, it is direct experience, through such means as acquisition of skill and other forms of active participation that increases self-efficacy, and research has shown that wilderness therapy can have lasting effects in this area (Paxton & McAvoy, 1998). Russell (2004) refers to this as "promotion of self-efficacy through task-accomplishment" (p. 141).

The Wilderness Setting: A Unique Therapeutic Environment

According to Gass (1993), change often occurs through a new and unique setting that "provides an environment where [students] possess few expectations or preconceived notions about their success" (p. 6). For some, this unfamiliar environment may be a result of the activity; for others, it may be a drastic change in actual location. Many consider the wilderness to be a novel setting because it increases "pressure and intensity [and provides] rare opportunities for individual freedom ... to experiment with new psychological strategies or a fresh sense of identity" (Kimball & Bacon, 1993, p. 26). According to the literature, the wilderness setting can help facilitate positive stress to help clients use different problem-solving abilities and reach desired goals (Gass, 1993). These ideas are similar to Cozolino's (2002) thoughts on the balance between nurturance and optimal stress and may help lead to neural integration in adolescents.

The literature provides ample evidence about the unique therapeutic environment provided by the wilderness. After all, there is a difference between wilderness therapy and adventure therapy (Gass, 1993). Adventure therapy can take place on a high ropes course in the middle of the city, but wilderness therapy most often involves an expedition in the context of a remote setting. At the very least, wilderness therapy involves an exposure to an unfamiliar, natural setting, which begs the question, why is a different environment important? Why the wilderness?

In John Miles' (1987) seminal article, "Wilderness as a Healing Place," he highlighted the psychological benefits of wilderness, how wilderness enhances self-worth, the connection between wilderness and the ability to learn, wilderness as a metaphor for life, and wilderness and physical fitness. All of these concepts make wilderness a unique therapeutic environment and are clinically relevant in adolescent treatment.

In looking at the psychological benefits of wilderness, Miles (1987) cites Kaplan and Talbot's (1983) extensive literature review looking at the varying psychological benefits of a wilderness experience. Kaplan and Kaplan (1989) first developed a model of understanding the wilderness therapy process in terms of a restorative environment. This type of environment is one in which a young person can restore their connections with self, others and the natural world and experience healing in a relational context. Their findings identified three main benefits. They found that the wilderness experience brings people *a greater awareness of relationship with the physical environment and increased attention to one's surroundings.* This attunement and connection with the natural world can help the client develop a sense of attunement and connection with others. They also found that people experience *a feeling of tranquility and greater self-confidence.* Kaplan and Talbot (1983) believed these gains were made in large part because the wilderness environment forces people to give up an illusion of control, thus paradoxically acquiring an internal locus of control that they are able to utilize in difficult situations.

Along with the psychological benefits identified by Kaplan and Talbot (1983), the wilderness experience is also one that can counter isolation and anomie (Miles, 1987). Miles defines isolation as a sense of powerlessness, indifference, estrangement and separateness from self and others. As people connect with the natural world and one another, as well as find compatibility in meeting the demands of the wilderness environment, they feel less isolated and more competent. Miles believes this leads to a *greater sense of personal worth.* Miles (1987) defined anomie as a state of overstimulation in which a person is overwhelmed by life and "moves rapidly through a set of unrelated experiences in a condition of separation from other people" (p. 47). He believed that the wilderness can help slow down some of the stimuli and offer people another chance at mastery and connection of their experiences. In this sense, the wilderness may provide the perfect respite for adolescent's suffering from depression.

Wilderness also enhances the ability of youth to learn by "engaging participant's senses and increasing receptivity to stimuli in their environment" (p. 49). Building upon Cozolino's (2002) theories on the neuroscience of psychotherapy, the wilderness environment may provide people an enriched environment filled with opportunities for neural integration.

Miles (1987) also points out that the unfamiliarity of the wilderness environment is evocative, and demands action to be taken. For example, a group should travel by canoe early in the morning when the lake is calm rather than later in the afternoon when the winds are blowing and the water is rough. If the group decides to work slowly and doesn't get onto the water until later, they will be subject to a harder day of travel. This connection between the environment and one's actions is a powerful teaching tool, even for those who would normally be resistant, because "learning is necessary to solve basic problems of comfort and survival" (p. 49).

Lastly, are the *implicit physical fitness demands of being out in the wilderness environment*. Without the conveniences of civilization, participants have more work to do to live comfortably, and have to expend more physical energy to get from one remote point to another. Aside from the obvious physical health benefits, there are again healing aspects of using one's body. Stich (1983) believed that "when a person gains control over his/her physical body, as must be done in wilderness travel, there may be a corresponding gain in control in other areas" (p. 53). As well, the physical intensity and corresponding release of emotion may provide participants with an outlet for their anxiety.

Kimball and Bacon (1993) also commented on the importance of the wilderness environment. They argue that the wilderness provides an ideal setting for clinical work with adolescents. First they discuss *the removal of distractions*. In the wilderness environment, technology and all its stimuli are non-present. Second, they highlight the natural consequences of the wilderness environment in which resistant adolescents cannot escape feedback from their environment. They give the example of adolescents whose gear gets wet overnight because they did not pay attention to the tarp-pitching lesson. For these adolescents, the consequences are immediate and directly related to their actions. In this way, Kimball and Bacon believed the wilderness helps break down "inappropriate defenses and denial" (p. 26). The therapeutic use of positive stress can bring out a level of authenticity and true emotion in adolescents who are used to maintaining a "false front" (p. 26).

In all of these ways, the role of the wilderness environment cannot be separated from the action and adventure it calls forth; however, without the wild and unfamiliar elements of this environment, these particular challenges would not be evoked. While challenge is ever present in the wilderness environment, especially due to its unfamiliarity to most people, the wilderness also provides what Kimball and Bacon (1993) referred to as a "rare opportunity for freedom" (p. 26). What they may have meant by this is an opportunity away from mainstream society for adolescents to try on new aspects of their identity. This is at the core of a positive therapeutic environment and is a vital part of having a corrective emotional experience.

Contemplation

Kaplan and Talbot's (1983) research also documents three main psychological benefits of the wilderness environment: increased awareness, increased self-confidence and tranquility, and contemplation. Contemplation is the ability to reflect on one's present situation clearly. According to Kaplan and Talbot, this occurs from compatibility among the demands of the environment on the individual and the individual's ability to meet those demands. This simplicity produces a contemplative state that may allow one to access a more spiritual dimension of the human experience. Norton's (in press) research reaffirmed the importance of contemplation in the treatment of adolescent depression and psychosocial health in particular.

In Norton's study (in press), youth reported "being far away from distractions," "having time to think and reflect," and "having huge epiphanies." This process is most evident during the solo experience, a program element that many programs use to give adolescents time alone away from the group, while still under the supervision of the trip leader or therapist. During this time, a youth must consider what brought them to the wilderness program and what they would like to change. They may also take time to write letters to their parents/guardians about how they are feeling about those relationships. This is often a powerful time in which youth face some difficult emotional issues. During this time, staff are never far away and take time to check on the youth, often doing one-on-one check-ins and giving youth journal assignments to help in the reflection process. Much has been written recently about the use of solo in wilderness programs (Knapp, 2005), and while a detailed inquiry into solo is beyond the scope of this chapter, solo is a hugely important course component, and leads to greater opportunities for contemplation.

Therapeutic Group Process

The role of the group in wilderness therapy is an essential component of the treatment process (Berman & Berman, 1994). Kimball and Bacon (1993) go so far as to say that "there is no such thing as 'individual' wilderness therapy" (p. 14). While this is no longer the case in some programs, the clinical norm is still participation in a small group in the context of a wilderness expedition. In this type of setting, the group relies on one another for physical survival in some cases, as well as emotional support. The group's intrapsychic functions of providing a holding environment, being a vehicle for the second phase of separation/individuation, and providing a rich environment for transference are complemented by the interpersonal components of the group process. The development of a cooperative interpersonal framework to facilitate positive group dynamics is a critical piece of the healing process.

Kimball and Bacon (1993) took a very relational stance on the process of healing. They believed that much the same way our personalities are first shaped by our interactions with others, they can also be *reshaped* through our interactions with others in the group process. In wilderness therapy, the group process is not just a therapeutic mechanism; rather it is a critical part of survival. Participants must navigate together, cook together, and set up shelter together. The impact of one person's actions, both positive and negative, is more evident in this intense context. Out of this context, Kimball and Bacon (1993) believed that group cohesiveness occurs. This sense of cohesiveness then allows the individual participant to confront challenges, both physically and emotionally.

The idea of establishing a safe, relational base is not new to wilderness therapy group theory. Kiewa (1994) wrote about the need for cooperation in groups, especially for women. She also noted the need for a humane environment (Knapp, 1988), which includes "factors such as respect, trust, high morale, opportunities for input, growth and renewal, cohesiveness and caring" (Knapp, 1988, p. 17). These are all components that fit with Schiller's (1997) relational model, and if not present can "restrict the group as a therapeutic medium" (Cohen & Schermer, 2002, p. 103). Russell (2004) reaffirmed this idea when he called for the promotion of a therapeutic social group (p. 142).

Likewise, when considering group development in wilderness therapy, it is essential to consider the role of the group leader within group dynamics. Brower (1989) affirms that the power differential in the group is especially highlighted between participants and the group leader in the early stages of the group as the group "turns to the leader" (p. 28). This is especially true in a wilderness therapy context, and is important to consider so that the group leader can empower participants and use her power to foster safety and growth. Cohen & Schermer (2002) reaffirm the importance of the role of the group leader by referring to group dynamics as "interactive communication with or among participants, including, usually with special weight, the therapist" (p. 91). This idea provides the perfect segue to consider the therapeutic relationship between the wilderness trip leader and the participants.

The Therapeutic Relationship

Wilderness therapy involves restructuring of the therapist-client relationship (Russell, 2004). The therapeutic relationship is one in which the trip leader or therapist lives alongside the participant in a wilderness context, sharing meals, being in the same weather and sharing some of the same physical challenges. The closeness and shared experiences of the trip leader/therapist and the group fosters a higher level of adult-adolescent communication and "minimize a sense of counter-therapeutic hierarchy" (Kimball & Bacon, 1993, p. 33). Still, the trip leader is automatically in a position of authority over the participants due to his/her knowledge of wilderness skills, the terrain, the route, etc. For this reason, it is doubly important for the trip leader to establish trust between him/herself and the participants, as well as to articulate that the goal is the gradual transfer of responsibility and authority over to the group.

Gass (1993) believed that some of the power of the therapeutic relationship in wilderness therapy comes from the metaphorical role of the wilderness trip leader as the good rapprochement mother. This role can help adolescents deal with unresolved developmental issues as they take on developmentally appropriate tasks. As adolescents confront opportunities in the face of uncertain outcomes, they build a sense of mastery that helps them create an identity not only through resolution of earlier developmental fixations, but through the reconstruction of the "dominant narrative or story the participant holds about themselves" (Stoltz, 1998). The creation of a new narrative increases the depressed adolescent's ability to transcontextualize, giving him/her a deeper sense of future. The wilderness trip leader or therapist plays a key role in helping the participant discover new evidence about him/herself to help create this new narrative.

As Will (1959) wrote, "Fundamental to all psychotherapy is the development of a relationship which makes possible a further evaluation of the past and an increased participation in new experience" (p. 86). This is true for wilderness therapy as well, and is based on a sense of connectedness and genuine caring on the part of the wilderness trip leader. This empathic attunement is at the core of the trip leader's or therapist's ability to both quell and adolescent's initial anxiety, as well as to confront the adolescent's past behavior as well as engage him/her in new possibilities for the future.

In order to build a genuine sense of connectedness, however, the wilderness trip leader or therapist must satisfy a variety of roles. As Kimball and Bacon (1993) pointed out, he or she must care for the physical safety of the group; have sufficient technical wilderness skills, judgment, and personal experience; be an effective teacher; and have training in working with at-risk youth. While the current debate rages over whether or not trip leaders or mental health professionals should provide services, it is certainly the case that regardless, they are responsible for "helping youths understand the profound implications of their course experience" (Kimball & Bacon, 1993, p. 32). They become a bridge for the youth, helping them to find the relevance between what takes place during the wilderness expedition and their lives at home.

It is also critical for the wilderness trip leader/therapist to consider that he/she is a role model for the group, as Kimball and Bacon (1993) write, "often taking on mythic proportions as hero, guide and exemplar" (p. 33). For this reason, the trip leader/therapist has to be even more conscious on the level of influence he/she can have on a participant and be "orchestrators" of the process more than in control of every outcome (Kimball & Bacon, 1993). As one who orchestrates the process, assessment of group and individual needs is critical. A focus on what is therapeutic should be the main focus, rather than simply focusing on wilderness travel and living.

Again, the relationship between the trip leader/therapist and the group, much like the relationship between adolescent depression and identity formation, is *not* one directional, rather, it can be seen as having deep transference and countertransference components as well. Every trip leader must be aware of his/her own emotional make-up and past experiences when it comes to working in a difficult environment with difficult youth. Participants can often trigger deep emotional reactions in trip leaders that require excellent supervision and guidance from outside staff.

In all of these ways, both the role of the group and the role of the trip leader/therapist emulate human relationships across many different situations. Participants can experience similar interpersonal challenges in the field that they do at home, yet have the opportunity to find new ways of responding. Likewise, wilderness trip leaders/therapists can provide a new type of response to the adolescent's acting out behavior, one that can lovingly challenge and confront, while still unconditionally accepting the youth.

Parent/Guardian Involvement

In order to secure changes that youth make during their wilderness experience, wilderness therapy programs have come to realize the importance of working with the entire family system. While adolescents remain the identified client, families are often responsible meeting with therapists in person or over the phone, completing homework assignments, and participating in some kind of seminar at the end of a youth's participation in the wilderness therapy program. Recent research has shown the importance of family involvement as well (Harper et al., 2007; Harper & Russell, 2008). Norton's (2009) study found that having positive family communication at the end of the wilderness therapy program was related to decreases in adolescent depression. Some programs have even incorporated family therapy interventions in a wilderness setting (Bandoroff & Scherer, 1994).

Transfer of Learning

Many wilderness programs take the participant out of his/her familiar environment. This has both pros and cons, as often an unfamiliar environment is necessary for an adolescent to break out of old habits and negative patterns of interaction (Berman & Davis-Berman, 1994). However, the downside of this approach is that the youth may have a meaningful, yet unconnected experience that he/she will be unable to utilize back home. For this reason, many wilderness therapy programs seek to anchor the youth's experience through reflection and preparation for the return home. This is often referred to as a transfer of learning (Kimball & Bacon, 1993).

Transfer of learning involves the integration of therapeutic learning into the client's everyday life (Gass, 1993). This happens on three levels through processing and reflection of the experience. These levels include: specific transfer, non-specific transfer, and metaphoric transfer (Gass, 1985). Specific transfer results when the actual products of learning (canoeing skills, belaying, etc.) are generalized to habits, and associations of these skills are applicable to other learning situations (Gass, 1985). Non-specific transfer occurs when the specific processes of learning are generalized into attitudes and principles for future use by the client (i.e., cooperation, self-awareness) (Gass, 1985). When parallel processes in one learning situation become analogous to learning in another different situation, it is called a metaphoric transfer (Gass, 1985).

All transfer of learning is implemented by appropriately framing or structuring each experience to directly assist clients with integrating functional changes in their lives. Focusing or front-loading the experience before the activity, and processing during and after the activity is crucial to its facilitation. Wilderness therapy provides the client with corrective emotional experiences involving new learning because of the framing done before the activity and the processing that follows. Both are essential conditions for therapeutic change to occur during the experience (Gass, 1993).

Another way wilderness therapy programs seek to help the youth transfer the experience back to his/her home life is by a gradual transition back into society. Some programs utilize a sequential process where the students spend time at a base camp following the wilderness portion of the trip. They then go on to spend time in an urban area participating in community service projects. At the end of the entire experience, many programs invite families to participate in parent/guardian conferences in which families and youth are reunited to discuss the youth's progress on the trip, as well as set goals for the future. Little research has been done on the impact of these strategies at helping the youth transfer their wilderness experience to their home environment, but it is clearly an important area for future research, given that the real power of the intervention is whether or not it helps the young person upon their return home.

Follow-Up

The best way of ensuring that a transfer of learning will occur is through intentional follow-up services for wilderness therapy graduates. The experiences that young people have on a wilderness therapy program must be linked to their larger context. Outdoor behavioral health care programs do this by creating collaborative partnerships with referring professionals, and working with aftercare services and families to ensure that progress made by the client can be maintained. Adjunctive wilderness therapy programs naturally link the young person's wilderness therapy experience back to their larger social context by embedding the intervention in a community mental health setting. Wilderness experience programs provide minimal follow up and need to improve in this area.

Kaplan (1979) asserted that social workers and other mental health professionals could help maintain the positive impact of the wilderness therapy programs by establishing community-based follow-up programs that would "reinforce and sustain the positive attitudes and behaviors developed" (p. 37). She believed that a community-based program for youth who completed these programs should include the following four components: ongoing outdoor programming, community service placements, alternative education programs, and counseling (pp. 44–45). The power of the wilderness therapy intervention and its influence on lasting change may be helped by this type of intensive follow-up. This could be an exciting prospect for mental health workers who are interested in using wilderness therapy with their clients while still engaging in community-based counseling as well.

Summary

The unique therapeutic components of wilderness therapy are as follows:

- challenge and adventure
- the wilderness setting
- contemplation
- therapeutic group process
- therapeutic relationship
- parent/guardian involvement
- transfer of learning
- follow-up

Table 3.2 Wilderness Treatment Program Process, Theory and Practice

Theoretical bases		*Elements of practice*
Program theory	Program design	• Integrate wilderness and treatment • Family systems • Alone time/reflection • Metaphor • Rites of passage
	Client approach	• Nurturing and empathy • Not force • Restructure client relationship • Time and patience
Program process	Program phases	• Cleansing • Social and personal responsibility • Transition and aftercare
	Therapeutic tools	• Wilderness skills • Educational groups • Therapeutic groups • Letters to parents • Ceremony and ritual • Individual and group therapy • Solo reflection time • Nature
	Treatment team	• Assess client • Establish rapport • Patience and support • Challenge therapeutically • Individualize process • Communicate process • Prepare aftercare plan

Source: as cited in Harper & Russell, 2008

This list of important therapeutic components is well-summarized in Table 3.2, and has been integrated with elements of the program process of wilderness treatment programs from Harper and Russell (2008). This table is a helpful way of concluding this section because it pulls together the various components and also includes the therapeutic tools involved, along with the role of the treatment team.

Ethical and Cultural Considerations

Although wilderness therapy has been recognized as a powerful intervention that promotes cognitive, affective and behavioral change (Gillis, 1992), leaders in the field of wilderness therapy admit that more research is needed to understand the impact of wilderness therapy on specific emotional and psychological issues (Berman & Davis-Berman, 1994; Russell, 1999). Research questioning the effectiveness of wilderness therapy is not as prevalent. As mentioned earlier, some believe that there is no scientific evidence that supports use of these programs. This argument, however, is becoming less accepted, as more and more research is being done in the field of wilderness therapy. Others cite research that suggests that wilderness therapy can actually harm teens, particularly sensitive teens with depression (Hait, 2002). This criticism, however, seems to focus more on boot camp style programs, in which adolescents are pushed towards changing behaviors in extreme ways, such as sleep deprivation, lack of food, and aggressive confrontation. Clearly, these things are not therapeutic, and do not represent the field of wilderness therapy as a whole. Other criticisms of wilderness therapy do exist. They focus less on effectiveness, and more on the limitations of the intervention. For example, it is the nature of the logistics of wilderness therapy to be enacted via programs that take youth out of their environments and family systems for the purposes of wilderness expedition and activities. This can have positive effects, but can also cause impingements to the transference of learning by removing the intervention from the youth's everyday psychosocial context (Russell, 2002).

Likewise, the effects of wilderness therapy may be short lived if they occur without follow up or ongoing treatment. Some wilderness therapy practitioners and researchers have emphasized the importance of follow-up procedures in ensuring the continual benefits of participation (Berman & Davis-Berman, 1994; Hutton, 1988, Marsh, Richards, & Barnes, 1986). For this reason, the intervention of wilderness therapy may best serve as an adjunct modality to other forms of treatment for adolescent depression.

Still, even as an isolated intervention, Russell (2001) found that there were long-term gains, and that these gains were no different between clients who utilized aftercare services and those who returned home post-program (Russell, 2002). Some researchers (Bandoroff & Scherrer, 1994; Russell, 2001, 2002), however, agree that, regardless of whether or not aftercare is required, certain follow-up components will aid in anchoring the benefits gained through the wilderness therapy program. These components include a positive family environment, strong interpersonal connections with peers and the continuation of some kind of physical activity. Unfortunately, these components are not always built in, but rather simply hoped for.

Another limitation to consider is that participation in wilderness therapy presupposes a certain level of physical capability and may not provide enough opportunities for people with severe physical disabilities. Traditional wilderness therapy programs are not set up to serve people with physical disabilities; however, more and more programs are developing to meet the special needs of this population, as well as with people with chronic illnesses.

Traditionally, wilderness therapy programs have been set up to deal generically with at-risk, problem, or emotionally disturbed adolescents. Russell (1999) reports that wilderness therapy programs are being regarded as an alternative treatment for more seriously disturbed adolescents who are not being reached by traditional therapies; however, little consideration has been given to the impact of lumping together participants with various mental health needs. Group composition is an area of wilderness therapy that needs more consideration. Little research has been done on diagnostic groups, such as groups specifically for depressed teens, substance abusing teens, etc. The only research on group composition in wilderness therapy is related to gender, and highlights the idea that single gender groups may contribute to a more therapeutic environment, especially among sexual assault survivors (Levine, 1994).

Although Russell (1999) sees a trend of seriously disturbed adolescents participating in wilderness therapy programs, there are possible limitations in serving people who are having serious psychological crises, such as severe eating disorders, suicidal ideation and gestures, or those with severely violent behavior. The wilderness environment is simply not restrictive enough to adequately protect these clients and those around them, and they may benefit more from traditional inpatient treatment (Berman & Davis-Berman, 1994). For this reason, effective screening of participants' mental health status is essential, and more research is needed in this area.

Along with effective screening, it is critical to gain informed consent from participants and their families. While many wilderness therapy clients are not mandated to attend treatment programs, they are often sent by their families, sometimes against their will. In certain programs, intake counselors work with families to create incentives or disincentives for youth to participate, which empowers parents/guardians to have more power in the family crisis. Some programs, however, refer families who are in even greater crisis to "escort services" that come and escort the youth to the wilderness therapy program, often when they are least expecting it. While this type of extreme intervention may be perceived as the only way to get the youth into treatment, wilderness therapy programs need to be cautious about respecting the client's right to self-determination in these cases. Likewise, research needs to be done to discern whether or not treatment effectiveness is diminished for youth who are sent to wilderness treatment programs against their will compared to those who go reluctantly, but willingly. Lastly, these so-called "escort services" need to be regulated and held accountable by local governing child welfare agencies to make sure the safety and rights of the client are being protected.

Wilderness therapy programs have also been criticized for not adequately meeting the gender specific needs of women with psychological disorders. Mitten (1994) warns that wilderness programs are not always empowering for women but that, in fact, the opposite occurs: female participants become dependent on leaders not only for therapy but also for survival skills. This takes away some choice in the process of building trust by forcing women to trust their program leaders, when perhaps they are not ready for that. This could be related to Brower's (1989) aforementioned theories about the imbalance of power that the group leader naturally has during the first stages of group development.

Along with gender, issues of race, ethnicity and socio-cultural views on nature, living in community, and risk must be considered. Wilderness therapy program goals may not be in accord with cultural beliefs surrounding these things. Too often programs are designed in advance without consideration of the demographics of the client population. Research on what is appropriate for specific populations in a wilderness therapy context is necessary for program implementation. For example, according to Asher, Huffaker, and McNally (1994), women of color have emphasized the need for groups which are made up only of women of their own race, to minimize the defensiveness they often experience when joining a mixed-race program. These limitations are important to consider when studying the effects of wilderness therapy on adolescent mental health because they may be variables that affect the efficacy of the intervention.

Finally, it should be noted that primary to the ethical implementation of wilderness therapy is the promotion of physical and emotional safety of all clients and staff. While much of the risk involved in challenge and adventure activities outdoors is what is termed "perceived risk," there *is* real risk inherent in participating in wilderness travel. Factors such as weather, hydration, equipment, navigation, etc. are all keey issues to keep in mind when promoting client safety. For this reason, it is critical to provide wilderness therapy clients with adequate supervision and monitor their physical and emotional states on an ongoing basis. Likewise, all wilderness therapy programs should have backcountry emergency medical and psychological crisis intervention response plans that have been well established and rehearsed. Consumers of wilderness therapy services *must* be able to trust that these interventions are physically and emotionally safe for participants.

Case Study

(Reprinted with permission from the *Clinical Social Work Journal*)

Jesse

Jesse was a 16-year-old, Caucasian girl of European descent who was raised with her older brother in an affluent home in Colorado. Her father was an oil executive and her mother a socialite. Her family was very close, though her father was often absent from the home for work. Jesse was given everything she wanted, and her parents routinely tried to placate her by ignoring her acting out behaviors. However, after one particular incident involving drugs and alcohol that Jesse's parents described as "scary," Jesse's parents decided they needed help. After talking with administrators at her school, they realized they could no longer ignore her behaviors and decided to send Jesse to participate in a wilderness therapy program because of her substance abuse, school failure and truancy issues.

Jesse reluctantly agreed to participate in a 28-day therapeutic wilderness program that involved camping, canoeing, and rock climbing. At the end of the program, Jesse participated in an urban community service project and a parent/guardian seminar in order to begin to transfer the learning from the wilderness experience back into her daily life.

When Jesse first came to the wilderness program, her entire identity was centered on being a "pot-smoking snowboarder." She was physically very capable and acted aloof and unphased by the challenges of the program. She made everything look easy, but only connected with other participants through surface conversations about drugs, boys, and snowboarding. Only when Jesse would talk one-on-one with the instructors did she allow her more vulnerable side to be exposed.

Jesse described herself to her peers as "spoiled" and almost seemed to take pride in this. She would roll her eyes and tell stories about how she was able to "get away" with so much with her parents. In discussions with the staff, Jesse admitted that she used to feel very close to her family, but that she no longer did. She said they used to "do anything for me," but that lately, they seemed to "not care" about her anymore.

After talking with Jesse, it became clear that her parents had overindulged her at times, and that they would often step in and rescue her by keeping her from experiencing the consequences of her failures. In Jesse's case, her parents' overindulgence took on the form of excessive gratification and a lack of parental control, a common occurrence in families that are struggling (Campis, Lyman, & Prentice-Dunn, 1986). Jesse's family tried to spare her from failure and disappointment, but in doing so, prevented her from developing the coping skills she needed to handle challenges on her own. This created a false sense of self for Jesse in which she believed she would always be rescued.

However, upon entering high school, Jesse was diagnosed with a learning disability and began to struggle in school. Though her parents tried, they could not protect her from the struggles she faced. According to Jesse, she had struggled in school her whole life, but it wasn't until high school that she was no longer able to compensate. She was failing classes and said she felt very stupid. Jesse became depressed, and her parents sent her to counseling where she was prescribed anti-depressant medication. For almost the first time in her life, Jesse experienced failure and disappointment; however, she had not developed the coping skills she needed to handle this disappointment.

Instead of facing her struggles, Jesse's depression worsened and she started smoking marijuana every day. She began failing her classes, and eventually started avoiding school altogether, skipping classes and going snowboarding instead. During this time, she would spend time with an older crowd that also used drugs. Jesse joined in until smoking marijuana was a daily occurrence. Because of her drug use, Jesse refused to take anti-depressant medication. Aware of the dangers of combining the two, she chose to smoke pot instead. Eventually, she stopped going to counseling, stating it was "a waste of time." Jesse began spending more and more time "on the mountain," dressing differently, listening to different music, and calling her snowboarding friends her "family." Sometimes, after a day of snowboarding on a school day, she wouldn't even go home.

Jesse had isolated herself from her family and her school. She was trying to separate from her family without having sense of self. Jesse's new identity was created in polarization to her parents' perceptions of her, rather than an adequate self-definition that integrated her role in her family and her role with her peers. Through the intervention of wilderness therapy, the goal was to help Jesse develop coping skills needed to handle challenges and rediscover her true self.

Jesse had a turning point one day when she was rock climbing as she faced her fear of failure as well as her fear of heights. On her first climb, Jesse slipped and fell. Although she was anchored on a belay safety system, she became very upset and afraid and was yelling that she couldn't go on. "I suck at this!" "I can't do this!" These and other expletives were flowing from her mouth.

Yet, her belayer, the holder of her safety system, remained calm and encouraged her to simply breathe deeply and listen to her body. As she began to calm herself, she was reminded that she may or may not be able to complete the climb, but that it didn't matter. What mattered was the present moment of anxiety and fear, and whether or not she could move past it—because if she could move past that moment, she could move past other moments.

At that moment, Jesse started to cry, "This is exactly what happened to me when I first started snowboarding. I sucked at it, and I kept falling, but it didn't scare me. I just kept trying because it made me feel so alive, and now I don't feel alive at all. I do it to get away, to get high. Those people aren't even my friends. They don't even know the real me. No one knows the real me. I just want to finish school, but I can't. I'm stupid. I need help." Jesse was at a moment of crisis in which she faced the realization that by her true self had become hidden by an overreliance on the party girl image she had worked so hard to create.

All this time, Jesse was standing on a ledge about 30 feet up in the air; however, her belayer did not offer to lower her immediately, which would've mimicked the rescuing behaviors of Jesse's parents. Instead, her belayer asked her what she needed right then. Was she feeling okay being up there after such a long time? Did she want to come down and talk more about things? Did she want to keep climbing? Her belayer reassured her that she was still okay holding her there, that it wasn't too much weight, and that she (the belayer) was fine. Eventually, Jesse wiped off her face, and looked up. "No, I want to go on. I just need to go slowly." Jesse proceeded to ascend the cliff, and made it to the top where she turned around to relish the view. "I've never seen anything like this!" Jesse said as she looked out over the forest and the lake.

That night Jesse took time by herself and wrote a letter to her family. She told them about her experience rock climbing and the impact it had on her. She told them she was sorry for letting them down and that she knew that they sent her to the wilderness program because they cared for her. She also began to write about her hopes for how the future could be different. Jesse continued to reflect on her climb and other meaningful challenges she faced throughout the entire program. As Jesse faced her fears, she experienced her true self—one of a strong and courageous young woman who could overcome challenges, including the ones in her own life.

Discussion

Wilderness therapy is not a panacea, yet it does provide a holistic approach that can begin to address the adolescent mental health issues experientially through challenge and adventure in a unique therapeutic setting. In this case study, the issues of adolescent depression, substance abuse, family conflict and learning disabilities are highlighted as salient treatment issues that may be effectively addressed in a wilderness therapy context.

Certainly adolescent substance abuse is a chronic problem that is on the rise. Research indicates the increased risks for severe depression and suicide for many adolescents who have been diagnosed with a learning disability (Huntington & Bender, 1993). Some believe this is related to a limited range of coping skills which leave many youth like Jesse vulnerable to psychiatric illness (Bernal & Hollins, 1995). While Jesse's depression was largely related to her learning disability diagnosis, the situation was made worse by her substance abuse and isolation from her family and school.

In Jesse's case, the coping skills that she employed in grade school, no longer worked in high school, and her parents were no longer able to protect her from these failures. This changed Jesse's entire self-concept, and she began to feel so inadequate after entering high school that she avoided failure by avoiding school, and was unable to ask for help. Over time, Jesse's feelings of helplessness and dependency led to extremely negative feelings about herself, key issues that have been identified in depression (Blatt, Quinlan, Chevron, & Zuroff, 1982; Seligman, 1975).

Likewise, Jesse's identity was still fused with the illusion of perfection she had been given by her parents. To attend school and fully engage in the learning context would mean relinquishing that illusion, which would produce both guilt and grief. Instead of facing up to failure in the school environment, Jesse immersed herself in snowboarding, at which she eventually excelled. Although the negative peer culture that accompanied snowboarding contributed to her false sense of self, this was Jesse's attempt at mastery of her situation. However, Jesse's feelings of hopelessness continued because she felt that she could not move past her inadequacies and had little to no vision for her future.

While the whole of Jesse's experience in the wilderness therapy program was very influential, it is important to consider what it was that made her rock climbing experience such a turning point. In many ways Jesse's belayer became a type of parent figure; however, unlike her parents, Jesse's belayer did not rescue her in a time of crisis. Instead, she encouraged Jesse to express her feelings, ask for what she needed, and make a calm decision about whether or not to continue climbing. This support, along with the actual activity of rock climbing, provided Jesse with a holding environment, a form of ego support necessary in helping her develop coping skills and a strong sense of self.

During Jesse's participation in the wilderness therapy program, she began to attempt and complete tasks that were difficult for her. Whether it was learning how to build a fire in the rain or rock climbing, Jesse was supported in not giving up even when things were hard and failure seemed imminent to her. Each time Jesse mastered something real, she experienced a new context of hope for her future. As Jesse accomplished these tasks, her role in the group shifted as well. Jesse became a leader and received positive peer feedback from the group that they liked this "new" Jesse. Others in the group began to rely on her for help and support, and this helped build Jesse's confidence even more.

At the end of the wilderness therapy program, Jesse felt very proud of her accomplishments. She began to share other parts of herself more authentically with the group, and she was able to start talking about what she wanted from her life in the future. Jesse was able to begin a dialogue about her true self, and continued to use snowboarding as a healthy metaphor for dealing with failure, anxiety, and depression. She reflected on her strengths in learning how to snowboard, as well as everything she accomplished on the wilderness therapy program. She began to say things like, "If I can do that, I can do anything!"

Jesse's new attitude helped her parents realize the value of allowing Jesse to face challenges on her own, while still providing her the appropriate level of support. For the first time, they began to talk openly about Jesse's strengths and areas for growth and what the best learning environment would be for her. Upon returning home, Jesse and her family decided that she should transfer to a boarding school that specialized in working with students with learning disabilities. This school also had an outdoor adventure program in which Jesse hoped to participate. Jesse made a commitment to lessen her marijuana usage and started taking anti-depressant medication. She engaged in family meetings with the administration of her new school, and was able to communicate her struggles to her parents without feeling ashamed.

In order to provide follow up for Jesse, a narrative of Jesse's progress and growth during the wilderness therapy program was sent to Jesse's new school so they could help her maintain the positive changes she had made. Three months after the wilderness therapy program ,Jesse's trip leader also sent her a "letter to self" that Jesse had written during her course to remind her of her that during her climb and in her life, Jesse could persevere; she just had to go slowly, making sure to ask for what she needed along the way.

This narrative provides a good picture of some of the therapeutic outcomes of the wilderness therapy intervention; however, it is also important to understand how the various therapeutic components of the intervention influenced Jesse's situation. Table 3.3 shows the application of the therapeutic components of wilderness therapy to Jesse's case.

Summary

This chapter presented wilderness therapy as an innovative intervention in the treatment of adolescent mental health issues. Wilderness therapy has a long history in the United States of helping youth make positive changes in their lives. Wilderness therapy is still being defined, but the wilderness therapy continuum includes a variety of different models and approaches. This chapter presented various theoretical explanations of the wilderness therapy intervention and prior research with mental health issues and specific therapeutic populations. A case study was provided to give the reader a clearer picture of the wilderness therapy intervention, and how the various therapeutic components work together to affect positive change.

Wilderness therapy is a multi-faceted intervention that addresses various aspects of development and pathology on physical, affective, cognitive, behavioral, existential, and systemic levels. Wilderness therapy creates a context of hope for young people by creating space for them to begin to imagine different possibilities for their lives. It has been said that adolescence is a time in which one world is disappearing and the other has yet to appear (Deutch, 1945). Perhaps wilderness therapy can be a bridge between these two worlds, a rite of passage of sorts, in which youth can discover a new sense of self.

Activities to Extend Your Learning

- Google "wilderness therapy programs" and see what types of programs you find.
- Review the program websites and write down what theoretical approaches are used.
- Write down if any of the websites include outcome research on their effectiveness and what that research states.
- What population of youth do they serve? What types of clinical issues do they claim to address?
- Do any of the websites give testimonials from youth or parents? If so, what do people say about these programs?

Table 3.3   Application of Therapeutic Components of WT Intervention

Therapeutic Components	Application Examples
Challenge and adventure: task accomplishment	Jesse faced an intense physical and emotional challenge while rock climbing. Not only did she overcome her fear of heights, she overcame her fear of failure.
The wilderness environment: being in nature	More than conquering the cliff during her climb, Jesse experienced the rock face as a learn and grow. When Jesse got to the top of the climb, the beauty of nature was a reward for her perseverance that far exceeded her expectations or past experiences. Jesse grew to love the outdoors during her WT program and decided to join the outdoor club at her new school so she could continue to have time in nature.
Contemplation	Jesse took time to write a letter to her family after her rock climbing experience. In this letter, she reflected on what the climb meant to her and what she wanted her life to be like when she got home. As Lightfoot (1997) might have said, this experience became a sort of "talisman" for her that she reflected on over and over during the program.
Therapeutic group process	Jesse's group provided her with positive peer feedback as she made changes in her attitude and behavior. They allowed her to try on a new role as a leader and reaffirmed this role by going to her for help and support.
The therapeutic relationship	Jesse's trip leader, who was her belayer during her climb, held her safe, but did not replicate the patterns of Jesse's parents by rescuing her. Instead, she empowered Jesse to make a courageous choice on her own. In this scenario, the therapeutic relationship was greatly restructured because Jesse and her trip leader were "in it together."
Parent/guardian involvement	Jesse experienced "meaningful separation" from her family and was able to take on a new role in the family system (Harper et al, 2008). This opened up new conversations and possibilities for Jesse and her family.
Transfer of learning	Jesse was able to use her experiences during the wilderness therapy program as a metaphor for her life back home. She realized that if she could face her fears and not give up while rock climbing, perhaps she could do the same at home, especially in the school setting.
Follow up	Narrative of Jesse's progress sent to Jesse's new school where she will receive after care services and educational and emotional support for her learning disability. 'Letter to self' mailed home 3 months after program to remind Jesse of her accomplishments.
Ethical and cultural considerations	In this case scenario, Jesse was struggling with a learning disability. It is important to consider special learning needs and how they may play out in a wilderness context. Youth with learning differences may need a higher level of support and instruction in order to learn and grow in a wilderness context. Gender issues are also important to consider in this case. It was essential not to coerce Jesse into continuing her climb, as that would have been disempowering. Giving her a choice, and helping her calm herself down proved to be the best therapeutic option.

- Visit a wilderness therapy program if there is one nearby you. Take a tour and ask to talk with the staff about their program.
- Discuss any controversial issues you think are important to address in wilderness therapy.
- Make a list of therapeutic components of wilderness therapy that could be used in a community-based setting.
- Take a walk in your favorite outdoor place and take time afterwards to journal and contemplate how being outdoors made you feel.
- How might this same activity help clients?

Recommended Resources

Websites

Association for Experiential Education Therapeutic Adventure Professionals: http://tapg.aee.org/
National Association of Therapeutic Schools and Programs: http://www.natsap.org/
National Association of Therapeutic Wilderness Camping: http://natwc.org/
Outdoor Behavioral Health Care Industry Council: http://www.obhic.com/
Wilderdom: http://wilderdom.com/adventuretherapy.html

Readings

Bandoroff, S., & Newes, S. (2004). *Coming of age: The evolving field of adventure therapy.* Boulder, CO: Association for Experiential Education.

Davis-Berman, J. & Berman, D. (1994). *Wilderness therapy: Foundations, theory and research.* Dubuque, IA: Kendall Hunt.

Davis-Berman, J. & Berman, D. (2008). *The promise of wilderness therapy.* Boulder, CO: Association for Experiential Education.

Ferguson, G. (1999). *Shouting at the sky: Troubled teens and the promise of the wild.* New York: St. Martin's Press.

Gass, M. (1993). *Adventure therapy: Therapeutic applications of adventure programming.* Boulder, CO: Association for Experiential Education.

Loughmiller, C. (1998). *Wilderness road.* Austin, TX: The Hogg Foundation for Mental Health.

Louv, R. (2006). *Last child in the woods: Saving our children from nature deficit disorder.* Chapel Hill, NC: Algonquin Books.

Schoel, J., & Maizell, R. S. (2002). *Exploring islands of healing: New perspectives on adventure based counseling.* Beverley, MA: Project Adventure.

Notes

1. Loughmiller started the Salesmanship Club Youth Camp in East Texas. The camp served youth and families from the Dallas/Ft. Worth area. Today, the camp no longer provides residential therapeutic wilderness treatment, but is used by the Salesmanship Club's Youth and Family Center for shorter, school-based programs. The therapeutic camping movement is still alive and well, however, and is affiliated with the National Association of Therapeutic Wilderness Camps (see http://natwc.org/).

2. For a list of significant historical events in wilderness therapy, see http://leegillis.com/AT/2IATC/advthe.htm.

3. Outward Bound uses an expeditionary progression that involves four phases of the expedition: Training, Main, Solo, and Final which mirrors the developmental stages of life and allows for the gradual transfer of freedom and responsibility to the youth, with the goal of preparing him/her for life's responsibilities after the wilderness program. Many wilderness therapy programs have adopted similar models.

4. For a more complete overview of clinical theories in wilderness therapy go to the Association for Experiential Education's Therapeutic Adventure Professionals Preferred Practices website: http://tapg.aee.org/tapg/bestpractices/.

5. The Outdoor Behavioral Healthcare Research Cooperative is based out of Western Washington University and consists of a group of practitioners and researchers whose mission is to carry out a comprehensive research program on outdoor behavioral healthcare programs operating in North America. For more on OBHRC, go to http://www.obhrc.org/

4.
MUSIC THERAPY WITH HIGH-RISK YOUTH
An International Perspective
Carol Lotter

Overview of Chapter

This chapter presents an international perspective on utilizing music therapy with high-risk youth and includes the following sections:
- Introduction
- International Context
- Music and Adolescents
- Music Therapy: History, Definition, and Overview
- Theories of Music Therapy
- Research on Music Therapy with Adolescents
- Case Study
- Ethical and Cultural Considerations in Music Therapy
- Summary
- Activities to Extend Your Learning

Introduction

Music is …
the key of success
my hero
our culture

For me music …
is fun
is a message

When I do music …
I start writing my own words
I get rhythm
I guide people
I feel like dancing
I concentrate on it

Music …
rocks my world

makes me feel
relieves my stress
give us a message
makes me want to scream.

These powerful statements were made by high-risk adolescents who participated in a group music therapy process and are evidence of the impact that music can have on young people. This chapter focuses on music therapy as a resource and intervention with adolescents at risk with specific reference to adolescents in conflict with the law in South Africa. Tumbleson (2001) defines at-risk adolescents as: "Adolescents who are at risk of failing in some major task that is necessary to assure a happy and productive life and of being failed by one or more adults or adult driven system or institution" (p. 1). Mendel (1996) identifies the following risk factors that contribute to youth's propensity for violence and delinquency:

- They are more likely to come from families where parents are abusive and neglectful and who provide harsh or erratic discipline
- They tend to live in communities rife with drugs, crime, guns and poverty where positive role models and safe constructive recreational opportunities are scarce.
- They are likely to associate with peers who are delinquent or drug abusing.
- They are "tracked" at school into classes dominated by low achieving and trouble-making students.

This population of young people is desperately in need of innovative interventions that are developmentally appropriate. For this reason, this chapter will discuss the role of music during adolescence with reference to existing literature. From there, six music therapy approaches and a survey of relevant literature will be presented and this will form the basis from which to present a variety of examples of clinical work drawn from group music therapy with these adolescents.

International Context

The context for this chapter is the National Youth Development Outreach (YDO), a non-residential, community based organization in Eersterust, South Africa. Like many other communities in South Africa, Eersterust is dealing with the dilemmas of contemporary African society—a highly complex mixture of developed, developing, modern and traditional lifestyles. Eersterust is referred to as a *previously disadvantaged community* and is, in part, characterized by socioeconomic problems such as poverty, unemployment and crime (Ryan, 1997).

It is estimated that 15% of all criminal offences in South Africa are committed by youth under the age of 18 years. In 1999 a total of 114,773 youth were arrested for criminal offences in South Africa. This figure increased by 55,000 in 2002 to 170,224 youth arrested (Steyn, 2005). According to Steyn (2005), most accounts of anti-social behavior, including youth offending, is due to the interaction between risk factors occurring at three levels: the individual, family and community (Loeber & Dishion

1983; Rutter, Giller, & Hagell, 1998; Patterson, DeBaryshe, & Ramsey, 1997; Moffitt 1993). It is quite obvious from these statistics that the number of adolescents at risk is on the increase. YDO is, thus, attempting to respond to this growing need within its own community. YDO offers social rehabilitation to adolescents at risk, and its primary focus is adolescents in conflict with the law who have been referred by the courts. In addition to court referrals, YDO responds to community referrals via social workers, schools, community organizations and parents. In this way YDO is catering for the broader category of adolescents at risk and not just those who are in conflict with the law.

Adolescent development is one of the components of the South African National Child and Youth Care system. YDO has incorporated this component by offering the Adolescent Development Programme (ADP) as part of the social rehabilitation of adolescents at risk. Music Therapy is one of the components of the ADP.

Music and Adolescents

In order to consider music therapy as an intervention for adolescents at risk, it is important to first discuss the role that music plays during this developmental phase in a young person's life. One of the means through which adolescents explore their place in the world is through music (MacDonald, Hargreaves, & Miell 2002). According to Laiho (2004), music appears to have its strongest relevance in adolescence, and Christenson and Roberts (1998) argue that possibly the clearest marker of adolescence is a passion for popular music. MacDonald et al. (2002) refer to the media as providing important sources of information and advice upon which decisions about identity can be made. Adolescents' involvement with music in particular has attracted considerable attention in this regard. Popular music is especially prominent during adolescence as listening to music is the most preferred leisure activity and many regard music as one of their most important possessions. Tarrant, North, and Hargreaves (2002) quote Larson and Kubey (1983) as saying that "the appeal of music during adolescence stems from its ability to address salient developmental issues" (p. 135). Roscoe and Peterson (1984) state that these developmental issues include acquiring a set of values and beliefs, performing socially responsible behavior, developing emotional independence from parents and achieving mature relations with peers.

In a study by North, Hargreaves, and O'Neill (2000), three factors were identified as to why adolescents listen to music:

1. to fulfill emotional needs
2. to express oneself.
3. to create a particular self-image (impression management needs)

Tarrant et al. (2002) refer to Social Identity Theory (SIT) to explain the adolescent connection to music (Tajfel, 1981). SIT starts from the assumption that we are all members of social groups, whether these are large scale social categories (e.g., gender or race) to which one is automatically ascribed, or smaller scale categories for which membership is usually earned. The categorization of the self as a member of the in-group necessarily excludes individuals categorized as the out-group. According to SIT this categorization instigates a sense of social identity which guides behavior.

This is reinforced by Pavlicevic (2003) who refers to music as intimately connected with our sense of social self. Drawing from social psychology, Pavlicevic contends that "music contributes to our sense of being a part of a social group as witnessed not only by the music but also the dress code and behaviors" (p. 198). MacDonald et al. (2002) suggest that engagement with music is one of the means by which adolescents portray their own peer groups more positively as well as sustaining positive self-evaluation.

Laiho (2004) identifies various ways in which music acts as a resource during adolescence. These include improving coping and mental health, the ability to influence moods and psychological functioning. Music also deals with the concerns of adolescence by exploring themes such as sexuality, autonomy, love, family, identity, behavior, drugs, religion, dress code, poverty and violence (Christenson, DeBenedittis, & Lindlof, 1985; Laiho, 2004: Pavlicevic, 2003; Tervo 2005).

While music as a commodity constitutes an important aspect of adolescence, this chapter employs the term *music* in a far broader way. In recent years there has been a shift away from considering music purely as an object or commodity or as something which can be concretely defined, analyzed and described. Rather music is regarded as being socially constructed. It is context specific, a process rather than a product and an action rather than a "thing" (Pavlicevic & Ansdell, 2004; Cook, 1998; De Nora, 2000, Martin 1995, Small, 1998). Small (1998) uses the term *musicking* which he defines: "to music is to take part, in any capacity, in a musical performance, whether by performing, by listening, by rehearsing or practicing, by providing material for performance (what is called composing), or by dancing" (p. 9). All participants and processes in the musical event are connected and reciprocally shape each other (De Nora, 2003). Any musical event involves both the social and the musical and affords different possibilities according to the musical situation and how it is appropriated.

Wyatt (2002) and Zimpfer (1992) place emphasis on the unique relationship between adolescents and music and suggested specifically that juvenile treatment programmes integrate music as a means to aid offenders in working through their issues. For this reason, this chapter focuses on music therapy as an innovative intervention with adolescents at risk.

Music Therapy: History, Definition, and Overview

History of Music Therapy

The notion of music as a therapeutic medium has been both understood and practiced through the centuries in different contexts since antiquity (Gouk, 2000). On the continent of Africa, traditional communities have embraced the healing power of music over many centuries. Music therapy as an established profession, however, has been in existence for the past 50 years. In South Africa music therapy is an emerging profession; 2009 marked 10 years of music therapy as a recognized health care profession.

Ansdell (2002) describes the evolution of music therapy from its early beginnings to the present. Table 4.1 identifies Ansdell's four stages.

Table 4.1   The Four Stages of the Evolution of Music Therapy

Stage 1 (1890–1940)	Stage 2	Stage 3	Stage 4
Musicians played to patients in hospital settings	2nd World War Entertainers performed for the wounded troops; Musicians played both to and with patients	Formal establishment of the profession as a recognized health care profession.	Current review of music therapy practice … a move towards an ecological, culture-centered approach to music therapy practice. Community music therapy is an emerging discourse in the profession of music therapy.
Medical model	1968: Pioneer Juliette Alvin founded the Society for Music Therapy and first training for music therapy at Guildhall School of Music in London	Establishment of training programmes around the world	
Recreational model	1960/70s Mary Priestly pioneered her work in psycho-analytic music therapy introducing a psychological model		
Addressing social and psychological aspects of illness	1970s pioneers Nordoff and Robbins developed Improvisational music therapy through their work with handicapped children		

Defining Music Therapy

There are numerous definitions of music therapy and not one that would necessary stand as a definitive statement. Let us first consider a broad definition of music therapy. A comprehensive definition of music therapy provided by the World Federation of Music Therapy (1996) states:

> Music therapy is the use of music and/or musical elements (sound, rhythm, melody and harmony) by a qualified music therapist with a client or group, in a process designed to facilitate and promote communication, relationships, learning, mobilization, expression, organization and other relevant therapeutic objectives, in order to meet physical, emotional, mental, social and cognitive needs. Music therapy aims to develop potentials and/or restore functions of the individual so that he or she can achieve better intra- and inter-personal integration and, consequently, a better quality of life through prevention, rehabilitation or treatment. (cited in Wigram, Pedersen, & Bonde, 2002 p. 30)

Theories of Music Therapy

Music therapy is not a one size fits all profession. Rather, it is dynamic, evolving and informed by, inter alia, musicology, ethno musicology, psychology, music psychology, sociology, medical, educational, and anthropological discourses. For the purposes of this chapter, and to lay the foundation for the clinical work described later, six music

therapy approaches, i.e., Creative Music Therapy, GIM: The Bonny Method, Analytically Oriented Music Therapy, Behavioral Music Therapy, The Drum/Improvisation
Treatment Group Model, and Community Music Therapy are presented.

Creative Music Therapy

Creative Music Therapy is a music centered approach developed in the 1970s by Paul
Nordoff, an American composer and pianist and Clive Robbins, a British special needs
educator. They developed an improvisational model of music therapy. Improvisational
Music Therapy has as its departure point the innate capacity for each person to communicate in a musical way. "This innate musicality, often subsumed by the emergence,
and eventual primacy, of words is tapped in music therapy, precisely because its essential nature is emotional" (Pavlicevic, 1997, p. 118). Referring to Nordoff and Robbins
(1977), Pavlicevic (1997) speaks of the 'music child'. "Music therapy improvisation
addresses the music child—by inviting the person to express him or herself through
sounds and by reading the child/adults capacity for flexibility in organizing rhythm,
melody, tempo—as portraying the person's expressive and communicative, reciprocal
capacities" (Pavlicevic, 1997, p. 118).

    Ansdell (1995) identifies specific processes in clinical improvisation which details
how music works in creative music therapy.

- **Meeting**: Ansdell (1995) draws from Martin Buber in his work on the nature of dialogue. He draws attention to the difference between what he terms "I-it""and "I-Thou"
  relationships. In an I-Thou relationship there is a real meeting within an intimate relationship. Applying this to Improvisational Music Therapy the therapeutic relationship
  and process begins with client and therapist being very distinctly I and You. The goal
  is to move from I/You to We—a shared encounter where there is a flow of musical
  interaction. This takes place when the therapist matches the music of the client and
  allows the client to hear and experience him/herself in relation to the therapist. This
  could take many sessions to arrive at this point and there is no formula attached to
  this process. Intrinsic to this process is the client being heard and hearing themselves
  in the music.
- **Quickening**: The effectiveness of music therapy is the fact that music moves us both
  emotionally and physically. Our human bodies are organized in terms of rhythm, pulse
  and cycles. What is important to understand about many clients is that the rhythm,
  phrasing, and pulse of their bodies is disturbed through pathology. It is the basic elements of music, rhythm, melody and phrasing which help to give back to the client
  what was lost or weakened, or, in the case of adolescents at risk, under developed.
- **Creating**: Pavlicevic (1997) refers to Winnicott who formulated the concept of primary creativity. From birth humans begin creating their world. This innate capacity
  for creating includes spontaneous play and imagination. The notion of playing and
  experimenting are a natural part of a child's world. The emphasis for the child is on
  exploration and through which learns to distinguish between self and other. How the
  infant creates is largely dependent on the mother's ability to creatively adapt to the
  infant. Winnicott suggests, also that primary creativity is not confined to infancy but
  is part of life for the duration of one's life. How does this apply to Improvisational
  Music Therapy? "Winnicott's (1971) understanding of playing is a useful analogy for

extending our understanding of clinical improvisation. In playing within the potential space between itself and the mother, the baby develops the capacity for receiving ideas introduced by another.... In a similar way, when a music therapist and patient are able to create a shared musical space between them, then an intimate and dynamic inter-subjective relationship is possible" (Pavlicevic, 1997, pp. 150–151).

Ruud (1998), who talks about improvisation as play and fantasy, says that through play we enter into dialogue with outside reality, role play, and change it symbolically. In clinical improvisation, the use of music metaphorically as representing an external reality can assist the client to face and deal with that reality within the context of a supportive relationship and being known in their musical metaphor.

- **Listening**: The importance of listening in clinical improvisation cannot be emphasized enough. For the therapist, listening to the person and music of the client is perhaps more important than playing. Mention was made earlier of the therapist providing the right music for the client. Clinical improvisation implies a new way of listening where all that has been discussed thus far is brought together through the act of listening. The therapist tunes into the non-verbal cues provided by the client, listens to the emotional and musical rhythm of the client in order to relevantly give expression to their vitality affects. This in turn will invite the client to listen in a new way, perhaps to themselves, but also to the therapist within the personal-musical relationship.

Guided Imagery and Music (GIM: The Bonny Method)

GIM is a receptive music therapy approach developed by Helen Bonny, a trained music therapist and violinist, in the 1960s during her participation in a research study at the Maryland Psychiatric Research Centre. Helen Bonny's role in this research study was to select music during the experimental psychotherapeutic treatment of substance abuse and cancer patients with hallucinatory drugs such as LSD. Her curiosity was aroused, and she began to experiment solely with music with patients in an altered state of consciousness and discovered that music without the aid of drugs was powerfully evocative (Bonny, 2002). As a result of rigorous research, Helen Bonny developed over 40 classical music programmes for specific clinical intentions. These programmes are 25 to 50 minutes in duration and comprise between 3 and 5 pieces.

Bonny (1990) describes GIM as "a process where imagery is evoked during music listening" (cited in Wigram et al., 2002, p. 115). Wigram et al. also cites Goldberg (1995) in his comprehensive definition of GIM: "GIM is a depth approach to music psychotherapy in which specifically programmed classical music is used to generate a dynamic unfolding of inner experiences ... (it is) holistic, humanistic and trans-personal allowing for the emergence of all aspects of the human experience: psychological, emotional, physical, social, spiritual, and the collective unconscious" (2002, p. 115).

The premise of GIM is that music is a projective tool, and that through the images which are evoked, material from clients' unconscious world can be brought to consciousness and processed during clinical sessions (Bonny, 2002). A GIM session comprises the following structure:

1. **Pre-talk**—during which the client talks about their presenting issues and the thera-pist guides the client in setting an intention, or focus for the session. The therapist then selects the music programme appropriate to the agreed intention.
2. **Induction**—the therapist invites the client to lie in a comfortable position and guides the client through a relaxation process towards a deepened state of consciousness. At the conclusion of the induction, the therapist will inform the client that the music is about to begin and reiterates the clinical intention for the music listening
3. **Music travel**—through the use of guiding questions the therapist works with the imagery which is evoked by the music. The therapist assumes a non directive approach, guiding the client through a series of non-leading questions. The premise is to allow whatever emerges through the music and to allow that to be developed. The music can evoke powerful imagery and emotions. Clients are encouraged to confront whatever is necessary for their growth and transformation. The music is regarded as the co therapist and GIM programmes are structured in such a way that, at the conclusion of the music travel, the music is able to contain difficult experiences.
4. **After talk**—the client is invited to symbolize their experience through drawing a mandala. The therapist witnesses this silently. Only once the client has completed this do client and therapist verbally process imagery or salient issues arising from the music travel. The mandala is very often the point of departure for the processing and often provides valuable insights to unconscious dynamics at work within the client.

GIM is a very specialized technique but illustrates in a sophisticated manner the evocative power of music listening. There are numerous creative ways in which music listening can be employed in clinical work where music can be regarded as a projec-tive tool. I will refer to this later in the chapter with specific clinical examples from my work at YDO.

Analytically Orientated Music Therapy (AOM)—The Priestly Model

AOM is a developed form of Analytic Music Therapy which was founded by Mary Priestly, trained music therapist and violinist, in the 1970s. She defines AOM as:

> "the analytically-informed symbolic use of improvised music by the music therapist and client. It is used as a creative tool with which to explore the client's inner life so as to pro-vide the way forward for growth and greater self-knowledge (Priestly, 1994, p. 3)

In AOM clients are involved in active music making in the form of clinical improvisation.

The music therapist, the music and the client are jointly analyzed in order to deter-mine clinical goals and ongoing clinical work. Creative Music Therapy typically does not include verbal processing during or after improvisations with clients, whereas in AOM emphasis is placed on the salience of verbal processing after improvisations between client and therapist, which provide meaning and insight for the client. What is emphasized in AOM is the transference phenomena and the relationship between the client and the therapist (Wigram et al., 2002). An AOM session typically includes the following:

1. **Pre-talk**—client and therapist discuss what is relevant for the client in the here and now. This serves as the basis for identifying a working topic formulated into a playing rule for the joint improvisation between client and therapist.
2. **Improvisation**—the working topic is non-verbally explored through music and the therapist supports the client's music and may introduce a variety of musically interventions as and when clinically appropriate. The music can be tonal or atonal and it can include sections where either client or therapist play alone.
3. **Verbal reflection**—the role of verbal reflection is to bring to consciousness inner dynamics of the client that may have been present or evoked during the improvisation. This provides the insight necessary for the growth and transformation of the client.
4. **Final improvisation**—an AOM session is typically concluded with a clinical improvisation based on insights gained during the verbal reflection between client and therapist.

In this model we see a combination of a music centered approach similar to that of Creative Music Therapy, and a psycho-analytic approach employing music as a projective tool which serves as a canvas for the landscape of the client's inner world.

Behavioral Music Therapy (BMT)

Behavioral Music Therapy focuses on the concrete use of music for the purposes of behavior modification, including physiological, motor, psychological, emotional, cognitive, perceptual and autonomic behavior. BMT can address a variety of non musical goals such as social engagement, physical activity, communication, cognitive processes, attention and concentration, enjoyment, reduction and elimination of antisocial behavior and independence skills (Wigram et al., 2002, pp. 134–135). Wigram et al. (2002) refer to Bruscia's (1998) definition of BMT as "the use of music as a contingent reinforcement or stimulus cue to increase or modify adaptive behaviors and extinguish maladaptive behaviors" (p. 134).

Wigram et al. (2002) refer to Madsen and Cutter (1966) who identify four ways in which music is used as treatment in BMT: (a) as a cue, (b) as a time structure and body movement structure, (c) as a focus of attention and (d) as a reward. In BMT music can be regarded as a stimulus and reinforcer of non-musical behavior. It can involve teaching a client a musical skill, the use of music listening or improvisation. The primary focus of BMT is to achieve changes in the client's behavior.

The Drumming/Improvisation Treatment Group Model

Watson (2002) created the Drumming/Improvisation Treatment Group Model which was developed based on the work of Loth (1996) and Reuer and colleagues (1999). Loth used improvisation music therapy groups in a forensic setting to:

- provide opportunities for self-expression
- decrease denial of feelings associated with the client's offenses
- decrease denial of uncomfortable or difficult feelings

- provide an opportunity for a cathartic release of tensions in a safe environment
- provide a sense of control through decision making

The objectives of the drumming improvisation treatment group model include:

- to engage in group improvisation and structured music tasks independently while making appropriate choices within guidelines;
- to demonstrate a balance between leading and following by matching peers volume, tempo and style;
- to use non-verbal self-expression by use of musical elements and to verbalize their physical and psychological changes due to the improvisation.

The format of the drumming/improvisation treatment group model includes:

- a warm up/focus activity
- free improvisation
- a closing task

Community Music Therapy

Community Music Therapy is an approach to working musically with people in context: acknowledging the social and cultural factors of their health, illness, relationships and music. It reflects the essentially communal reality of musicking and is a response both to overly individualized treatment models and to the isolation people often experience within society.

In practice Community Music Therapy encourages music therapists to think of their work as taking place along a continuum ranging from the individual to the communal. The aim is to help clients access a variety of musical situations, and to accompany them as they move between 'therapy' and wider social contexts of musicking, including performances in public arenas.

Ansdell (2002) highlights a distinction between traditional Improvisational Music Therapy and Community Music Therapy. Improvisational Music Therapy works traditionally in a limited and protected manner, the work being mostly private and behind closed doors. These working practices are based mainly on psychoanalytic theoretical assumptions:

- the individual intra-psychic focus of therapeutic work
- the ethics of confidentiality
- the primacy of the therapeutic dyad
- the metaphor of the containing space

The Community Music Therapist typically works wherever music or music making is needed. "The work can be 'closed door work' where a protected space is needed for the client but more commonly there is an 'open door' approach, with a natural yet safe 'permeability' to the therapeutic frame, the safety residing as much with the therapist as the 'space'. The underlying belief in this approach is that the people music therapists work with primarily live in circumstantial communities of some sort (hospitals, clinics, schools etc.) where people's health and illness is located between and amongst the personal, social, communal and institutional context they find themselves in" (Ansdell 2002, p. 29).

As such, Community Music Therapy involves extending the role, aims and possible sites of work for music therapists—not just transporting conventional Music Therapy approaches into communal settings. This will involve re-thinking not only the relationship between the individual and the communal in Music Therapy, but also taking into account how physical surroundings, client preferences and cultural contexts shape the work (Ansdell, 2002, pp. 12–13).

Stige (2002) does not regard community music therapy as a new *paradigm* for music therapy but considers community music therapy as a concern with real world challenges, related to questions such as "What is the relationship between music therapy, community, and society?" Stige (2002) further regards community music therapy as something that is closer to an area of practice and cites Kenneth Bruscia (1998, p. 157) who defines an area of practice in the following way: "An *area* of practice is defined by what the primary clinical focus is, or what is the foreground of concern for the client, the therapist, and clinical agency" (Stige 2002, p.1). He continues by specifying that of particular relevance are: the priority health concern of the client and of the agency serving the client, the goal of the music therapist, and the nature of the client-therapist relationship" Stige (2002) offers a definition of community music therapy which is drawn from Culture-Centered Music Therapy (Stige, 2002):

> Community music therapy practices are linked to the local communities in which clients live and therapists work, and/or to communities of interest. Basically two main notions of community music therapy exist: a) music therapy *in* a community context, and b) music therapy *for change in* a community. Both notions require that the therapist be sensitive to social and cultural contexts, but the latter notion to a more radical degree departs from conventional modern notions of therapy in that goals and interventions relate directly to the community in question. Music therapy, then, may be considered cultural and social engagement and may function as community action; the community is not only a context for work but also a context to be worked with. (p. 2)

These theoretical approaches to music therapy have laid the foundation for further discussion which highlights examples of research from literature in which music therapy is employed as an intervention with at-risk adolescents in a variety of contexts.

Research on Music Therapy with Adolescents

Rio and Tenney (2002): Music Therapy with Troubled Youth in a Residential Treatment Setting

Rio and Tenney (2002) designed a music therapy programme for troubled youth in a residential treatment setting. This study, conducted through Arizona State University, sought to design a music therapy process to improve social interaction and relatedness, increase self expression and self esteem, and decrease hostile and disruptive behavior. According to attachment theory, developing relationships using music as a catalyst offers adolescents new opportunities to form healthy attachments with another in that it allows for non threatening reciprocal interaction. Residents received a varied music therapy programme that consisted of improvisation, listening to recorded music, singing, movement to music, drumming and percussion, and discussion. The music therapy treatment was organized according to five stages which could be applied to a single session or to the entire treatment process:

- focus
- trust
- leadership and identity
- group cohesion
- closure

Rio and Tenney (2002) concluded that music therapy provides an effective alternative to traditional verbal therapies and that being able to adapt music experiences to the strengths and needs of the individual is crucial in helping the adolescent develop self confidence. They stated that "there is no one music therapy method or technique that taps into adolescents' needs better than another except that which is meaningful to the person receiving treatment. Meaningful musical experiences can contribute to the development of interpersonal relationships, even significant attachments in adolescents who may not have experienced these previously" (p. 97).

Cohen (1987): Music therapy as an Intervention with Over-Controlled Offenders

Janice Cohen (1987) employs music therapy as an intervention for over-controlled offenders, adolescent as well as adult clients. These clients have fewer socially acceptable outlets. For these clients increased anxiety from non-expression of anger results in increased potential for violence. Cohen cites Bruscia (1987) as saying that "Music therapy offers the language of creative musical expression as a vehicle for therapeutic growth and change. The work of therapy can take place in the actual process of playing music through associations to the music or in the relationships that develop as a result of the music" (1987, p. 216). She employed the primitive nature of musical rhythms as the basis for providing a non-verbal pre-memory relationship with her clients. Once a sense of safety was established, music allowed the flexibility to introduce challenge while sustaining support. This could be achieved within a single musical piece alternating between steady consonants and syncopated dissonance. The active nature of music provided the opportunity to practice assertive behavior that might be discouraged on the cell block and music provided a safe container for the expression of intense emotions. A dilemma encountered by Cohen was that clients may easily have altered their behavior to please the therapist whereas this positive behavior was not generalized in their day to day functioning.

Camilleri (2002): Use of Drumming in an At-Risk Neighborhood in Manhattan

Vanessa Camilleri, a music therapist based in New York City, works with adolescents in an at-risk neighborhood in Manhattan. The use of drum circles is proving to be a valuable intervention with these adolescents. In working with students with self-esteem issues, or an inability to express feelings, she says that "Drumming can give a student a voice, amplify emotions, such as anger and help them with assertiveness" (2002, p. 262). Some of the techniques employed are:

- Once a child becomes comfortable with the tools of drumming they can use the drum to introduce themselves. Each child says their name whilst drumming and the group listens and then mirrors back.
- Listening and imitating games where one person makes a sound on the drum and the group copies it back.
- The echo game. One person makes a drum sound and then one person at a time around the circle copies the rhythm. Every sound is accepted for what it is. There is no right or wrong.
- Challenging game. Groups of children will time how fast a rhythm travels around the circle, each time discussing methods of speeding up and trying to beat their previous time.

Fouche and Torrance (2005): Music Therapy with Adolescent Group Involved in Gangs

Fouche and Torrance (2005) are the co-founders of the Music Therapy Community Clinic on the Cape Flats in Cape Town, South Africa. Their work as music therapists covers a spectrum of projects, one of which is a music therapy group with adolescents at risk of becoming immersed in gang culture. Gang activity is prevalent on the Cape Flats due to the socially fragmented nature of the community rife with social problems such as high levels of unemployment, drug and alcohol dependency, family fragmentation, overcrowded living conditions, school truancy and high levels of violence. Gangs provide a sense of belonging and provide emotional support for these boys (Dissel, 1997; Pinnock, 1998).

The music therapy work with these groups of adolescents comprises weekly sessions consisting of musicking and talking. Unstructured improvisations enable members of different gangs to explore new identities and social roles through being musicians on an equal footing making music together. "The music energizes them, gets them moving, and gives them purpose … music therapy provides an opportunity to explore different ways of relating, creating and expressing" (Fouche & Torrance, 2005, pp. 2–3). The talking component of the sessions involves the boys being given space to relate stories of their gangs and share about life in their communities.

Wyatt (2002): Music Therapy at the Seattle Children's Home with Juvenile Offenders

Wyatt (2002), who works at the Seattle Children's Home with juvenile offenders, refers to several authors who have suggested that creative arts therapies, including music therapy, add another dimension to the verbal treatment of at-risk youth.

- Skaggs (1997) describes a music centered creative arts programme for male juvenile sex offenders.
- Gardstrom (1996) suggests using music therapy interventions with juvenile offenders including group song writing, listening to music with lyrics forming the basis of

discussion and states that performance groups encourage responsibility and cooperation thus improving pro-social skills. Group music therapy presents opportunities for
at-risk youth to learn interpersonal problem solving and conflict resolution skills.

- Cohen (1987) uses song writing to help adult offenders express themselves creatively
  rather than destructively.
- That (1987) suggests that music therapy interventions allow the imprisoned individual
  to express and release feelings.

Wyatt (2002) offers 10 clinical guidelines for music therapy intervention with this
population.

- Keep the attention and motivation of troubled youth by using a variety of
  interventions.
- Incorporate music listening into the sessions.
- Use caution when selecting recorded music.
- Set consistent limits on behavior for the protection of the group members.
- Utilize proportional interventions to redirect behavior.
- Adolescents generally enjoy percussive instruments such as the djembe, conga, and
  metallophone.
- Reframe negative exchanges to engage the adolescents in the therapeutic process.
- Avoid power struggles.
- Provide structure.
- Be honest.

Wyatt (2002) concludes "that music therapy interventions for this population that
are designed to improve impulse control, challenge and stimulate thought, develop
pro-social skills and encourage meaningful self-expression will become the basis for
the effective clinical music therapy treatment of juvenile offenders" (p. 87).

*Watson (2002): Music Therapy at a Community Protection and Treatment Centre for
Adult Male Sexual Offenders*

Watson (2002) developed the Drumming/Improvisation Treatment Group Model at
the Arizona Community Protection and Treatment Centre (ACPTC). This model was
highlighted in the theory section of this chapter, and though it was designed for residential adult male sexual offenders, could equally apply to adolescents at risk. Techniques draw from rhythm-based music therapy, drumming circles and music therapy
improvisation with offender populations. Watson found that the use of this model was
effective for increasing self expression and awareness of emotions; appropriate social
interaction, cooperation; and coping skills among residents.

Watson (2002) proposes a rationale for drumming/improvisation in treatment
and refers to the following authors:

- Boyle (1988) and Gardner (1990). Drumming creates sound waves which directly
  affect the body. This direct impact of sound and vibration on the body may result in
  the sexual offender becoming aware of body sensations which thus may result in emotions being awakened or released.

- Loth (1996) emphasizes the non-verbal aspect of improvisation, especially for clients with lesser cognitive abilities.
- Hoskyns (1988) describes a model of improvisational music therapy with repeat criminal offenders on probation. A primary goal was to promote the use of *non-verbal expression* to complement the other treatment groups which were largely verbal.

The research presented in this chapter illustrates the varied music therapy techniques which can be employed when working with adolescents at risk. A case study highlighting clinical examples from group music therapy at the National Youth Development Outreach (YDO) will further demonstrate the efficacy of music therapy with at-risk adolescents.

Case Study: Clinical Examples of Music Therapy at the National Youth Development Outreach (YDO)

These clinical examples are drawn from my work at YDO over a 4-year period. The groups I worked with consisted predominantly of male adolescents between the ages of 13 and 18, who were referred to music therapy as a result of involvement in petty crime, school truancy, themselves, victims of domestic violence or arrest due to assault charges. I worked with each group referred by the courts for a period of 6 to 8 weeks. Each group process consisted of the following components: drumming and improvisation, story creation through music listening, paint what you hear and song writing.

Drumming and Improvisation

First, each session started and ended with a drumming circle using djembe drums. This provided an entry and exit point to the sessions, creating a contained space in which to work with the boys. Each boy is acknowledged by name and the same 'drumming ritual' is used each week to mark the beginning and ending of sessions.

  Drumming activities included:

- *Leader-follower* games where the boys experience how their music impacts the rest of the group as their rhythms are reflected back by the rest of the group, thus giving each participant the experience of being heard in the music.
- *Listening activities* were developed in order to address clinical goals such as developing social skills, attention and concentration.
- *Building team rhythms* where the larger group is divided into smaller groups in which participants co-operate with each other negotiating and developing rhythms.
- *Drum as container* for which participants are encouraged to view the drum as a container for any feelings they may bring to the session. During this activity the boys are encouraged to play as they wish and to 'play out' their feelings onto the drum. Here the participants experience the drum as a stress reliever and anger management tool.
- *Group improvisations* during which each participant is invited to play a rhythm whilst listening closely to the pulse of the group. There are no rules during these improvisations and the development of the music is dependent on how the group functions together. Concrete musical elements such as tempo, meter, dynamics, rhythm,

phrasing and, at times, when voice is added, melody and harmony are uniquely woven together to create music which reflects who the group is as they sound *their* music. At times other percussion instruments as well as piano and guitar are added to create a space for free improvisations providing the opportunity for self expression through a range of musical choices.

Story Creation through Music Listening

This component illustrates the use of music as a projective tool. The group engages in jointly creating a fictional story whilst listening to 5 pieces of music. The group negotiates the title, theme or subject matter of the story before the music begins. The therapist then plays the first piece of music and invites the group to think about how their story begins. At the conclusion of the music, the group then begins to create their story. The role of the therapist is to simply transcribe the story as it unfolds. Pieces 2–4 are used to allow the story to deepen and develop and the 5th piece is used to conclude the story.

The following story was created by a group who chose to have as the theme of their story, their home town, Eersterust. This is the story as it unfolded (the text is a direct transcription of the group's story).

> CD 1 (Mountain Retreat, Kogi Bridge)
> It was a small, restful town, as the new generation's children grew up. Life was lived, going with the flow. It was a quiet night, and scary.
> CD 2 (Saint-Saens: Carnival of the Animals: Wild Asses)
> There is drama in the village. They start shooting each other while there was a party. There was a mysterious feeling. They were drunk and started shooting each other. There was a car chase, the police were chasing them.
> CD 3 (Rachmaninov, Piano Concerto no. 2)
> People were hiding, they were scared. Bodies were lying helplessly. Someone was looking for them with a gun. There's blood all over the place. The police ran away—they were being shot.
> CD4 (Saint-Saens; Carnival of the Animals: The Swan)
> There was a funeral. People were crying—they want them back. Tragedy. They were upset and lost the ones they loved.
> CD5 (Rhythm of the Night: Moulin Rouge)
> Celebration of the dead—those who are dead were once in the world of crime and sin and now they can rest. People were excited. After-tears. After the celebration the village again was quiet.

From Product to Process

At the end of this process, one group member commented that 'Eersterust is not quiet and restful'. What followed was a discussion where themes from the fictional story, which had been created and negotiated by the group, became the basis from which to relate stories from their own experiences. Issues such as shooting, crime, mafia-bosses, drugs/alcohol, gangsters and glamour boys were discussed with reference to their own lives.

As the music therapist, my role in the above process was that of facilitator and scribe. The group members constructed the story in its entirety. What is important to state is that the *process* of listening, negotiating and storytelling is more valuable than the *product* itself, as it enables group participants to relate the subject matter to their own personal story.

Music Listening and Visual Representation

This activity combines music listening with visual and symbolic representations of what the music elicits.

> A long strip of newsprint is placed on the length of the floor. (A large space is required for this activity.) One can either use buckets of paint with different sized brushes, or one can provide pastels and wax crayons as well as magazines and newspaper clippings. 6 contrasting pieces of music are played in quick succession, during which the group is invited to draw, write down words or symbols and paste pictures or headlines to visually represent how the music speaks to them. Once the all the music has been played, the group is invited to walk around the piece of newsprint and identify what stands out for them. This is then used as the basis for discussion and personal story telling.

Songwriting ... Process, Product and Performance

This particular example illustrates three aspects of songwriting and why it is a valuable technique to include in a music therapy process with adolescents at risk. I will firstly describe the *process*. I invited the group to write a song as a message to their peers to reflect a different value system as a result of their participation in the Adolescent Development Programme. Dudu arrived the following week with the words of a song entitled "Working for a Brighter Future."

He presented the song to the group, and I suggested that they work together on composing the music for the lyrics. Over the next three sessions, the group began to create the song with each group member contributing ideas and playing a role. The group decided to rap the song and each person was assigned their part in the performance of the song.

As I reflected on the words in preparation for the next session, Nike's slogan "Just do it" flashed before me and with a slight play on words suggested to the group the phrase "Just don't do it" as this seemed to encapsulate the message of the song. The group embraced this and during the next rehearsal of the song the group asked me to add a piano part whilst they sang "Just don't do it". We negotiated this until it felt right for all involved. The process was about everyone in the group being affirmed for their contribution, it was about collaboration and it was about working towards a common goal.

Second, it is necessary to state that the *product emerged from within the process* I have just described. This resulted in every group member owning the song as theirs, although the initial idea was Dudu's inspiration and contribution. The group re-titled the song as "Just Don't Do It" after they had re-worked it and made it their own.

Just Don't Do It (Working for a Brighter Future)

> *Dudu's[1] Song*
> **Verse 1** (said by the group)
> This message is from our future leaders, our young stars, our youth, US!
> Just don't do it
> Just don't do it
> Just don't do it
> Just don't do it
> **Verse 2**
> Please guys, drugs and crime are no solution to any problem in life,
> Instead they lead one to end up in jail or dead
> Just don't do it
> Just don't do it
> **Chorus**
> Today's youth have no future
> Due to the use of dangerous substances
> It leads them to steal and commit a lot of crime
> Just don't do it
> Just don't do it
> **Verse 3**
> Parents, teachers, the police and the community
> Must stand together to fight against evil deeds
> Just don't do it
> Just don't do it
> Said: Please guys, just don't do it
> **Message**
> We as the youth are ignorant of things that destroy our lives.
> Peer pressure is our enemy.
> When you go down friends won't be there to lift you up

In our final session, we invited musicians from the community to *perform* the song with the group. A keyboardist, vocalist and drummer worked with the group and, after further developing the song, they performed it together. At one stage one of the musicians invited the soloist (Dudu) to improvise on the line "Just don't do it" while the keyboardist played a predictable chord sequence. This was one of those magical moments when the music simply happens and spontaneously takes on a life of its own.

While music therapy often takes place in a contained clinical space shared only by clients and therapist, here we see the process of creating a song, moving beyond the boundary of the therapy space into a wider space, sharing and collaborating with the wider community resulting in their voice being heard, performing new identities and social roles and impacting their community in a positive, productive manner. According to Derrington (2005):

Songwriting increases confidence and independence. The production of a song can provide a real sense of achievement. It can help turn around negative ways of relating to others into positive interactions because the work is a shared process and based on the therapeutic paradigm of listening and supporting. The subject matter in songs can be negative and sometimes violent but the structured and interactive work of putting ideas into song is a therapeutic intervention, which is managed in the confidential and containable therapy setting. (p. 71)

Ethical and Cultural Considerations in Music Therapy

Music therapy practice and research occurs across a range of institutional, private practice, community and public settings. Music therapy clients are diverse in terms of background, culture, age, level of functioning, diagnosis, level of education and other demographic and social markers. Of fundamental importance to any therapeutic process is the respect of each client in terms of privacy, confidentiality and respect of client rights. Music therapists are bound by the rules and ethical code of each country's health regulation body. In South Africa music therapists are governed by the Health Professions Council of South Africa.

The culturally diverse reality of the South African context offers many challenges and opportunities for music therapy practitioners. Brown (2002) highlights the ethical responsibility of music therapists to be aware of their own beliefs and values, to research the culture and context of clients and therapy settings, as well as the responsibility to not engage in culturally insensitive behavior. This awareness impacts not only on the inter-personal relationship between client/s and therapist but on the inter-musical relationship between client/s and therapist.

Due to the powerful visual and audio qualities of music, clinical work is often video or audio recorded. This is most often used for analysis purposes as micro moments in improvisations cannot be recalled after an improvisation. Recordings are also played to clients to enable them to hear themselves and the impact they have on the music. In this regard, it is standard practice for music therapists to obtain the informed consent of clients. Where clients are unable to personally grant consent, due to impaired functioning or being under age, it is imperative that a guardian or institutional representative sign on their behalf.

The term *schizophonia* has been used to refers to 'musics which have been disconnected from their original contexts of use and produced for consumption in other contexts' (Stige, 2002 p. 67). This refers specifically to World Music, which is becoming increasingly popular and available to the consumer. There is some debate around whether Therapy Music could be removed from its therapeutic context, considered an art form and listened to for its own value. Stige (2002) highlights the ethical considerations of this notion in terms of who this benefits, the rights and position of the client and the tendency of therapists to select musically interesting clients for their own benefit. Whilst this is not standard practice amongst music therapists it is important to consider and could become more relevant in the future.

Increasingly music therapists are including performance as part of the music therapy process with individuals and groups. This is particularly relevant to community music therapy. Turry (2005) highlights potential pitfalls of performance: "If success is measured on how the performance is perceived rather than on the effect on the client's overall progress, it could be harmful to the client" (p. 21). At all costs, performance within a music therapy process should protect the rights and well-being of clients. Turry identifies the following assessment questions to consider:

- How does the client relate to others?
- How does the client relate to the therapist and/or peers after the performance?
- Does the history of the client give any indication of the possible effect of performing as part of the therapy process?
- Does the performance process enhance the therapeutic relationship? (p. 23)

It is equally essential that music therapists develop critical self-awareness in order to recognize when performance is included in the therapy process to benefit the therapist instead of the client (e.g. there is often the need for music therapists to showcase the efficacy of the work for funding and employment purposes). Critical evaluation is required under these circumstances to ensure the well-being of the client.

In addition to the above-mentioned considerations the role of the music in the therapy process requires scrutiny. This chapter has highlighted the benefits of music as a therapeutic medium. It may be important, then, to consider when music may be considered harmful to clients.

Ahmadi (2009) in discussing the role of so-called *hard and heavy music* as a coping method highlights the following considerations: ' A variety of problems like teenage pregnancy, alcohol and drug use, homicide and suicide are thought to be either directly or indirectly dealt with or strongly implied in hard and heavy music genres, such as heavy metal music. In some cases, the lyrics in this kind of music communicate potentially harmful health messages' (p. 1). This is not to say that this genre may not offer value to the therapeutic process, but it does highlight the necessity for therapists to exercise caution when music is selected for sessions and to monitor, in the clinical setting, when music is not beneficial to clients and make the necessary adaptations.

Music created with clients in any music therapy process, whether it be in a traditional therapeutic setting with an individual client or in a public performance as part of the music therapy process for an individual or a group, is primarily for the benefit and well being of the client.

Summary

This chapter presented music therapy as an intervention with youth at risk. The history of music therapy was briefly described and various music therapy approaches were discussed. The clinical examples drawn from a variety of music therapy settings from existing literature as well as my own music therapy work in South Africa illustrated the efficacy of music as a resource for working with youth at risk. These examples demonstrated how music therapy affords psycho-social benefits to youth at risk as it provides a non-verbal, creative medium for self-expression in a safe, contained therapeutic space.

Activities to Extend Your Learning

- Consult YouTube for video clips of music therapy sessions and drumming circles
- Attend drum circle facilitation workshops
- Participate in creative arts therapies workshops
- Watch the following films and reflect on the impact of music on the central characters' lives:
  - *Music of the Heart*
  - *As it is in Heaven*

Recommended Resources

Websites

The American Music Therapy Association: http://www.musictherapy.org/
New England Region of the American Music Therapy Association: http://aboutmusictherapy.com/
World Federation for Music Therapy: http://www.musictherapyworld.net/

Books

Camilleri, V. (2007). *Healing the inner city child: Creative arts therapies with at-risk youth*. Philadelphia: Jessica Kingsley.
Gardstrom, S. (2007). *Music therapy improvisation for groups: Essential leadership competencies*. Gilsum, NH: Barcelona.
Oldfield, A. (2006). *Interactive music therapy: A positive approach: Music therapy at a child development centre*. Philadelphia: Jessica Kingsley.

Journals

The Journal of Music Therapy
Music Therapy Perspectives
Voices: Music Therapy Online Journal (http://www.voices.no/index.html)

Notes

1. Participant's name was changed to protect his identity.

5.

ANIMAL-ASSISTED APPROACHES TO CHILD AND ADOLESCENT MENTAL HEALTH

Jennifer Boggs, Phil Tedeschi, and Frank Ascione

Overview of Chapter

This chapter will cover animal-assisted interventions (AAIs) with children and adolescents and includes the following sections:
- Introduction
- A Brief History of Animal-Assisted Interventions
- Definitions
- Theoretical Perspectives in the Literature
- Equine-Assisted Growth and Learning Association vs. Equine Facilitated Mental Health Association
- Cognitive Behavior Therapy and Animal-Assisted Interventions
- Solution Focused Therapy and Animal-Assisted Interventions
- Prior Research on Treatment Efficacy of AAI
- General Benefits of Animal-Assisted Interventions with Adolescents
- Trauma
- Therapeutic Applications with Specific Child and Adolescent Populations
- Therapeutic Components of Animal-Assisted Interventions
- Important Ethical Considerations in Animal-Assisted Interventions
- Cultural Considerations
- Case Study
- Summary
- Activities to Extend Your Learning

Introduction

Why do humans keep companion animals? They serve no practical purpose. They cost money to keep, add burden to our already hectic lives, damage household objects, and create messes on the floor. Boris Levinson described human companion animal keeping as something that is done for psychological not practical reasons:

> Because of the close relationship between the pet and the human being, some writers have gone so far as to posit the "theory" that the pet domesticated the human being. It could very well have been that when man first began to modify his environment and hence to lose contact with it, he felt a great need to strengthen his contact with nature through the adoption of pets. (Levinson & Mallon, 1997, p. 3)

Dogs literally walked out of the cave with man and have been an integral part of human history and the evolution of civilization (Vila et al., 1997). Today, people have contact with a wide variety of companion animals that provide recreational opportunities and emotional support. In addition, the therapeutic community has designed animal-assisted interventions (AAIs) that enhance a wide variety of treatment modalities. These range from walking a dog, riding a horse, stroking a cat, holding a hamster, and feeding a tank of fish. Every day people perform all of these activities with their companion animals outside a therapeutic environment. The difference between the common person conducting these tasks and the performance of these tasks in a therapeutic environment is the application of a sound theoretical model that justifies the inclusion of animals in the therapeutic environment. These theories are not entirely psychological change theories such as cognitive behavioral, psychodynamic, or solution focused, but also includes theories of humane education, physical and recreational therapy, and building rapport and engagement. AAIs can be delivered by a spectrum of mental health professionals from a master's level therapist to a local horseback riding instructor with a high school education. Currently, the field is in the infancy of empirically justifying the inclusion of animals in the therapeutic environment. The field is replete with stories such as the one below about Steve.

Steve was 3 years old when child protective services removed him from his biological mother's care for neglect. Steve knew very few words, was dirty, and unaccustomed to wearing clothing. His first foster mother described him as a "wild animal" because he would tear off any piece of clothing she tried to put on him while running around the house screaming. His foster mother slowly won the battle of the clothing, but was unable to find a way to keep Steve safe in her home. "He is into everything all at once, he is the most hyperactive child I have ever seen," she said. Steve was diagnosed with ADHD and medication interventions were attempted with little success. He was replaced in a foster to adopt home with his younger brother, Reilly, when he was 5 years old. His new parents tried several different types of traditional talk therapy to help Steve with limited success. They decided to try something different at the recommendation of their caseworker: equine-assisted psychotherapy. After hearing about Steve's history, the therapist had some concerns about Steve remaining safe around a horse. However, she knew that her horses were accustomed to these types of kids and instructed one of her horse handlers to watch Steve very closely. During the first session, Steve ran around the arena like a "wild animal," but slowed down and walked when he got close to a horse. The therapist saw this reaction and was hopeful that the horse's intimidating presence may provide Steve with the motivation to slow down and think. As the weeks went by, the transformation from a "wild animal" to a settled, calm, and thoughtful child was remarkable. By week 9, Steve was leading a horse independently around the arena and showing an ability to plan ahead when an obstacle was placed in front of him. His parents were in tears when they saw Steve's progress.

Despite the lack of empirical evidence to support AAIs, these types of stories are in the many case studies and qualitative assessments that currently comprise the AAI field. It can be postulated that this is the reason animal-assisted approaches are experiencing tremendous growth around the nation. In the United States there are over 2,500 animal-assisted programs (Benda & Lightmark, 2004). Countless case studies have described similar scenarios of children and adolescents experiencing tremendous therapeutic improvements following animal-assisted interventions. Students in social work, counseling, or psychology programs who hear these types of stories or experience these types of benefits themselves with their own animals are drawn to a number of national programs designed to provide professional training for those who will be working in a therapeutic setting. There are currently several graduate programs offering animal-assisted therapy education in United States.

One example of such a program is the University of Denver's Institute for Human-Animal Connection, Graduate School of Social Work (GSSW), which offers a specialized training program and research center. The program includes two courses, Integration of Animals into Therapeutic Settings and an advanced course, Animal-Assisted Social Work Practice. The courses expose students to practice guidelines for animal-assisted activities (AAA) and animal-assisted therapy (AAT), integrating national standards of care, proper safety, ethical guidelines for animals and clients, experiential and alternative therapy theory, participation in experiential learning events including the elective opportunity to participate in international travel courses, seminars, field experiences, and specialized animal-assisted social work field placements. Some students elect to train a certified therapy dog during their second year of graduate school, which becomes their professional therapy dog. They graduate from GSSW together as a specially trained human-canine team. Other students may emphasize training as a nationally certified equine therapist or educator, humane educator or conservation social work specialist. Partnerships with American Humane Association, Colorado Animal Control and Care specialists, leading assistance dog organizations, and Denver Zoo expand the experiential and service learning opportunities. The primary focus of training remains on domestic dogs, horses, cats, small animals, therapeutic farm, humane education models, and conservation social work. Exotic animals are not utilized in direct contact with therapies.

Animal-Assisted Social Work (AASW) lends itself to interdisciplinary coordination in each of these areas and can be introduced into a number of therapeutic settings (with individuals, groups and families) in diverse communities. Often populations receiving social work services are those who have had minimal positive experiences in their lives. Put as simply as possible, when introduced properly into a therapeutic setting, animals make people feel good, improve quality of life, and assist in healing. For individuals with a troubled history of human interactions, an AAI animal can serve as a nonthreatening partner in the treatment and support process, creating an initial trust connection that later may be transferred to the professional. The quiet, calm presence of an animal in a therapeutic situation with those who have experienced trauma can remediate some of the episodes' effects, enabling the individual to benefit more from the intervention. In addition, an animal's loyalty and authentic nonjudgmental willingness makes our relationships with them some of the most enduring and safe interactions possible. AASW is a powerful therapeutic approach that can have multiple impacts, aiding in physical, social and emotional healing through a dynamic of relationship and connection with others.

A Brief History of Animal-Assisted Interventions

The first record of animals used in a psychotherapeutic setting was in England at the York Retreat during the late 1700s. This retreat, founded by the Quakers, is touted as one of the first facilities to treat the mentally ill with compassion rather than brutality. Patients were encouraged to care for small animals including chickens and rabbits that resided at the retreat. This practice was thought to encourage self-care, responsibility, and self-control by providing the patients with animals who were dependent on them for care (Bustad, 1979).

The roots of modern AAI are credited to child psychiatrist Boris Levinson who was the first modern credentialed mental health professional to bring animal assisted (or pet animal-assisted as he called it) approaches under scientific inquiry. Levinson found that having a dog present in his therapeutic sessions assisted him in engaging resistant clients. He wrote that the dog's presence seemed to break down defenses and allowed him to build trust with the child faster, particularly adolescents (Levinson, 1964).

Since Levinson, several authors noted the positive influence companion animals have on the stress levels and lifespan of the physically ill. Longitudinal studies have found that those diagnosed with cardiac conditions who owned a companion animal, lived longer than those without companion animals (Friedmann, Katcher, Lynch, & Thomas, 1980). Friedman and Thomas (1995) found that the presence of an animal reduced blood pressure and heart rate, but only for a short time. One rationale for this phenomenon is that animals garner our attention and focus away from ourselves and onto them, thereby inducing a state of relaxation, if only for a few moments (Katcher, Friedman, Beck, & Lynch, 1983). Anybody who has ever held a puppy or a kitten is probably familiar with this effect.

Definitions

Animal-Assisted Therapy (AAT)

The Delta Society has an excellent description of animal-assisted therapy:

> AAT is a goal-directed intervention in which an animal that meets specific criteria is an integral part of the treatment process. AAT is directed and/or delivered by a health/human service professional with specialized expertise, and within the scope of practice of his/her profession. Key features include: specified goals and objectives for each individual; and measured progress. (n.d., p. 1)

Animal-Assisted Activity (AAA)

The Delta Society also has a good description of animal-assisted activity (AAA). It should be noted that the term *animal-assisted learning* (AAL) is used synonymously with animal-assisted activity (AAA).

AAA provides opportunities for motivational, educational, recreational, and/or therapeutic benefits to enhance quality of life. AAAs are delivered in a variety of environments by specially trained professionals, paraprofessionals, and/or volunteers, in association with animals that meet specific criteria. Key features include: absence of specific treatment goals; volunteers and treatment providers are not required to take detailed notes; visit content is spontaneous. (n.d., p. 1)

Equine-Assisted Learning (EAL)

EFMHA defines EAL as an: "educational approach that includes equine facilitated activities incorporating the experience of equine/human interaction in an environment of learning or self discovery" (EFMHA, 2010, p. 1). EAL does not use a licensed mental health professional (MH) or treatment planning. Additionally, EAL plans generally have a set program that doesn't change according to participant characteristics. EAL programs are usually run by people with extensive horse knowledge and often focus on goals involving self-esteem, self-confidence, and sense of responsibility

Therapeutic Riding (TR) and Hippotherapy

Therapeutic riding involves mounted activities for children or adults with mental, emotional, and physical disabilities (NARHA, 2010). EAL and EFP can use both unmounted and mounted work, whereas therapeutic riding includes primarily mounted activities. Therapeutic riding is normally considered a recreational activity with emotional and physical benefits to participants. Instructors are not required to be certified mental health professionals. NARHA has an extensive instructor certification program and riding center certification program that include many safety standards. However, there is no legal requirement for an instructor or a center to be certified through NARHA to provide therapeutic riding.

The term *hippotherapy* is often confused with therapeutic riding, but it is actually quite unique. Hippotherapy includes a physical, occupational, or speech therapist who incorporates the movement of the horse into traditional therapy techniques. The goals of hippotherapy are entirely physical, occupational, or speech therapy treatment goals. Hippotherapy, specifically the movement of the horse, has been shown to increase muscle symmetry in children with spastic cerebral palsy (Benda, McGibbon, & Grant, 2003). Hippotherapy is currently one of the most well-researched animal-assisted therapy approaches in the United States. It is actually reimbursed by most U.S. health insurance companies. For more information on hippotherapy including a thorough review of the literature, visit the American Hippotherapy Association's website (www.americanhippotherapyassociation.org).

Theoretical Perspectives in the Literature

Role of Animals in the Therapeutic Environment

One important element of animal-assisted approaches is whether the animal plays a central or auxiliary role in the environment. Therapists such as Teri Pichot, therapist and program manager at Jefferson Country Deptment of Health in Denver, Colorado, would indicate that the primary mode of treatment is talk therapy where the dog is used as a therapeutic tool to build rapport, equalize the power differential between therapist and client, encourage clients to engage in a positive activity, and assist clients in focusing their attention on something other than themselves (Pichot & Coulter, 2006). Therapy in this environment could occur without the therapy dog's presence; the dog's role is supportive and auxiliary to treatment. There are days when Teri brings one of her dogs, Rocky and Jasper, to work with her and days when he stays home. Teri uses a solution focused talk therapy approach with her clients with or without Rocky and Jasper's assistance.

Philosophically, Pichot's approach to animal-assisted therapy is starkly different than the Equine Assisted Growth and Learning Association (EAGALA) model where the horse is viewed as an equal co-therapist who must be present. Where Pichot uses a traditional theoretical orientation, solution-focused therapy, EAGALA created their own theoretical orientation that incorporates the horse. They describe their orientation as a team approach between a mental health therapist (MH), equine specialist (ES), and horse. This experiential learning approach will have the client interact with the horse by doing some sort of game or activity. During the performance of this activity, the MH and ES will make objective observations of the client's behavior. Following the activity, the MH and ES will ask questions about their observations in an unbiased manner with the intention of creating a metaphor between the client's behavior with the horse and their real life behavior. For example, a question could be: "I noticed that the horse walked away from you when you lifted the halter. What was that about?" The idea here is that the client can make up their own meaning for the horse's behavior that will be informational to the client in solving a problem in their own life (EAGALA, 2006). A follow-up question may be: "Do you feel that the way (however they describe current feeling when horse walked away) at any other time in your daily life?"

Equine-Assisted Growth and Learning Association vs. Equine Facilitated Mental Health Association

In addition to the aforementioned EAGALA model, an alternative model for incorporating horses into the therapeutic environment was created by the Equine Facilitated Mental Health Association (EFMHA). Both models use a collaborative approach between a licensed mental health professional (MH) and an equine specialist (ES). EFMHA is an extension of the North American Riding for the Handicapped Association (NARHA) and EAGALA is a standalone organization. Where EAGALA is primarily process oriented and utilizes ground work only, EFMHA uses mounted exercises and focuses on the relationship between clients and equines that develops during riding, longing, grooming, driving, or other handling activities. EFMHA teaches horsemanship or proper ways of interacting with a horse as well as horse behavior education. EAGALA does not teach any horsemanship. EAGALA has their own theoretical orientation that they describe as solution oriented, experiential, non-directive, and client centered (EAGALA, 2006); EFMHA encourages psychotherapists to use the horse as a tool in applying their preferred theoretical orientation. EFMHA uses the term *Equine Facilitated Psychotherapy* (EFP) to describe their approach whereas; EAGALA uses the term *Equine Assisted Psychotherapy* (EAP).

Diamond vs. Triangle

A major consideration in practicing any form of AAI is whether the clinician will play the role of handler or if another person will fulfill this role. Figure 5.1 shows

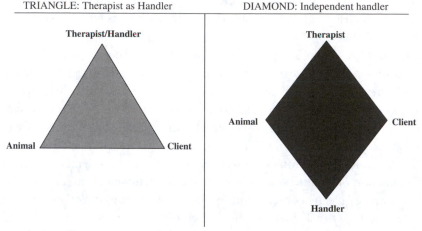

Advantages of Triangle

- Client views therapist as trustworthy and safe because of their affiliation with the animal.
- Therapist knows animal well and is aware of their body language for use in therapeutic interventions with the client.
- Therapist has more control of the therapeutic environment and does not have to worry about the handler doing or saying something that could interfere with treatment.

Disadvantages of Triangle

- Therapist has dual responsibility to the health and well being of both the client and animal during the session that could become problematic if the client loses control of self.
- Therapist has added responsibility to care for animal as part of their daily work routine, which could be problematic to work environments that are less animal-friendly.

Advantages of Diamond

- Therapist has sole responsibility for client during session and does not have a dual role with animal.
- Therapy animal has a single person with the responsibility of watching out for their needs during session. Animals have stress signals like pacing, yawning and panting in dogs that indicate that they may need to take a break.
- There are less likely to be hurdles in work environments with animals that come for a short stay with the handler. For example, in hospital settings, the animal assisted sessions may take place in a certain area of the hospital. If the therapist needed to travel to other areas of the hospital throughout her workday, this could be problematic if she has her therapy animal with her that day.
- With larger animals, such as horses, the physical safety of clients can be attuned to by the handler.

Disadvantages of Diamond

- Client must develop trusting relationship with two people and may develop a closer relationship with the handler who they associate with the animal.
- Handler must be trained in basic counseling skills and not interfere with the therapist's treatment plan by interjecting at inappropriate times.
- Therapist, handler, and animal must spend large amounts of time developing their relationship, boundaries and flow during sessions.
- Therapist will need to spend time extensive amount of time with animals in order to understand their non-verbal communication for use in the therapy session.

Figure 5.1   Diamond vs. Triangle

the differences between these two arrangements in terms of the relationships that are present in the therapeutic environment.

There are animal-assisted therapy organizations that support each of these models and some that support both models (e.g., the Delta Society). EAGALA supports the Diamond Model. EAGALA believes that the therapist must be responsible for the client's emotional safety during sessions whereas the equine specialist must be responsible for the client's physical safety during the session. This approach makes sense considering the potential risk of physical harm that a horse presents to a client who is inexperienced in horse handling. However, EFMHA recognizes the use of the triangle model during equine-assisted learning activities.

Cognitive Behavioral Therapy and Animal-Assisted Interventions

Cognitive behavioral therapy is a widely accepted form of talk therapy that focuses on the connection between emotions, thoughts and behavior. Frame (2006) conducted a qualitative study of 15 psychotherapists who used EAP/EFP to treat adolescent depression. The interaction between the client and horse was thought by several therapists to produce a feedback loop for the client's behavior. We have observed this effect several times in our clinical work with adolescents where a client will approach a horse very quickly resulting in the horse moving away from them. They may say, "That horse doesn't like me," to which I would respond, "That horse doesn't even know you." From there we can explore the reasons that the horse may have moved away from them (horse is shy, horse doesn't trust new people, horse doesn't like quick movements), which will challenge their initial automatic thought that "the horse doesn't like me." The client would then be directed to approach the horse again to test one of the "theories" for the horse moving away.

The therapist's ability to intervene and alter behavior and thought processes in the moment followed by the client's ability to test out these new patterns of thought and behavior are of great benefit. Traditional talk therapy using CBT would ask client's to describe their thoughts, feelings, behaviors, and then homework would be given to try out at home (Beck, 1995). The integration of CBT is not exclusive to equines and may also easily be incorporated into environments with other animals.

Solution Focused Therapy and Animal-Assisted Interventions

This section will summarize two chapters on the integration of animal-assisted interventions with solution focused therapy from Teri Pichot and Marc Coulter's book *Animal Assisted Brief Therapy: A Solution Focused Approach* (2006). There are several similar values between Solution Focused Therapy and AAI (pp. 104–107).

- "If something is working do more of it": If having a therapy dog present makes the clients experience a more positive one, then more therapy dog visits please!
- "If it is not working, do something different": If your current approach is not working, try adding a therapy animal, maybe it will change something.

- "Small steps can lead to large changes": Having an animal in the therapy room or waiting room is not a cure-all, but if that dog makes the client more willing to open up, it can be an essential small step towards recovery.
- "The solution is not necessarily directly related to the problem": Solution focused therapy does not explore a client's problem, but instead encourages clients to only consider and implement solutions. Therefore, if the therapy dog puts the client in a better mood that encourages more positive thinking about solutions, this is a helpful outcome.
- "No problem happens all the time. There are always exceptions that can be utilized": Interactions with a therapy dogs create an exception behavior to depression, anxiety, or other symptoms. For example, the client may smile, laugh, or relax when visiting with the therapy dog, but may complain about feeling sad and lonely.

There are two goals of AAI at Pichot and Coulter's agency: creating a sense of community and challenging the client's preconceived negative ideas about the agency. Rocky, Pichot's therapy dog, has a reputation as the greeter in the waiting room. "Rocky's ability to give a warm greeting that includes a 'kiss' and a snuggle serves to give warmth and a personal touch that would be deemed inappropriate by a human therapist" (Pichot & Coulter, 2006, p. 110). Clients who are visiting the county health department are not usually excited about being there. They may be there to receive inoculations, testing for sexually transmitted diseases, or to participate in a substance abuse program. Rocky's mere presence can change this preconceived idea that this is a scary place by simply not being expected. Additionally, visiting with Rocky can offer clients an opportunity to interact with staff and discover that they are friendly and welcoming.

Including an animal in a solution focused therapy session is more involved and requires specific rationale for their inclusion (Pichot & Coulter, 2006). The benefit derived from including a therapy animal in the session must be carefully thought out for each individual client. Even when a client may request the therapy dog's presence, the benefit must go beyond this request. Some adolescents may be so distracted by an animal that they do not focus on the therapist's questions. In these instances, the animal can become more of a hindrance than a help. On the other hand, if the adolescent seems to be more engaged, less anxious, or in a better mood when the animal is present, AAI would be recommended. Pichot and Coulter recommend offering the use of a therapy dog to a client and then measuring the non-verbal response the client gives to this suggestion. Many clients may simply agree with the inclusion of a therapy dog out of politeness towards the therapist or a vague sense that this could be helpful. If the client revisits the subject at a later time without the therapist prompting the topic, this may be an indication that they are genuinely interested in incorporating the therapy dog.

There are several treatment goals that consistently benefit from the inclusion of a dog using solution focused therapy. These include improving depression, parenting skills, and lessening anxiety. Client's who are depressed often have a very difficult time describing anything positive. The presence of a therapy dog can create a positive interaction that the therapist can use as a starting off point to help the client think of other positive interactions. The parallels between parenting a child and training a dog are numerous and include the need for consistency, a child/dog's desire to avoid unpleasant things, and needing affection. Within the solution focused framework, positive interactions with the dog, such as properly rewarding good behavior and punishing bad behavior, can be complimented by the therapist. Finally, goals involving anxiety can be realized when the client is allowed to touch and play with the dog's fur, nose, or paws during the session. This idle distraction can relieve anxiety, encourage the client to open up more, and provide the therapist with an avenue of inquiry for the future use when the client is in a relaxed state.

Prior Research on Treatment Efficacy of AAI

Research on AAIs is in its infancy. While the majority of research indicates a positive impact of AAIs, much of the work includes dissertation thesis, conceptual articles, and qualitative pieces by therapists on their own work. Within the past 10 years, there have been quantitative contributions to some corners of the field including trauma, depression, anxiety, social supports, humane education, and self-esteem. However, the majority of the quantitative work has had small sample sizes with several design flaws that prohibit extensive generalizability.

Kruger, Trachtenburg, and Serpell's (2004) review of AAIs in adolescent populations identified several key problem areas in the field that need to be addressed: the absence of a clear definition, practice guidelines, or well-accepted terminology; lack of a theoretical foundation or empirical study; and a prevalence of weak or poor research designs. Additionally, they identified several other key concepts: despite lack of evidence, AAIs are growing and gaining acceptance in the mental health field; AAIs have the potential to reduce the time spent in therapy, which can serve as a motivation to gain funding for research; future research needs to consider cultural and ethical issues and long-term effects of AAIs.

General Benefits of Animal-Assisted Interventions with Adolescents

Animal companionship is thought to fill needs of affection and connection to others (Friedman et al., 1980). Adolescents in residential care who were allowed to keep companion animals are described as improved in their sense of responsibility and ability to nurture others (Banman, 1995). Shultz (2005) found that psychosocial functioning scores of at-risk youth ages 12–18 on the Youth Outcome Questionnaire (YOQ) were significantly improved compared to a control group following participation in a 10-week equine facilitated psychotherapy group.

Self-Esteem

While there have been some studies that have shown increases in self-esteem using canines, the majority of clinical outcomes have been reported in equines. This is most likely due to the immense size of the equine and the sense of empowerment an adolescent gains from controlling a large animal. Several equine studies have indicated an increase in self-confidence following participation in an equine-assisted learning, therapeutic riding, or equine-assisted therapy program. Youth in residential care often feel a lack of control over their ability to influence their life's course (Cooper & Jobe, 2007). When these youth are able to see an increase in their abilities to control a horse, the observed result was increased self-confidence.

While the Cooper and Jobe (2007) study is informative, it lacks empirical rigor as the founders of the program conducted the qualitative study.

Quantitative work includes Preush (1997) and Iannone (2003), who both found an increase in self-esteem of emotionally disturbed adolescents (age 12–15) following participation in therapeutic riding programs using validated self-esteem inventories in a pre/post test design. Trotter (2006) found increases in self-esteem of school children using the Behavioral Assessment of School Children scale following participation in a 12-week equine-assisted psychotherapy program with limited mounted activities. On the other hand, Ewing, MacDonald, Taylor, and Bowers (2007) found no change on the Self Perception Profile for Children Scale following an equine-assisted learning program. The equine-assisted research on EAT (Equine Assisted Therapy) and TR (Therapeutic Riding) programs is favorable for increasing self-esteem however; equine-assisted learning programs have shown mixed results. This may be due to the absence of a psychotherapist during EAL programs or the lack of research on EAL programs.

Depression and Anxiety

Companion animals have been reported to decrease anxiety and depressive symptoms in children (Brickel, 1982). Trotter (2006) quantitatively compared a school-based life skills curriculum to an equine-assisted psychotherapy curriculum and found decreases in depression, social anxiety, and sense of inadequacy as reported by parents and adolescent participants, but not teachers following both curriculums. Parents in the equine-assisted psychotherapy group also reported decreased problems with externalizing behaviors and increased social skills and adaptability where parents in the in school curriculum did not report these differences.

Souter and Miller (2007) conducted a meta-analysis of quantitative work using animal-assisted interventions for depression (not specific to adolescents). They searched 19 databases using strict inclusion criteria for each study, which included use of a control group, random assignment, use of a validated depression measure, and participation in some type of animal-assisted intervention. Five articles met this criteria, many of them visiting canine programs. After analysis of these articles, it was determined that animal-assisted interventions had a "medium" effect size on depression. This was interpreted to mean that although patients who participated in animal-assisted interventions were unlikely to experience a dramatic decrease in depression, they still experienced a noticeable degree of relief. This would be congruent with Salotto's (2001) qualitative work with visiting canine programs that interpreted the clinical outcomes for AAI to be a crutch, not a cure for the isolation experienced in residential settings.

Animals as Social Support

The necessity of social support (animal or human) has been shown to be of great importance to physical and mental health (Esterling, Kiccolt-Glaser, Bodnar, & Glaser, 1994; Sherbourne, Meredith, Rogers, & Ware, 1992). There are several theories for animals acting as social supports under investigation. The first is that animals act as human surrogates with isolated individuals like older adults, those with mental illness, and children/adolescents in neglectful households. The most typical and studied type of AAI are visiting animal programs in residential settings such as treatment centers, psychiatric hospitals, or nursing home facilities.

Salotto (2001) quotes a client from a nursing home facility: "I know God brought you and DJ (therapy dog) here, because I didn't have the slightest idea what I was going to do for the next four hours until dinner" (pp. 46–47). While this is a humorous statement, the sense of isolation and loneliness experienced by this client is implicit. Salotto claims that visiting animal programs are currently one of the best remedies for social isolation but are by no means a cure. A better solution may be facilities that allow residents to keep their companion animals with them as it has been shown that there are differences in one's physiological response to their own companion animal versus a strange companion animal. Heart rate and blood pressure reductions have been shown to be decreased significantly more when someone is interacting with their own dog versus a strange dog (Baun, Bergstrom, Langston, & Thoma, 1984). Adolescents in residential setting report more favorable attitudes towards companion animals compared to those in public school settings, which could suggest that their sense of isolation could be alleviated by a companion animal (Wilbanks, 1989).

Trauma

Childhood trauma and a diagnosis of PTSD are common occurrences among adolescents in the mental health system. One of the most common sources of trauma is childhood sexual abuse; approximately 10% of boys and 25% of girls in the general population experience childhood sexual abuse (Whealin, 2009). Among youth in residential treatment, the prevalence of childhood sexual abuse increases to as high as 67% for girls (Kumar, Steer, & Deblinger, 1996) and 24% for boys (Hawke, Jainchill, & De Leon, 2000).

There are two perspectives that will be explored here on AAIs with relation to trauma. The first is the use of a therapy animal in recovery from trauma by incorporating the animal into a traditional clinical approach of Prolonged Exposure. The second perspective is that a previous relationship between a trauma victim and a companion animal can assist them in recovering from their trauma. These two perspectives for AAIs with victims of trauma are not exhaustive in the field, but are most applicable to treatment with adolescents. Using AAI in trauma work is ideal when the client has a positive history interacting with animals. Instances where there has been an abusive relationship from the child to the animal, which is more common in households where interpersonal violence is prevalent, are not well suited to this approach. This is mentioned in the context of childhood trauma because the sources of child hood trauma including physical abuse, sexual abuse, neglect, and inter-family violence are also predictors of animal abuse by either parents or children (Ascione, Kaufmann, & Brooks, 2006). Therefore a careful assessment of the adolescent's history of interacting with animals, including abuse must be undertaken prior to the use of AAIs. However, it should be understood that a history of animal abuse does not necessarily contraindicate the use of AAIs. This decision must be undertaken by the clinician who must weigh the potential danger the child may present to the animal, the clinicians ability to keep that animal safe, and the potential benefit the child could realize from working with the animal.

Animal-Assisted Prolonged Exposure

Traditional treatment using prolonged exposure involves psycho-education, relaxation techniques, and progressive exposure to feared memories and situations. Lefkowitz, Paharia, Prout, Debiak, and Bleiberg (2005) identify PE as one of the most successful treatments for PTSD, but highlights the 25% drop-out rate. Exposing suffers of PTSD to the very thing that they fear would be an extremely arduous undertaking. Lefkowitz et al. (2005) proposes the addition of a therapy animal (dog) to help decrease the physiological stress response experienced by clients during therapeutic exposure to triggering events. For more information on this approach, see Lefkowitz et al. (2005), which describes in detail how to introduce a therapy animal along with a procedure for each session in a 10- to 12-week treatment plan.

Using A Previous Companion Animal Relationship in Recovery from Trauma

As described above, companion animals are often an integral part of a child's development. Children will often talk about their companion animal's experiences in the household before they will talk about their own (Fine, 2006). Children who experienced abuse in the household may describe abuse from their parents to their companion animals. When there is co-occurring animal and child abuse, it may be easier for the child to discuss the animal's feelings regarding the abuse. The therapist can use this as a bridge to the child's inner world. For example, the adolescent may say something like, "Sidney (dog) whimpers when he gets hit." The adolescent may also describe their companion animals as an ally in escaping violence or comforting them after a traumatic event. Fine (2006) describes a boy who said that his dog would lick the tears from his face after his stepfather had physically abused him.

Therapeutic Applications with Specific Child and Adolescent Populations

Interventions in Residential Settings

There have been several methods for using AAIs in residential settings: the farm environment, therapist's incorporating their own therapy animals (triangle model) or visiting animals (diamond model), and participation with community resources such as equine programs, zoos, or animal shelters. The Green Chimney's program in Brewster, New York, is a residential and outpatient facility for children with emotional, behavioral, and learning challenges that utilizes a therapeutic farm environment on their campus. Residents care for farm animals, rehabilitate wildlife, participate in horticulture therapy, and also have the opportunity to train assistance dogs for the physically disabled (Green Chimneys, 2009).

Residential centers also have the opportunity to partner with therapeutic riding facilities where residents can learn to ride and care for horses. Aspen Hollow Young Ranchers, an equine-assisted learning program located just outside of Denver, Colorado, partners with Denver area residential treatment centers. Aspen Hollow runs a 6- to 8-week program that begins with adolescents choosing and catching a horse in a herd of 8 to 10 horses. They are then encouraged to build a relationship with this horse through grooming, leading, and performance of ground work for several weeks before they learn to ride this horse. Aspen Hollow's facilitators use a strength-based approach utilizing interactions with the horse as a metaphor for their attitudes, relationships, and behaviors in their real lives (personal communication, A. Gardner, 2008). Finally, residential centers can join with local animal shelters to create programs like the Behavior Reduction in Kids (BARK) program at the Mental Health Center of Denver (2009). Adolescents and therapists help to train and rehabilitate dogs for adoption at the Denver Dumb Friends League while working on their individual treatment goals.

School-Based AAI programs

> When the children were changing the water of the goldfish, Frank had a sudden impulse of cruelty, and said to the others, "Shall we stamp on it?"… Before she [the teacher] could stop them, they had thrown the fish out into the sand and stamped on it. They stood round and looked at it, rather excited, and obviously wishing they hadn't done it, and Frank said, "No let's put it into water, and then it'll come alive again." (Isaacs, 1930, pp. 204–205 as cited in Melson, 2003, p. 1)

AAI programs in schools must be closely monitored, and all children should be educated on proper handling techniques (Chandler, 2005). It should not be assumed that children will automatically treat a classroom animal appropriately, as some children have had cruelty modeled in their homes. While the quote above is meant to show intellectual development of young children, adolescents possess the same risk for animals. The student/teacher ratio in a classroom is quite high (30:1), indicating the necessity for procedures to keep animals safe in classrooms. The benefits of having animals in the classroom are numerous including the opportunity for humane education that encourages empathy development (Ascione, 1997), inclusion in math and reading programs (Chandler, 2005), and as a motivation and reward for learning or doing assignments (Fine, 2006). School-based programming may also include school counselors keeping therapy animals in their offices. Children who would otherwise be intimidated to talk to a counselor, may just stop by to visit with the therapy animal (Chandler, 2005).

Family Approaches Using the Equine Herd Dynamic

Equine herds are especially well suited for work with adolescents and families because they offer an experiential parallel process for many family dynamics, along with several other important characteristics:

- Equine interactions offer an intimidating challenge to all members of the family and therefore create a shared experience for the family. This shared experience could be powerful for disengaged families that may lack common activities or interests. Alternatively, enmeshed families can also benefit by focusing on the individual relationships that members develop with individual horses. Equines are challenging to work with, but also very forgiving and accepting. Experiential theory posits that individuals change and grow when they are challenged (EAGALA, 2006). Interacting with equines is challenging even for people who have years of experience.
- Equine herd behaviors offer a metaphor for family interactions. Equine herds have leaders, followers, protectors, coalitions, and triangles. In the family therapy world a triangle occurs when two family members unite against a third member (Nichols, 2009). This happens most often when a parent and child align themselves against another parent. People who are participating in this behavior are often unaware that they are doing it. Horse herds have similar behaviors when two horses are close buddies. They may get upset when their buddy interacts with another horse. Equine herds also have dominant leaders who serve as protectors, taking on the responsibility of keeping the followers safe. This is similar to the role parents play with their children. Interestingly, unlike many human relationships, horses are assertive and direct in their communication style without any hidden agendas. Joe Camp, an authority on equine herd behavior, illuminates this concept well:

  > When a leader horse swells up and pins her ears and moves toward a follower's butt, it means move that butt. Now! And that such a move doesn't mean *I don't like you.* Or *I want you out of my pasture.* It simply means, *I am the leader here and I want you to move your butt over.* That's it. A few minutes later the same two horses will be huddled next to each other, head to tail, swishing flies out of each other's faces. (Camp, 2008, p. 39)

- *Equine/human interactions offer a metaphor for parent/child interactions.* A healthy parent/child interaction occurs when the parent has more power than the child. The child should respect but not fear the parent's authority. Similarly, in a healthy equine/human relationship, the human has more power, and the equine respects but does not fear the human. Even though the horse is 1,100 lbs, hundreds of thousands of years of evolution have designed horses as prey animals and humans as predators (Camp, 2008). The domesticated horse succumbs to the will of the human voluntarily without fear, the wild horse flees the human for fear of being hunted. In order to successfully impose your will on a domesticated horse (so that they accept it), you have to be assertive, consistent, fair, and patient in your demands (like a fellow horse). Does this sound like a skill set that a good parent would have? Interactions with horses can illuminate parental problems as well as provide a practicing ground to improve parenting skills.
- *Equines are engaging for clients, especially adolescent youth.* Fine (2006) discusses the use of animals as an engagement tool for adolescents with strong barriers to therapy. Engagement is the first process that must be accomplished by any therapist if they wish

to be successful with any client. Fine (2006) discusses animals as a "social lubricant" used to aid therapists in developing rapport with clients. Animals provide a sense of comfort and acceptance, thereby increasing the likelihood that the client will trust the therapist.

* *Equines are honest mirrors of human behavior.* Equines are very in tune with body language and social cues as their survival as prey animals depends on it (Camp, 2008). EAGALA (2006) indicates that moments when horse behavior mirrors human behavior are observations the therapist should try to recognize and point out. Examples of this include a herd of horses standing far apart when the family members are standing far apart in the arena, but coming closer together when the family members are closer together. Another example is a horse pacing or stomping the ground around a client who is nervous and fidgety.

Therapeutic Components of Animal-Assisted Interventions

Engagement/Motivation

Starting with Levinson (1964) and continuing on from there, the ability of animals to engage children and adolescents in a therapeutic process is one of the most reported effects of AAIs. This effect has been empirically shown in two studies (Corson, Corson, & Gwynne, 1975; Wesley, Minatrea, & Watson, 2009). Engagement is an especially important topic when working with an adolescent population where motivation to trust a therapist and participate in a change process are often problematic (Garcia & Weisz, 2002).

One study specifically examined the effect a therapy animal had on a counselor's credibility with institutionalized and non-institutionalized adolescents. They found trend level differences in reported counselor credibility with the addition of a pet for both institutionalized and non-institutionalized groups (Wilbanks, 1989). Interestingly, those in residential treatment settings reported significantly more favorable attitudes towards pets than those in public school or detention settings. Further research is needed to confirm this finding and to explore differences in attitudes towards companion animals of adolescents in various types of settings.

This AAI is almost too easy for some people to accept, the mere presence of a therapy animal automatically gives the therapist a step towards engaging the client without any real "work" being done by the therapist. To the naysayers of AAIs, consider that engagement is the most important and vital step in therapy. Without engagement, no future intervention will work, no matter how brilliant and creative it may be.

Companionship and Attachment

Gail Melson (2003) theorizes that animals and the natural world play a role in child development that has been largely overlooked. Most scientific work in child development has been largely anthropocentric (human only) where Melson suggests a theory that is biocentric (living things). This theory indicates that living things not only play a role in social and emotional development, but also in cognitive, perceptual, and language development. Studies of perceptual development have shown that infants attend significantly more to live animals (smiling, tracking with their eyes, making noise) than stuffed animal toys, or even robotic, animated toys (Kidd & Kidd, 1987; Ricard & Allard, 1992). Socially, Melson reports that 42% of 5-year-old children spontaneously mention a companion animal when asked "Who do you turn to when you are feeling sad, angry, happy, or wanting to share a secret?" (Melson & Schwarz, 1994). Other studies have mentioned rates as high as 78% of children referencing companion animals in their social support system (Covert, Whirren, Keith, & Nelson, 1985). The rationale for this strong affinity towards companion animals as important resources in the social support system has been postulated to occur because children view companion animals as everlasting, non-judgmental, and completely accepting. The family dog or cat doesn't care if you break a glass or spill your juice box on the expensive rug. It is unknown how companion animal-human relationships develop over the life-span, specifically how they change as a child matures into an adolescent.

Crawford, Worsham, and Swinehart (2006) would like to make a distinction between human-human attachment and human-companion animal attachment. This suggestion seems to contradict Melson's biocentric theory to children's development that seeks to include attachments with companion animals in developmental models. The literature on the human-animal bond uses the term *attachment*, and Crawford et al. (2006) would like a distinction made between this use of the term and "attachment theory" put forth by John Bowlby (1958). Attachment theory says that healthy development occurs when a child forms secure attachment with a stable adult figure. Secure attachment involves the primary caregiver meeting a child's primary physical needs (food, water, shelter, bathing, and medical care) as well as their social needs (responding to a child's facial expressions, moods).

It may be farfetched to suggest animals could meet a child's physical needs, but how extraordinary is it to suggest that animals could be responsive to a child's social needs? As children grow up, they begin to explore their world and gain independence with the knowledge that there is a secure figure to return to when the world gets too scary (Bowlby, 1988). In most cases the biological mother forms secure attachment with their child, but in their absence, secure attachment is possible with other adult figures (fathers, grandmothers, nannies, etc.; R. Bowlby, 2007). When children do not securely attach to a primary caregiver, they may experience a multitude of social and emotional problems later in life. These problems include the negotiation of healthy boundaries with others; for example, some children/adolescents may attempt to anxiously attach themselves to others who are not appropriate attachment figures like peers or youth workers.

Many children in residential treatment have problems with healthy attachment from unhealthy parental relationships that may have been abusive or neglectful (Moses, 2000). Crawford et al. (2006) point out several similarities and differences between human-human attachment and human-companion animal attachment in the areas of: goodness of fit, secure base, emotional bond, seeking proximity, and representational models. However, each of these differences is not well explored and further work in this area is needed to understand differences of attachment between human-human and human-companion animal relationship, especially in children.

Important Ethical Considerations in Animal-Assisted Interventions

Therapist as Role Model for Treatment of Animals

Therapists who use therapy animals in their practices have the responsibility to be role models for treatment towards those animals. This includes rewarding good behavior, showing empathy towards animals, employing proper caretaking techniques, and also disciplining bad behavior. Disciplining does not imply that you smack or yell at your animal for chewing up your favorite sweater, but that you punish in a humane way. A stern "no" and the removal of the sweater, followed by ignoring the animal's attempts at attention would show a parent a proper response to poor behavior. This parallels a parent's optimal response to a 2-year-old child throwing a temper tantrum.

There is a responsibility to be familiar with proper training techniques for specific types of animals. Horses require more physical contact and can be physically pushed as they are 10 times larger than a human, however this behavior would not be appropriate with a cat. For example, during an equine therapy session with a family of four, we were working on empowering a mother who used a very passive parenting style. Her adolescent children walked all over her, and the horse was literally walking all around her despite her efforts to make him stand still while we talked. Horses like strong leaders and do not mind being dominated in a humane manner, in fact this is how horse herds operate with a pecking order of dominance. During the following session, the therapist was holding this same horse and was attempting the same behavior with the horse as he had with the mother the previous week. She stood directly in front of him and pushed him back several feet using the lead rope, a move to show him her dominance. He stood perfectly still for the rest of the session. They did not talk about the therapists' actions, but the following week, the mother did exactly this same thing, except she said, "I'm not going to take this anymore." She wasn't just talking about the horse.

Appropriate Client Attachment to Animal

Start with the end in mind. This is a good motto when beginning a therapeutic journey with a new client. It is especially important when incorporating an animal with whom the client could potentially become attached. For example, at a local equine-assisted learning program for adolescents in residential treatment, some clients would cry and show other emotional reactions on the last day of the 8-week program. This may sound strange, but it is important to maintain proper therapeutic boundaries between the animal and the client. Saying something like "Fluffy loves you too," may sound like a nice sentiment, but it encourages a level of unhealthy attachment between a therapy animal and a client. This can be a difficult boundary to negotiate when one of the advantages of AAIs are the animal's ability to hug, cuddle, or maintain some other form of physical contact with a client that may be inappropriate with the therapist. In the local equine-assisted learning program mentioned above, adolescents would lean on their horse or place an arm around their necks or backs. A good rule of thumb is to avoid statements regarding the animal/client relationship that would be inappropriate for the client/therapist relationship.

Prior Assessment of Client's History with Animals

It is extremely important to evaluate the client's history with animals prior to introduction of an animal in the therapeutic environment. Items that should be assessed include: history of animal abuse, allergies, phobias or fears, and behavioral or medical concerns (Delta Society, 1996). Several ethical questions arise in this area including: Should animals be used with adolescents who have a history of animal abuse? Should animals be included with adolescents with severe hyperactivity, psychosis, or explosive histories? How should these histories be assessed, and are certain types of animals more suitable for certain symptoms? Small animals have an increased risk of injury compared to larger animals. There are currently several studies that report positive findings with adults who have psychotic symptoms (Beck, Seraydarian, & Hunter, 1986; Kovacs, Kis, Rozsa, & Rozsa, 2004), indicating the potential benefit of AAIs with individuals who experience psychosis. A careful examination of the client's current symptoms, including their connection to reality and triggers of negative behaviors, should be understood by the handler. Additionally, as mentioned earlier those with histories of animal abuse should be evaluated according to the potential danger the child may present to the animal, the clinicians ability to keep that animal safe, and the potential benefit the child could realize from working with the animal.

Assessing for Animal Abuse

As we have already noted, a young person's history of animal abuse may not necessarily preclude animal assisted interventions. A first step is recognizing that animal abuse may stem from varied motivations (Ascione, 2005). Motivations that may be particularly relevant for adolescents include imitating peer models, engaging in animal abuse during gang initiation activities, modifying a negative mood state via the "excitement" of harming living creatures, involving animals in sexual activity, and retaliation against an animal's owner. Exploring an adolescent's motivation for harming animals can help the clinician judge whether the adolescent is ready for animal assisted therapeutic activities or if such activities should be delayed until animal abuse issues have been resolved.

Fortunately, the science around the assessment of animal abuse has improved dramatically in recent years. Ascione and Maruyama (in press) provide an overview of developments in this field and recommend a relatively easily administered assessment that can be completed by an adolescent's parent or caregiver and by the adolescent as a self-report (Dadds, 2008). Other, more extensive and detailed assessments are also available (Boat, Loar, & Phillips, 2008) that could be adapted by a clinician into a guided script to engage adolescents in an exploration and discussion of past animal abuse experiences. Resources related to both assessment of and therapeutic interventions for animal abuse (Phillips & McQuarrie, 2009; Randour & Davidson, 2008) can be accessed at American Humane's website (www.americanhumane.org).

Since, as we noted, adolescents in therapy may have histories of maltreatment, it behooves the clinician to become familiar with the links between animal abuse and adolescent physical abuse, sexual abuse, and exposure to intimate partner violence (Ascione, 2008, 2009; Ascione & Shapiro, 2009). Empowered by this knowledge, clinicians are in a better position to make decisions about adolescents' readiness for animal assisted interventions. Even extremely troubled youth may benefit from such well-timed therapeutic work. We are reminded of Gendon Swarthout's (1995) wonderful story, *Bless the Beasts and the Children,* in which youth at risk rescue wild buffalo from slaughter. "Beasts and boys considered each other. They smelled each other. And suddenly boys of fifteen, fourteen, and twelve were children once more. The breath of innocent animals blessed them" (p. 142).

Animal Selection and Responsibilities of Handlers

There are several factors for a clinician to consider in the selection of the appropriate animal type to use in one's practice including: physical location, occupational limitations, culture of clientele, handler responsibilities, therapeutic goals, financial considerations, and level of comfort/experience with animals. The Delta Society has standards of practice for handlers that include knowledge about caring for one's animal of choice, continuing education, ability to advocate for one's animal, and necessary veterinary documentation. Additionally, the Delta Society has several behavioral standards that every therapy animal should meet reliability, controllability, predictability, and suitability (Delta Society, 1996).

Almost any domesticated animal can be a therapy animal if it possesses the right qualities including dogs, horses, cats, fish, pocket companion animals (hamsters, rats, mice), and farm animals (cows, chickens, sheep, goats).We will describe the two most common therapy animals used with adolescents: dogs and horses.

Generally speaking, dogs are advantageous therapy animals because they adapt well to new situations, enjoy affection from humans, are easily transportable, learn new commands easily, and are relatively safe when socialized and trained. The handler (therapist or not) has the responsibility of knowing their dogs' stress signals that could indicate the need for action by the handler during a session. For example, you are working with a hyperactive child who is moving very quickly around your therapy dog. Prior to the child entering the room, your dog was quietly snoozing on the floor. Now your dog is showing some stress signals: yawning, panting, and pacing the room. Your dog is stressed out by this child and needs you to intervene. This could be an excellent therapeutic teaching moment for the child to become more aware of the effect their behavior has on others. You could simply point out to the child that your dog seems to be feeling upset at the moment and needs everyone to be very still and calm. The child may be more motivated to calm down if they believe that it will help the dog.

Most adolescents have had a history interacting with dogs as family companion animals, which can be a great place to start a conversation in order to build rapport. While this intervention would be more powerful with a therapy dog present, it is possible to show a picture of your dog as a starting off point. Pichot describes an intervention she used to increase an adolescent client's awareness of their aggressive tone. This client entered her office and very curtly instructed her dog Rocky to "come here!"

Rocky did not come and Pichot indicated that she respected Rocky's opinions and thoughts just as she respected the clients. If Rocky didn't want to come, she wouldn't force him. The client sat down and Pichot started the session, eventually the client calmed down and Rocky came over to visit. This greatly pleased the client, and Pichot asked the client to consider the reason for Rocky's interest in visiting with her now. The client said, "I'm not so angry (now). He probably knew I wouldn't be so fun to be around" (Pichot & Coulter, 2006, p. 179).

There are several seldom mentioned issues that should be taken into account when working with dogs: breed biases (particularly breeds that are thought to be aggressive); a dog's opportunistic nature; a well-tuned olfactory system; dogs are predators who enjoy chasing grabbing, chewing, and holding; no dog is 100% safe; dogs do not like loud or high pitch sounds; and, finally, dogs do not enjoy being left alone (Pichot & Coulter, 2006). While a dog can be trained to control these natural tendencies, they will always be present and must never be ignored. Less experienced or educated dog handlers will say that their dogs are "totally kid safe." Most dogs are "kid safe" to a point, and this point must not be tested or pushed. Therefore, it is always a good practice to not put your dog in any situation where it could potentially be tested, such as leaving the dog alone with children. These drawbacks may seem insignificant for the family companion animal, but they are quite important when bringing the dog into a occupational setting such as a hospital, mental health center, nursing home, or residential treatment center that are not set up to be animal friendly. For example, while visiting a local residential treatment center, a student was meeting with a therapist who had her therapy dog with her that day. During the meeting, the fire alarm went off in the building, and the dog became extremely agitated, pulling her handler out of the building as fast as her little legs would carry her. Once outside the building, the alarm could still be heard, even when they were several hundred yards from the building. The handler was trying very hard to comfort the dog, but the dog was still quite agitated.

Equines also offer a tremendous opportunity for a creative therapist to develop meaningful activities for adolescent clients, but there are several disadvantages to using horses. First, there are increased risks of physical safety when working with horses. Anyone who has had extensive experience working around horses has been stepped on, bitten, received rope burn, a head injury, and/or potentially broken bones. EFMHA and EAGALA both take safety very seriously and have extensive literature on this subject in their manuals. Second, horses are more expensive to keep then most other therapy animals which, in turn, causes an increased session fee. A modest 1 hour EAP session costs $120, where part of this fee goes to the therapist and the other part to the horse handler (EAGALA, 2006). Some programs gain funding from grants, foundations, and private donations to cover the equine expenses, which can then make EAP a more affordable practice. Third, while the horse's intimidating size may be therapeutically beneficial for many clients, it could also be disadvantageous for others. Fourth, equine therapy facilities are not easily accessible or available in all areas including urban areas with some exceptions. For instance, the Horses in the Hood program works exclusively with children of color in South Central, Los Angeles (Horses in the Hood, 2009).

Cultural Considerations

While conducting an assessment of a client's history with animals, cultural consider-ations for the treatment and role of companion animals should be assessed. Just as ther-apists' values, beliefs, political, and religious views may differ widely from their clients, views and practices regarding treatment of animals may also clash. Cultural differences in animal treatment practices creep into the AAT environment in unexpected ways. For example, during an equine-assisted psychotherapy session a boy from Mexico took his horse's lead rope (leash for horses), and placed it underneath a pole on the ground. The therapist was stunned for an instant before she realized that he was securing his horse so that he could assist another student with her horse (she was having some trou-ble). When the therapist asked him about this, he indicated that this was how his family in Mexico had secured their horses, by placing their leads under a large rock. She com-plimented his helpfulness, as well as his attempts to secure his horse so that she would be safe while he helped another. Then, the therapist explained the normal practice for securing horses in U.S. culture was the use of a quick release knot and explained that this was the method he needed to use from now on as the horses were trained to this method and to secure them in another way could jeopardize their safety.

Other cultural considerations that must be taken into account are history of involvement with dog fighting, cock fighting, interactions with police dogs, use of dogs for protection, cultures where dogs, cats, horses, or other therapy animals are consumed, and cultures where dogs are used by authorities in brutal ways. This list is not exhaustive as was evidenced by the example above. Every client will have a dif-ferent history interacting with animals that will influence their interactions during therapy sessions.

Risley-Curtiss, Holley, and Wolf (2006) did an exploratory study using phone interviews of ethnic diversity in the human-animal bond. The 587 completed phone interviews included 37 questions regarding care and beliefs about companion ani-mals. Overall, 63% of respondents reported owning a companion animal, where 77.2% of companion animal owners were White, and 79.1% of owners had dogs. Those who identified as American Indian (73.5%) were most likely to have a companion animal, followed by White Non-Hispanic (65%), Hispanic/Spanish heritage (56.9%), African American (40.9%), Pacific Islander (40%), and Asian (37.5%). Interestingly, a compar-ison study, which included a significantly higher representation of non-White eth-nicities, produced a similar breakdown of companion animal ownership: White 74%, Latino 47%, African American 37%, and Asian 43% (Siegel, 1995).

Analysis for possible predictors of types of animals (dogs, horses, birds, cats, rab-bits, fish, small animals (rats, mice, etc), and turtles) by ethnic diversity revealed that those of Hispanic/Spanish heritage were significantly less likely to own cats or birds, and that those identifying as American Indian were significantly more likely to own fish (Risley-Curtiss et al., 2006). Additionally, those who identified as Hispanic/Spanish origin were significantly less likely to have a veterinarian, 3.41 times more likely to not have their companion animal neutered or spayed, and 55% more likely to get a "sense of personal safety" from their companion animal. One of the most interesting findings in this study was that there were no significant differences between ethnicities regarding a companion animal's ability to offer emotional support, unconditional love, and companionship. Additionally, 97% of respondents with companion animals considered them "members of the family," indicating the need to further study the role of companion animals in family structures. Limitations of the study include generalizability to the African American population as this group was underrepresented in the sample compared to generally accepted population information in the area.

Siegel (1995) found that White adolescents reported a closer attachment to their companion animals compared to non-White adolescents (Latino, African American, and Asian). Other significant findings include the increased likelihood of companion animals in households with mean annual incomes over $40,000 and households that are detached homes. Additionally they found that only children (no siblings), regardless of ethnicity, reported a stronger attachment to their pets then those with siblings. This would support the role of companion animals in family systems according to Melson's (2003) biocentric development theory.

Case Study

Background and Placement History

Jason is a 13-year-old White male from an urban midwestern city. He has a mild developmental disability and also experiences attachment difficulties, but does not have a diagnosis of reactive attachment disorder. Jason was born with fetal alcohol syndrome. He lived with his biological mother for the first few years of his life, was removed to a foster home from ages 5–6 due to neglect, went back to live with his biological mother from ages 6–10, was removed again due to neglect, and placed in a foster to adopt home with Suzanne and Fred. Suzanne and Fred were very welcoming parents who Jason reported liking very much. Several months after he went to live with Suzanne and Fred, one of their other children reported that Jason would watch him change clothing and had tried to touch him in a sexually inappropriate manner. Child protective services attempted to mediate this situation with in home family and individual therapy. However, Jason continued to act in a voyeuristic manner towards his younger siblings. Child protective services ultimately removed him from this home because of the risk he posed to his younger siblings and placed him in a foster home with several older boys at age 11. When Jason was introduced to his new foster mother, she asked him, "Do you like animals?" He responded with a very excited "Yes, I love them, we used to have a dog when I lived with my real mom, but he didn't act right and we had to get rid of him." His foster mom, Jessica, replied, "That is good to hear that you like animals because I have a dog, a cat, 4 horses, and 2 goats."

Presenting Problem

Jason continued with in home individual and family therapy in his new placement. He had a very difficult time bonding with his foster brothers who described him as: "extremely annoying," "he never shuts up," and "needs all the attention." However, he bonded very well with the animals in Jessica's home. It was for this reason that Jessica found a program that offered animal-assisted therapy for Jason. This particular program offered equine-assisted psychotherapy and canine assisted psychotherapy using agility training. After 2 years of in home individual and family therapy, Jason had made little progress towards his treatment goals. Jessica reported that the other children resented Jason during family therapy because the majority of the time was spent dealing with one of his issues. Jessica also reported that Jason was extremely needy of her attention and was constantly creating negative means to gain this attention (i.e., verbal and physical fights with foster brothers, dismantling household appliances, refusing to follow directives, and shouting obscenities and insults at other members of the household). Regarding his bond with the animals in Jessica's household, Jason said, "Whenever I'm feeling upset about something, I just got hang out with the horses and pet them, they are my friends." Jason's strengths included his helpfulness, resilience to insults, and his caring nature towards animals.

The therapist determined that Jason was anxiously attached to Jessica (a form of insecure attachment) and viewed any attention she gave to other children as a threat to him. Additionally, Jessica was Jason's only ally in the family, as all of the other children in the household were vehemently opposed to Jason living with them and would often tell him. One foster child would routinely tell Jason, "You should have never been born."

Goals for Therapy

- Goal 1: Create healthier attachment between Jason and Jessica using family therapy with equines as evidenced by Jessica reporting increased independence and decreased attention-seeking behavior from Jason.
- Goal 2: Increase Jason's sense of self-efficacy using canine agility as evidenced by self-reported and parent-reported accounts of Jason taking healthy risks in new activities.
- Goal 3: Create a less triangulated family dynamic using equine family therapy where Jason has other allies in the household besides Jessica as evidenced by Jason or Jessica reporting increased empathy from at least one foster brother towards Jason.

Animal-Assisted Interventions with Jason Using Equines and Canines

Equine-Assisted Family Therapy   Jason participated in 1 year of equine and canine therapy with a licensed clinical social worker. The therapist brought in a structural and Bowenian family therapy approach to her equine-assisted psychotherapy work. The equine family therapy included Jessica, Jason, and Jeffery, Jason's oldest foster brother (17 years old) who was a strong role model in the household, for 12 weekly sessions. Jeffery had participated in the foster brothers' coalition against Jason. The therapist decided to include Jeffery in therapy because of his ability to influence the other brothers and also his strong ability to empathize with others. The hope was that Jeffery could influence the other brothers to be more accepting and empathetic towards Jason.

The first few sessions of equine therapy involved silent activities where the family had to perform a task with the horse as a team without speaking. One such activity, extended appendages, asks the family to linked arms and then perform a task such as catching a horse, leading a horse through an obstacle course, or placing a saddle or bridle on a horse (EAGALA, 2006). The therapist's rationale for this approach was to help the family find a more healthy way to communicate with one another. This worked very well as Jeffery was able to show some empathy and caring towards Jason during the processing of these sessions.

The following equine sessions involved several riding sessions. All members of the family had riding experience and basic riding skills. Therefore the family was able to do more complex activities than clients without riding experience. The therapist created challenging activities that included elements competition (i.e., two partners holding a rope and trying to steer their horses through an obstacle course without dropping the rope). These activities brought out conflict between Jeffery and Jason, Jason and Jessica, but not between Jeffery and Jessica that the therapist was able to use as a metaphor for their dynamic in the household. Specifically, neither Jessica nor Jeffery were able to find a way to work through the activity in a positive way with Jason, whereas Jessica and Jeffery were able to do this activity quite easily. Additionally, the horses reacted to their escalated voices during the activity by walking faster and taking a few trot steps, which made it more difficult to steer them through the course. The therapist was able to use the horses's reaction to create a metaphor for the level of anxiety that conflict creates in the household. Anxious feelings that were unpleasant to live with resonated strongly with all members of the family. It also seemed to create some motivation to address the issues from all members of the family as they reported a healthier dynamic directly after this session.

The final few equine sessions had an increased focus on Jeffery. Jessica brought up some concerns about Jeffery moving out soon and his readiness to return to his biological mother's care. Interestingly these sessions involved ground activities where the family choose to have a talk therapy type session in the pasture with the horses. Jason held a horse and played with the mane, scratched the neck and leaned on the horse for these last few sessions. This activity seemed to soothe Jason during the sessions. For most of these sessions, Jeffery and Jessica just stood and talked with the therapist while Jason simply stood by silently interacting with the horse. Jeffery would occasionally walk around the pasture when he became angry or frustrated with something. The family dynamic had decentralized from Jason to a broader focus on all members of the family. Thus, Jessica's desire to discuss Jeffery's move was embraced by the therapist as it allowed decentralized the family's focus on Jason. Additionally, during one of these sessions where Jeffery became angry and started to attack Jason verbally, Jason started to cry and revealed some deeper feelings of guilt and fear concerning his inappropriate sexual behavior that lead to his potential adoptive family "giving up on me." The entire time he was talking about these feelings, he was holding a horse. When he stopped talking, he placed the horse between himself and his family while he cried. The horse seemed to act as a shield that allowed him to be vulnerable. After this tough session, the family reported some drastic changes in the way everyone was interacting. There was still conflict, but it wasn't just between Jason and everyone else, the conflict was between everyone in the family.

Canine-Assisted Therapy Using Agility   Canine-assisted therapy was individual with Jason only and occurred concurrently with the equine-assisted therapy. There were two focuses in this therapy, understanding behavioral reinforcement used in training canines and increasing self-efficacy through performance of agility activities. Two border collies, Tux and Sherman, who were agility trained, were used for every session. Both dogs were high energy, fast, and excitable. Therapy started by simply creating ground rules for interacting with the dogs in appropriate ways, including lessons around appropriate times to reward/not reward behavior.

The majority of the sessions were spent performing agility activities with Tux and Sherman. Jason greatly enjoyed this activity and showed confidence when he was able to take the dogs through a whole set of obstacles without a mistake. The therapist had to negotiate two different roles during these sessions: trainer and therapist. In her trainer role, she instructed Jason on the proper commands, corrected his mistakes, and encouraged him when he did something correctly. At the end of the session she would switch back into her therapist role where she would process the session with him and try to ask questions that would link behavior she saw in session to his behavior outside of session.

A theme throughout the sessions was a focus on some attention-seeking behaviors that Tux would often use to get affection. Tux would walk up to a person and nudge their hand strongly with his nose. Jason thought that this was a very adorable behavior at first and would stroke Tux on the head when he would do it. However, after several sessions, he started to become annoyed by this behavior. The therapist had asked him in the beginning about his thoughts on this behavior, and Jason said he didn't mind it. Now, they were able to discuss the "annoyance" this behavior created (a theme from the family) and that Jason had inadvertently supported this behavior by giving him attention when he nudged. From there, the therapist was able to show Jason a behavioral modification strategy to reduce the nudging. Additionally, she was able to discuss with Jason the feeling of annoyance. The therapist decided to refrain from making a direct link between the annoyance dynamic with the canines and the annoyance dynamic in the family. She knew that it would be more powerful if Jason discovered this link himself.

Level of Goal Achievement

Goal 1 (increase healthy attachment): Progress towards this goal occurred when Jason discussed his feelings of guilt and fear during the equine family sessions. There was a discussion around Jason's fear that nobody would ever care for him and that he would always do something negative to push people away from him. This created insight for Jason around his attention-seeking behavior from Jessica. Several weeks after this session, Jessica reported that Jason was making friends at school and that he had expressed some desires to participate in extra-curricular activities with friends. He still used some attention-seeking behaviors, specifically when there was conflict between him and his foster brothers, but these behaviors were about 50% reduced from when he started therapy.

Goal 2 (increase self-efficacy): Jason's participation in extra-curricular activities can be viewed as a positive risk. Jessica reported that Jason has been telling her, "No I don't want to," when she asks him to do a household chore. While this is creating some conflict between Jessica and Jason, it does give evidence to Jason's sense of confidence, independence, and control of himself. Previously, Jason would perform any chore without question that Jessica asked of him. During the adolescent stage of development, the child begins to ask for more independence, which, in turn, creates some conflict between parent/child. Therefore, this type of conflict may be considered fairly normal and healthy.

Goal 3 (decreased triangulation): The family has reported that there is no longer a central focus on Jason as the "problem child," which would indicate a decrease in triangulation. However, he still has not bonded with any of the foster brothers which is troubling. Even though Jason has bonded with some friends from school, a positive factor in his life, the absence of another ally in the family is a risk factor for a return of the triangulation dynamic.

Summary

There is an extensive history of anecdotal writings, a plethora of case studies and unpublished work, and several quantitative pilot studies that tout the benefits of AAIs, which include social support, calming effect, ability to uplift mood, and increasing self-esteem. Unfortunately, there is less empirical evidence to support these benefits. Despite this, there are university programs that teach/study the human animal bond and numerous private programs that use AAIs with adolescent populations. These program and organizations are active in promoting new research in the field of AAI. Clinicians use AAIs in a variety of settings (schools, residential treatment centers, outpatient clinics, and farm environments) for a variety of purposes including: engagement, to build self-esteem, reinforce boundaries, as an object to project feelings and thoughts, to practice parenting skills, to address attachment difficulties, and many other purposes. Prior to initiating any AAI, there are several areas that need to be assessed in the interest of safety to the animal and client (e.g., history of animal abuse, history of interactions with animals, cultural beliefs about animals, allergies, and level of self-awareness/control). AAIs can compliment traditional forms of talk therapy including solution focused or cognitive behavioral therapy or stand alone as their own form of therapy, dog training, or horseback riding. Animals-assisted interventions offer a broad array of therapeutic tools for a creative clinician to adapt and utilize with adolescent clients.

Activities to Extend Your Learning

- Explore two unique residential treatment programs, Green Chimneys and Gaitway High School, that have a vast variety of animal assisted activities and therapies: http://www.greenchimneys.org, http://www.fieldstonefarmtrc.com/GaitwayMain.php

- Create a curriculum that addresses a common treatment area in the adolescent population (anxiety, depression, attachment) using animal-assisted interventions.
- Volunteer for an animal assisted program. Potential opportunities include an educational program at a local animal shelter or as an assistant in a therapeutic riding program.
- Interview a clinician that uses animal-assisted interventions in their practice.

Recommended Resources

Websites

American Hippotherapy Association: http://www.americanhippotherapyassociation.org/
Delta Society: http://www.deltasociety.org/Page.aspx?pid=183
Equine Assisted Growth and Learning Association (EAGALA): http://www.eagala.org/
Equine Facilitate Mental Health Association (EFMHA): http://www.narha.org/SecEFMHA/WhatIsEFMHA.asp
International Society for Anthrozoology: http://www.isaz.net/
North American Riding for the Handicapped Association (NARHA): http://www.narha.org/
Therapy Dog International: http://www.tdi-dog.org/
University of Denver Institute for Human Animal Connection: http://www.humananimalconnection.org/
University of Denver Graduate School of Social Work, Animal Assisted Social Work Certificate: http://www.du.edu/socialwork/programs/msw/concentration/certprograms/aaswcertificate.html
University of Pennsylvania School of Veterinary Medicine, Center for the Interaction of Animals and Society: http://research.vet.upenn.edu/Default.aspx?alias=research.vet.upenn.edu/cias

Readings

Chandler, C. K. (2005). *Animal assisted therapy in counseling.* New York: Routledge Taylor & Francis Group.
Fine, A. H. (2006). *Handbook on animal assisted therapy: Theoretical foundations and guidelines for practice* (2nd ed.). San Diego, CA: Academic Press.
Katcher, A. H., & Beck, A. M. (1983). *New perspectives on our lives with companion animals* (pp. 351–359). Philadelphia: University of Pennsylvania Press.
Kellert, S. R., & Wilson, E.O. (1993). *Biophilia hypothesis.* Washington DC: Island Press.
Mandrell, P. J. (2006). *Introduction to equine-assisted psychotherapy: A comprehensive overview.* Author.
Turid, R. (2006). *On talking terms with dogs: Calming signals.* Wenatchee, WA: Dogwise Publishing.

6.

BIBLIOTHERAPY AS AN INTERVENTION APPROACH FOR CHILDREN AND ADOLESCENTS WITH EMOTIONAL DISABILITIES

Karen Gavigan, Stephanie Kurtts, and Megan Mimms

Overview of Chapter

This chapter presents bibliotherapy as a supportive intervention in child and adolescent mental health and includes the following sections:
- Introduction
- Definition and History
- Theoretical Perspectives in the Literature
- Prior Research on Bibliotherapy
- Therapeutic Applications with Specific Children and Adolescent Populations
- Therapeutic Components of the Intervention
- Examples of Bibliotherapy Interventions
- Ethical and Cultural Considerations of Bibliotherapy
- Case Study
- Summary
- Activities to Extend Your Learning

Introduction

Bibliotherapy is an intervention that has been used to treat mental illnesses and emotional disturbances for many years and across different groups of individuals. This has included populations such as war veterans, individuals seeking counseling for emotional needs, and children and adolescents in need of social skills instruction (Regan & Page, 2008). Bibliotherapy has been long been considered a strategic healing tool for addressing healthy social and emotional development of individuals with disabilities as well as helping those without disabilities to understand the issues associated with children and youth with special needs (Kurtts & Gavigan, 2008; Pardeck, 1994).

The use of children's and adolescent literature is a way to share powerful examples of how people may or may not relate to individual differences. This can be especially true for understanding how disabilities impact the lives of individuals and their families and friends. For professionals who serve children and adolescents with mental health issues, exposure to the use of children's literature about disabilities can offer an effective instructional tool to not only help students develop empathy and understanding of diversity, but also to inform their own professional practice as they prepare to meet the individual educational needs of children in their classrooms.

Bibliotherapy may also be considered as a tool for collaboration amongst professionals who provide support and intervention for children and youth with emotional disturbances and may be considered to be at-risk for potentially negative outcomes or behaviors (McCarty, & Chalmers, 1997). This a particularly significant point when considering how many professionals may be involved in the treatment of and intervention approaches used with children and youth with mental illness and emotional disturbances.

In order to better understand the role and purpose of bibliotherapy in addressing the treatment of children and adolescents with mental health issues and potentially at-risk behaviors, this chapter includes the following topics:

- definitions and history of bibliotherapy
- theoretical perspectives and related research presented in the literature on bibliotherapy
- therapeutic applications and components of selected bibliotherapeutic interventions
- ethical and cultural considerations of the use of bibliotherapy
- a case study depicting bibliotherapy as an intervention for adolescent mental health issues

Definition and History

We read to discover that we are not alone.
—C. S. Lewis from the movie, *Shadowlands*, as cited in Herbert & Kent, 2000, p. 171

Herbert and Kent (2000) define bibliotherapy as an attempt to use literature in a way that helps children understand themselves and to cope with problems relevant to their personal situations and developmental needs at the appropriate time. Others define bibliotherapy as a process that leads youth toward emotional wel-being through a facilitated dialogue about literature (Hynes & Hynes-Berry, 1986; Schlicter & Burke, 1994). The ultimate goal of bibliotherapy is not to evaluate whether or not an individual comprehends the text. Rather, it is used to help the reader evaluate their feelings and the ways in which they respond to the literature.

Specifically, Aiex (1993) delineates nine reasons for using bibliotherapy with children and youth:

- To show an individual that he or she is not the first or only person to encounter such a problem;
- To show an individual that there is more than one solution to a problem;
- To help a person discuss a problem more freely;
- To help an individual plan a constructive course of action to solve a problem;
- To develop an individual's self-concept;
- To relieve emotional or mental pressure;

- To foster an individual's honest self-appraisal;
- To provide a way for a person to find interest outside of self; and
- To increase an individuals' understanding of human behavior or motivations.

Using literature to help young people develop emotionally and socially has evolved over thousands of years. In fact, the history of bibliotherapy can be traced back to ancient times. For example, the Greeks referred to *biblion* (book) and *therapeia* (healing) (Rudman, Gagne, & Bernstein, 1993). As early as the 19th century, doctors began prescribing books to hospital patients so that they could become familiar with their medical issues (Warner, 1980). In 1916, Samuel McChord Crothers was one of the first American authors to use the word *bibilotherapy*. However, it wasn't until the 1930s and 40s that lists of therapeutic books were prepared and other articles began to appear about bibliotherapy (Rudman et al., 1993).

Currently, there are two types of bibliotherapy. The first is *clinical bibliotherapy*, a technique used by trained mental health professionals to guide clients through problems by directed reading. Clinical bibliotherapy is "a mode of intervention in aiding persons severely troubled with emotional or behavioral problems" (Lack, 1985, p. 29).

For the purpose of this chapter, the emphasis will be on *developmental bibliotherapy*, which focuses on needs that are developmental in nature rather than relying on a clinical approach (Doll & Doll, 1997). It is the approach used most often in school and library settings as well as in other community service agencies that serve children and youth. The objective of developmental bibliotherapy is *to promote and maintain mental health and to foster self-actualization through the interaction between an individual and literature* (Rudman et al., 1993). Developmental bibliotherapy attempts to help individuals deal with stressful social and emotional issues such as abuse, adoption, bullying, death, and divorce. It has also been used successfully to address self-concept and physical disability issues with children and adolescents.

Theoretical Perspectives in the Literature

Sociocultural Perspective of Literacy Learning

Bibliotherapy is based on a sociocultural perspective of literacy learning (Bakhtin, 1986; Rosenblatt, 1978; Vygotsky, 1978). Vygotsky's sociocultural lens is centered on the belief that "human leaning presupposes a specific social nature and a process by which children grow into the intellectual life of those around them" (1978, p. 88). His theory stressed the role of language in the learning process. During bibliotherapy sessions, students use language to facilitate their interpretations of text, exposing their ideas to the influence of conversations with service providers and/or peers.

Many of today's literacy theorists and practitioners share Vygotsky's belief that learning is a social process. They feel that students should interact with teachers and peers using oral and written language to construct meaning about what they have read (Alvermann, 1987; Daniels & Steineke, 2004; Guthrie, 2008; Raphael et al., 2001). Bibliotherapy is a natural extension of the theory that language learning is socioculturally based since sessions allow readers opportunities to respond to literature through facilitated dialogue. Furthermore, these sessions enable readers to identify, discuss, and analyze the meaning of text about developmental issues.

The sociococultural theories of Vygotsky are extended through the work of Bakhtin (1986), a Russian philosopher and linguist who believed that meaningful learning occurs when speakers engage with one another in a social interaction. It was Bakhtin's belief that we need others to respond to the thoughts we express in order to help us understand ourselves. In terms of bibliotherapy, Bahktin's work supports the theory that students need frequent opportunities to become active participants in discussion-based literacy settings. It is through discussion that students find meaningful ways to negotiate their understandings of literature and to deal with tensions that often exist in their lives. Bibliotherapy sessions can enhance readers' development by offering an environment in which children and youth can develop both socially and intellectually as they interact with their teacher and/or peers.

Rosenblatt's reader-response theory echoes many of the ideas of Bakhtin and Vygotsky (Rosenblatt, 1978). It is a school of literary theory that focuses on the reader and his or her experience of a literary work. For example, Rosenblatt stated that reading is a transaction, a two-way process between the reader and the text at a special time and with certain circumstances. She made the case that "understanding literary reading is a process whereby personal responses are continually transformed to create an ever widening net of relations connecting individual readers with the world at large" (cited in Faust, Cockrill, Hancock, & Isserstedt, 2005, p. 166).

Prior Research on Bibliotherapy

There are several studies examining the use of bibliotherapy with children and young adults dealing with difficult issues. One of the more recent studies examined the ways in which 20 graduate students used 16 literature selections to facilitate the social-emotional learning of at-risk youth (Regan & Page, 2008). The graduate students used an online forum to exchange ideas and experiences regarding their bibliotherapy sessions. Using the Circle of Courage model (discussed later in this chapter), they aligned their novels with the four dimensions of Belonging, Generosity, Mastery, and Independence. The graduate students found that the literature they used with at-risk youth provided these adolescents with positive and powerful experiences.

In another study, Ackerson, Scogin, McKendree-Smith, and Lyman (1998) found that bibliotherapy was beneficial for adolescents struggling with depression. The results of the study showed that bibliotherapy may prove to be an effective treatment for adolescents who are reluctant to use psychosocial or pharmacological treatments. Another bibliotherapy study dealing with adolescents found that literature was effective in supporting gay and lesbian youth (Vare & Norton, 2004).

Additional studies on bibliotherapy have addressed the social and emotional concerns of students with disabilities. For example, studies by Moody and Limper and Zaccaria (as cited in Lenkowsky, 1987) demonstrated that bibliotherapeutic instruction was an effective process for improving the self-efficacy, feelings, and productivity of children with disabilities. Cornett and Cornett (as cited in Borders & Paisley,

1992) demonstrated that the use of bibliotherapy improved students' perception of self worth and achievement and had positive effects on students' social behavior, interpersonal relationships, and acceptance of people different from themselves. In terms of physical disabilities, bibliotherapy was discovered to be helpful in easing the social concerns and physical problems experienced by children who were blind.

Research Limitations

There is currently a limited amount of empirical evidence to support the use of bibliotherapy with children and youth. Additional research is needed to inform the policy and practice of service providers who serve this population. Furthermore, research regarding bibliotherapy can vary widely. In the past, researchers often used varying and wide-ranging definitions of bibliotherapy (Doll & Doll, 1997). Some researchers lack the experimental design skills needed to conduct rigorous research (Prater, Johnstun, Dyches, & Johnstun, 2006). Finally, other researchers struggle to prove that the effects of bibliotherapy are unique, and not the result of other interventions (Vare & Norton, 2004).

Perspectives on Bibliotherapy in Professional Literature

Although, there is a need for more empirical research in the field of bibliotherapy, many professionals continually advocate its use with children and young adults. Several of these non-clinicians have written articles encouraging the use of developmental bibliotherapy to address social and emotional issues faced by children and youth. For example, one librarian examined the use of bibliotherapy with students experiencing teasing and name calling (Duimestra, 2003). Similarly, two school nurses wrote an article recommending bibliotherapy as a strategy for helping students deal with bullying (Gregory & Vessey, 2004). Furthermore, Corr (2004) encouraged the use of bibliotherapy as a means for supporting students dealing with death. The concept of using bibliotherapy to help children facing bereavement issues was presented by a librarian who touted the benefits of using picture books to help grieving children (Manifold, 2007). In addition, Kramar and Smith (1998) described the benefits of using bibliotherapy with students whose parents are going through a divorce.

Forgan (2002) presented the steps for teaching problem solving through bibliotherapy in an article he wrote for *Intervention in School and Clinic*. This approach was also described by Doll and Doll (1997) who wrote that "problem solving provided by literature will cause young people to change the ways in which they interact with or behave toward other people" (p. 8). Additionally, Prater and colleagues (2006) presented a 10-step process for implementing bibliotherapy with at-risk students in the classroom. In a similar program, Schreur (2006) recommended the use of bibliotherapy for suspended at-risk students. These, and other, programs for at-risk students are based on the belief that bibliotherapy can help individuals develop an understanding of how the issues in the literature relate to their own challenging situations.

Several books have been written that add to the body of literature offering perspectives on bibliotherapy. For example, Greenwood Press published a series of books entitled, *Using Literature to Help Troubled Teenagers*. Some of the topics covered in the series include end-of-life issues, identity issues, societal issues, and family issues (Allan, 2002; Carroll, 1999; Kaplan, 1999; Kaywell, 1999). More recently, Prater and Dyches (2008) published the book *Teaching about Disabilities through Children's Literature,* which includes bibliographies and lesson plans about books dealing with attention deficit hyperactivity disorder (ADHD), as well as emotional and behavioral disorders. These and other titles, along with recommendations from librarians and counselors can help service providers determine which literature is appropriate for use in bibliotherapy sessions.

Therapeutic Applications with Specific Children and Adolescent Populations

The developmental bibliotherapy session can be part of a curriculum-based lesson or one that is specifically designed to teach children about an issue. These sessions are effective when they begin and end on a personal note with the reasons that the student found the literature either helpful or unhelpful (Gladding & Gladding, 1991). Forgan (as cited in Iaquinta & Hipsky, 2006) states that a quality bibliotherapy lesson contains the following elements, (a) pre-reading, (b) guided reading, (c) post-reading discussion, and (d) problem-solving and reinforcement activities. For example, a teacher in California developed a successful lesson using the book, *A.D.D. not B.A.D.* (Penn, 2003) with her first-grade students. Her pre-reading activity consisted of asking the students, "What does it mean to be different from everyone else?" After reading the book aloud, the students had the opportunity to role-play a few scenes. The teacher then conducted a post-reading activity and a culminating discussion of positive ways students can interact with A.D.D. students in their classroom (Iaquinta & Hipsky, 2006).

There are numerous other examples of children's and young adult literature that can be used successfully to provide bibliographic instruction. Many of the titles are award-winning literature such as Caldecott and Newbery award books. The Recommended Resources section, located at the end of this chapter, can aid service providers in the selection of appropriate books and informative websites dealing with developmental bibliotherapy.

Sridhar and Vaughn (2000) believe that the most important step when using bibliotherapy with children and youth is to match appropriate books with the reader and his or her problems. The reader must be able to relate to the character in the books whether they are real or fictional. It is also important to select quality literature that lends itself to discussion. Hynes and Hynes-Berry (1986) cite the following criteria when selecting literature used in bibliotherapy:

- thematic dimensions (powerful vs. trite)
- stylistic dimensions (clear vs. convoluted language)

Therapeutic Components of the Intervention

Whitney, a classroom teacher, writes about her experience using the book *Crazy Lady!* (Conly, 1993) with high school students.

> I thought, now that is a book that will help high school students understand and accept one another, just like the characters did! I wanted to read the entire book out loud to all of the students. (personal communication, January 20, 2007)

Typically, bibliotherapy sessions consist of reading the literature, or listening to it being read aloud, followed by a discussion led by a facilitator (Borders & Paisley, 1992).

Many of the professionals who use developmental bibliotherapy, recommend that it be conducted in stages. For example, Forgan (2002) advocates the use of a four-stage bibliotherapy framework. This instructional framework includes pre-reading, guided reading, post-reading discussion, and follow-up activities. During the pre-reading stage of bibliotherapy, the facilitator activates the reader's background knowledge and makes predictions about the book to set the stage for reading. This is followed by the guided reading stage in which the facilitator helps students identify with the character's problems at the same time they relate them to their own. During the post-reading discussion, students are encouraged to generate alternative solutions to the character's problems. Finally, role-playing, writing, interactive games and other follow-up activities are used to practice the problem-solving process. An example of implementation of this approach is addressed in the chapter section on therapeutic components of intervention.

Other service professionals believe that readers should encounter three stages; identification, catharsis, and insight (Afolayan, 1992; Kramar & Smith, 1998; Morawski, 1997; Sridhar & Vaughn, 2000). They believe that in an effective bibliotherapeutic intervention, the reader should experience:

- Identification: The main character should be close in age to the students and should exhibit behaviors and experiences similar to those of the reader.
- Catharsis: In addition to identifying with the main character, readers should relate to their actions in the story and feel emotional ties with him or her.
- Insight: The readers are provided opportunities to analyze the main character and situation and develop opinions regarding behaviors or actions adopted by the main character in his or her attempts to deal with the problem.

Examples of Bibliotherapy Interventions

The 10-Step Process

The 10-step process that has been described by Prater and colleagues (2006) suggests an effective approach to implementation of bibliotherapy in classroom settings. This approach can address behaviors of children who are at-risk for school failure by allowing them to deal with sensitive issues such as social, economic, and family stress factors that may impact school performance. In addition, Prater and colleagues suggest that the 10-step process to using bibliotherapy in a classroom setting also provides additional intervention to teach social skills that can help prevent school failure.

Step one. Develop a relationship with the student by establishing trust, confidence and rapport. It is important for students to feel comfortable with their teacher in order to share their innermost thoughts and goals. Sharing of personal experiences is necessary in defining specific aspects of a child's life that may need to be addressed.

Step two. Other school personnel that may help in the bibliotherapy process must then be identified in step two. Such personnel may include related service providers, administrators, or staff members that are involved in the well-being and day-to-day goings on of the educational life of the student.

Step three. Parents are an integral part of this process. They are an asset when determining a student's family and educational history, but they also may be part of the problem due to possible alcohol, drug, and other challenges that may have contributed to the student's educational issues. It is necessary to first determine what information you will be comfortable asking the parents to share.

Step four. After developing a relationship with the student and getting others, such as parents and/or related service providers, involved in the bibliotherapy process, it is necessary to clearly identify a specific problem that the student is having. This problem should be one that is directly affecting the student's educational, social, and/or emotional performance in school.

Step five. Teachers should then define variables necessary to solve the problem, keeping in mind that bibliotherapy is an option, but it might not be appropriate for the specific problem that has been identified. If it is appropriate, then specific bibliotherapy activities should be developed, either for the entire class, student groups, or individual students.

Step six. Books that appropriately address the defined issue must be located. These books could be chapter or picture books, depending on the age of the student, keeping in mind that there are many picture books that can be used to interact with students of all ages. The chosen books should also be interesting to the student and have an aspect of realism.

Step seven. The chosen book is then introduced to only the student or students who are participating in the bibliotherapy process. The teacher must use discretion when describing why the book was chosen, specifically relating the choice to behaviors she has observed in the classroom and how the book may help avoid similar behaviors in the future.

Step eight. After the introduction of the book, reading activities should be implemented. Such activities could include journal writing, compare/contrast activities, and question/answer sessions. Journal writing allows students to share their thoughts and feelings on paper. Teachers should respect students' privacy and only encourage those students who choose to read their writings aloud to do so. Comparing and contrasting allows the student to compare their own experiences to those of the character in order to observe their similarities and differences, hopefully, allowing them to make connections between their own behavior or experience and the behavior or experience of the character. Question and answer sessions allow children to further explore the chosen reading, possibly opening up more doors of understanding to their own behavior and personal interactions.

Step nine. Post-reading activities can vary depending on the strength of each individual student. For example, those students who are gifted in art can choose to make a collage, a poster, or a sculpture to represent an idea or concept of the story. Those students who are gifted writers may choose to write a letter to a specified character or rewrite part of the story.

Step ten. The final step involves evaluating the effectiveness of the bibliotherapy activity by revisiting each step to decide which steps were most effective and which steps were least effective. Teachers can then share this information with the parent and the student to discuss and reevaluate the student's progress.

Circle of Courage Model

In the American Indian culture, the Circle of Courage is based on values related to raising children and developing youth in a positive manner. The medicine wheel is used to represent belonging, generosity, independence, and mastery in order to nurture children to their fullest potential. The Circle of Courage can be used as a bibliotherapy approach to connect with children and youth with emotional disturbances (Regan & Page, 2008). The Developmental Therapy-Developmental Teaching Model will also be discussed.

Belonging. This term can be defined in the following statement, "It takes a village to raise a child." In this sense, belonging refers to the necessity of all adults in a community to take ownership of a child's development and help the child feel a part of that community. In literature, the lack of belongingness often contributes to feelings of anxiety for the characters involved. Choosing books with positive interactions between characters allows students to copy those interactions, thus improving their behaviors and sense of belonging.

Generosity. Generosity refers to the need to be of assistance to others. Through literature, involving bravery or sacrifice, students can observe that it is often more beneficial to give than to receive. Generosity can be shown by students working in groups and by assisting others during other types of activities related to the literature selection.

Independence. The more children are allowed to learn from their own mistakes, the more likely they will develop into an independent individual. Self-control is a contributing factor to those students attempting to become independent. Using appropriate literature can assist students in making appropriate choices and to learn from those mistakes made in the past.

Mastery. In the Circle of Courage, mastery is the belief that you must feel competent in a skill in order to obtain further success. Oftentimes, students who are at-risk struggle with accepting the fact that they have mastered a skill, largely in part to a history of failed attempts. Using literature to relate to characters can give students the ability to accept and incorporate their strengths in their educational careers.

As mentioned earlier, in the 10-step process, students must be given appropriate post-reading options in order to express and understand their talents.

Developmental Therapy-Developmental Teaching Model

The Developmental Therapy-Developmental Teaching Model relates to underlying issues associated with the problematic behavior of characters represented in the literature, and must be discussed with the Circle of Courage Model. It is important to realize the stages of development that children go through in order to represent their feelings and behaviors with appropriate literature. Such literature will surely bring students anxieties to light, and appropriate use of characters will enable students to relate their experiences to others, opening them up for a greater understanding of themselves, and therefore, a higher self-esteem.

Literature Circles

Stringer, Reynolds, and Simpson (2003) attempted to improve students' self-esteem in reading by incorporating literature circles through a collaborative partnership between a classroom teacher and a school counselor. Bibliotherapy trade books were chosen based on appropriate reading level and content related to self-esteem issues. Literature Circle training was provided for the teacher and the guidance counselor, and their roles were clarified by a university instructor of reading. Both participants were present during the Literature Circle, with the counselor able to assist with deeper student concerns related to self-esteem.

Although this study revealed no significant change in students' self-esteem as perceived on the pre and post-tests of the revised Tennessee Self-Concept Scale – Children's Form, Stringer and colleagues (2003) believe that continued collaboration, past the 2 months involved in this study, and the use of an alternate test would have shown a positive effect in regards to the students' self-esteem in reading (see Table 6.1).

Table 6.1   Recommended Approaches to the Use of Bibliotherapy

Approach	Who it Helps	Components of Intervention	How it Works
10 Step Process	Children with at-risk behaviors	10 steps to address at-risk behaviors and teach social skills that can help prevent school failure	Helps teachers address at-risk behaviors using literature
Circle of Courage Model	Children and youth with emotional disturbances	Medicine wheel, significant in American Indian culture, represents belonging, mastery, independence, and generosity. Used with the Developmental Therapy-Developmental Teaching Model	Nurtures children's potential, and they thrive
Literature Circle	Children struggling with self-esteem in reading	Appropriate books chosen by and discussed with a teacher and a guidance counselor	Builds self-esteem

Ethical and Cultural Considerations of Bibliotherapy

The literature on the effectiveness of bibliotherapy is mixed; while some studies point to challenges in determining long-term effects, others suggest that bibliotherapy can improve students' self-identity and self-esteem when used with appropriate books chosen with the following ethical and cultural guidelines (Vare & Norton, 2004).

It is essential to incorporate ethical practices when working with students with self-identity issues in order to elicit positive student growth. Drawing from Vare and Norton's (2004) guidelines for use of bibliotherapy with gay and lesbian youth who struggle with self-identity, the following issues should be considered in the ethical and culturally sensitive use of this therapeutic intervention for children and adolescents with emotional disabilities.

Guideline 1: Bibliotherapy is not an easy solution for challenging student issues (Warner, 1989). It is imperative to address student challenges appropriately, and bibliotherapy is one option. More serious interventions may be required depending on the needs of the individual student.

Guideline 2: When suggesting books, teachers must not appear to ignore the issue at hand (Warner, 1980). The bibliotherapy activity is not meant to replace having a discussion about the problem. Rather, it is meant to address personal issues in a more indirect manner.

Guideline 3: Students should not be forced to participate in the reading. Forced participation could contribute to further communication and self-perception issues for students. Presenting literature material via a visual source, such as poster, may encourage students' participation and interest.

Guideline 4: Books should relate to the students' needs and interests (Warner, 1989). Obtaining a selection of literature pertinent to the students' challenges and lifestyles is necessary in promoting understanding of their current life circumstances. Inappropriate material could cause students to be more confused about their identity.

Guideline 5: Teachers should not choose books that will impose values of the general community (Warner, 1980). In order to defer from criticizing a students' individual issue, books that allow students to feel safe and not alone in their challenge are considered appropriate selections.

Guideline 6: Nonfiction and fiction books should be made available. Both types of literature have the potential to contain information directly relating to a youth's situation, allowing them to relate to and benefit both forms of writing.

Guideline 7: Books should include realistic content. Books that inaccurately portray characters using stereotypes or unrealistic information are inappropriate and could contribute to a negative outcome.

Guideline 8: Fiction choices should consist of appropriately developed characters, plots, settings, and themes. Such literary qualities are necessary in accurately portraying resolutions to internal conflicts.

Guideline 9: Books should allow students to understand their challenge rather than be judged by it. Books that directly or indirectly relate to the students' challenges may be useful in promoting an understanding of self-identity. Such books may validate the students' feelings, encouraging them to accept their identity and grow as individuals.

Table 6.2   Suggested Bibliotherapy Titles for Emotional Disabilities and At-Risk Behaviors

Topic	Titles for Children	Publishing Information	Titles for Young Adults	Publishing Information
Anger	*When Sophie Gets Angry – Really, Really Angry* by Molly Bang	New York: Scholastic, Inc. 1999.	*Touching Spirit Bear* by Ben Mikaelsen.	New York: HarperCollins, 2001.
Anxiety	*The Kissing Hand* by Audrey Penn.	Terre Haute, IN Tanglewood Press, 2006	*Nature of Jade* by Deb Caletti.	New York: Simon & Schuster Books for Young Readers, 2007.
Attention Disorders	*Otto Learns about His Medicine* by Matthew Galvin	Washington, D.C.; Magination Press. Revised edition, 1995	*Joey Pigza Swallows the Key* by Jack Gantos	New York: Farrar, Straus, and Giroux, 1998.
Bullying	*The Recess Queen* by Alexis O' Neill & Laura Huliska-Beith	New York: Scholastic, Inc. 2002.	*The Chocolate War* by Robert Cormier	New York: Alfred A. Knopf, 1974.
Death	*The Purple Balloon* by Chris Raschka	New York: Schwartz & Wade, 2007.	*Kira Kira* by Cynthia Kadohata.	New York: Atheneum Books for Young Readers, 2004.
Divorce	*Fred Stays with Me* by Nancy Coffelt	New York: Little, Brown, 2007.	*Along for the Ride* by Sarah Dessen	New York: Viking Juvenile, 2009.
Mental Illness	*We'll Paint the Octopus Red* by Stephanie Stuve-Bodeen	Bethesda, MD: Woodbine House, 1998.	*Kissing Doorknobs* By Terri Hesser	New York: Doubleday, 1998.
Parents with Mental Illness	*Sometimes My Mommy Gets Angry* by Bebe Moore Campbell	NewYork: Viking Penguin, 2003.	*So B. It* by Sarah Weeks	New York: HarperCollins, 2005.
Self-Esteem	*Ziggie's Blue Ribbon Day* by R.W. Ally	New York: Farrar, Straus and Giroux, 2005.	*Chicken Boy* by Frances O'Roark Dowell	New York: Atheneum Books for Young Readers, 2005.

Incorporating such guidelines during the bibliotherapy process will heighten the possibility of positive outcomes regarding students who struggle with esteem and identity issues. Table 6.2 provides a selection of recommended books that could appropriately be used with bibliotherapeutic intervention for children with emotional disabilities and at-risk behaviors.

Case Study

This case study gives an example of a second grade boy who is struggling with ADHD, as well as recent grief and loss issues. In this case example, you will read about the interaction of the teacher and the child, as well as the teacher and the family system. This case study is typical of the type of situations in which bibliotherapy may be very useful, especially as applied in the classroom. A the end of the case study, several questions are posed to help the reader consider the ways in which bibliotherapy may be used to help this particular child manage his behaviors, cope with his grief and loss issues, and also work with the child's father.

(This case study is from the IRIS Resource Locator, *Case-based Activities: He Just Needs a Little Discipline.* Retrieved October 27, 2009, from http://iris.peabody.vanderbilt.edu/activities/case_based/ica004.pdf. It has been reprinted with permission from Vanderbilt University.)

He Just Needs a Little Discipline

Matt was diagnosed with attention deficit hyperactivity disorder in second grade. After he started eighth grade, his teachers became concerned about his frequent outbursts in class and tried numerous types of interventions. Ritalin was prescribed in the past and it helped, but Matt's father believes that his son should learn to cope without medication. Matt recently confided in Jill Gray, one of his teachers, that he thought he could focus better if he could go back on the Ritalin. The situation intensified after Matt's mother died and his teachers wondered what to do.

Matt Snyder jumped into the middle of the puddle, not caring that his pants and shoes would be soaked for the remainder of the long trek to his father's coffee shop. He dreaded this long walk every afternoon after school and wondered why his father insisted that it was good for him. Things had been different when his mom was alive. She would never have expected Matt to walk miles in the rain.

Matt had just finished hanging up his raincoat and putting his book bag behind the counter when his dad emerged from the kitchen. "Good grief, Matt, can't I ever count on you for anything?" his father demanded with a disgusted look on his face. "Didn't I tell you this morning to get here pronto because we needed to clean out the cooler? And look at your shoes and pants. They're all wet! I bet you were playing around again, weren't you?" Mr. Snyder grabbed Matt by the arm and pointed him toward the back of the shop. He did not understand why his son was so immature and irresponsible and his frustration with Matt was obvious to everyone. "Sooner or later Matt will have to grow up and learn to act like the rest of us!" he was often heard to say.

Matt was diagnosed with attention deficit hyperactivity disorder (ADHD) and a learning disability at the age of eight. When the family doctor suggested putting Matt on Ritalin to help him focus and stay on task, his mom and dad reluctantly agreed. After Mrs. Snyder's death, Mr. Snyder decided to stop giving Matt the medication, believing that with a little discipline his son could learn to cope without it. "I do not want my son being dependent on a drug to behave and learn in school," he explained to the teachers when they asked why Matt was no longer taking the Ritalin.

Jill had been a teacher for students with learning disabilities in a self-contained classroom for thirteen years; however, this was her first year teaching collaboratively on a multidisciplinary team. Jill, along with four general education teachers, was responsible for teaching social studies, science, English, and math to a group of eighty students. Ten of the students, including Matt, had learning disabilities, emotional handicaps, or both. Jill helped the team modify instruction for the students and also co-taught one class with each of the teachers throughout the day. The team approach was working well for all of the students except Matt.

Matt had difficulty with writing assignments, processing auditory information, and focusing and maintaining his attention. Jill developed lecture outline notes for Matt to follow in each class and paired him with a peer for writing assignments. He was also given additional time to complete his assignments. Even with these modifications, Matt became frustrated easily in class and often threw things on the floor, yelled and cursed at his peers, and pounded his fists on his desk. The team's approach to dealing with disruptive students was to provide them a quiet area away from other students where they could complete their assignments. Each class had several study carrels in the back for students who preferred to work in seclusion or who were placed there as a consequence of disruptive behavior. Matt usually found himself in one of those carrels almost every day during English.

Jill knew that Matt hated English, so she started working with him individually for half of each class. She also developed a contract with him to award extra computer and free time if he completed daily assignments without outbursts and disruptions. None of these interventions helped though, and Matt continued to be frustrated and disruptive.

Matt knew that he had a problem staying focused and believed that he could do better in school if he resumed taking the Ritalin. In a daily journal, Matt wrote "I didn't used to get in trouble all the time at school before my dad stopped letting me take my medicine." Jill was frustrated because Mr. Snyder absolutely refused to consider allowing Matt to resume his medication. In addition, the other teachers were running out of patience and ideas for how to help Matt be successful. His disruptive behavior was spreading to other students in the class.

Matt worked very hard to make the boys' eighth-grade basketball squad—something Mr. Snyder had celebrated proudly. Matt was happy to have finally gained his father's approval, but his explosive temper and lack of control on the court became a real point of contention for his coach. Game after game, Matt was sidelined for his aggressive, on-court behavior. Finally, Coach Levy felt he had no choice but to remove Matt from the team. Mr. Snyder was furious and grounded Matt for a month. But even worse, Matt knew he had let his dad down again. His self-esteem hit an all time low.

The teachers decided to meet as a team with the principal, Mr. George, to discuss what action to take to address Matt's disruptive behavior. Mr. George was very supportive of the teachers' concerns and suggested sending Matt to the office if his disruptions persisted. This meant Matt would have to call home to notify his parent of his office referral and the consequences.

The first time this intervention was tried, Matt expressed his anxiety about calling his father. Jill offered to make the call with him in hopes of buffering the situation at home.

"Hello, is this Mr. Snyder?" she inquired. "This is Mrs. Gray, one of Matt's teachers."

"Yes, Mrs. Gray. What's Matt done now?" he grumbled, anticipating the worst.

"Well, Mr. Snyder, I'm afraid Matt is in the principal's office with a behavior referral. He continues to have problems controlling himself in the classroom and from now on when that happens, he will have to report to Mr. George. We feel you need to be informed of these actions when they occur," Jill explained.

"Is my son there with you?" responded Mr. Snyder in a controlled but angry voice. "Please put him on the phone."

Jill handed the phone to Matt. "Your father wants to talk to you, Matt. Are you okay?" Matt nodded his head yes.

Matt didn't say a word for several minutes as he held the phone to his ear. Jill could hear Mr. Snyder yelling over the phone. As perspiration began to appear on Matt's face, Jill motioned him to hand the phone back to her. "Matt, I need to speak with your father in private. Please go to the lobby and wait for me there," she instructed.

"Mr. Snyder, our concern is that Matt's behavior will eventually lead to suspension. Sometimes he doesn't even realize when he is getting out of control. Your son really needs some help!" continued Jill.

"This is really a matter between me and my son, Mrs. Gray, and I assure you that he will control his behavior in the future."

Jill hung up the phone. When she returned to the lobby, she found Matt slumped in a chair with an anxious look on his face. She regretted that her team had handled this situation as they had, and feared for Matt as she considered what would happen when he reached home that afternoon. As she left the office to return to class, she wondered what more she could do to help Matt.

1. How could the use of one of the bibliotherapeutic approaches to intervention assist with managing Matt's behaviors? What might be the best approach for Matt's teachers to consider?
2. How could the Matt's teachers work with his father to implement the use of adolescent literature about emotional disabilities in helping Matt with managing disruptive behaviors, as well as coping with the loss of his mother?
3. How would bibliotherapeutic interventions be used in light of Matt's father's reluctance to continue with medication?

Summary

Examining social and emotional issues through children's and young adult literature provides a new perspective on understanding and acceptance of individual differences. It can also help them develop a deeper understanding of themselves. Effective bibliotherapy sessions require the selection and use of quality literature and appropriate intervention techniques. Therefore, in addition to learning about research in the field of bibliotherapy, service providers should be provided opportunities such as workshops, required readings, and discussion groups to develop expertise on how to effectively implement bibliotherapy with children and adolescents. Finally, additional empirical studies are needed to determine which literature and what types of strategies have proven to be the most effective in the field.

In this chapter, we have provided definitions and a history of bibliotherapy, theoretical perspectives and related research presented in the literature on bibliotherapy, therapeutic applications and components of selected bibliotherapeutic interventions, ethical and cultural considerations of the use of bibliotherapy, a case study depicting bibliotherapy as an intervention for adolescent mental health issues, and several suggested activities that can extend understanding and implementation of the use of bibliotherapy for children and adolescents with emotional disabilities. When compassionate and caring teachers, librarians, and counselors use bibliotherapy to help children and young adults make connections with literature, it can help those individuals understand that they are not alone.

Activities to Extend Your Learning

The following activities can be used with children and youth to enhance their understanding of issues associated with emotional disabilities.

- Use the book, *Fred Stays with Me* (Coffelt, 2007) to discuss divorce with 5- to 7-year-olds. After reading the book aloud to the children, ask them the following questions:
  - Why does the girl sometimes live with her mom and sometimes live with her dad?
  - Do you think it would be difficult to travel back and forth between your mom's house and your dad's house? Why or why not?
  - How does the girl feel when Fred is with her?
- Use the book, *The Recess Queen* (O'Neill & Huliska-Beith, 2002) to discuss bullying issues with 5- to 7-year-olds. After reading the book aloud to the students, ask students if they know what a bully is.
  - Show them the PowerPoint presentation, *What To Do If You are Being Bullied*, prepared by a kindergarten class, located at http://pirate.shu.edu/~jamesjan/Anti-Bullying_files/frame.htm
  - After viewing the presentation, have the students draw their own pictures that could be used in a similar presentation.
- Use the book, *When Sophie Gets Angry – Really, Really Angry* (Bang, 1999) to discuss anger with 5- to 7-year-olds. After reading the book aloud to the children, ask them the following questions:
  - What made Sophie angry?
  - What did she do when she got angry?
  - Have the students draw a picture showing how they felt when they have been angry about something.
  - Have the students share their pictures and then discuss ways to safely express their anger.
- Use the book, *Kira-Kira* (Kadohata, 2004) to discuss death with children ages 11–14. After reading the book, ask the students to respond in writing to the following questions:
  - As part of her eulogy to Lynn, Katie she tells a special memory of Lynn. Write about a special memory of Lynn that Katie might have included in the eulogy.
  - Lynn wakes up crying one night about a dream that she is swimming in the ocean. How does this dream foreshadow her death?

- Use the book, *Joey Pigza Swallows the Key* (Gantos, 1998) to discuss attention disorder issues with children ages 10–16. Have students prepare a KWL chart *(K for what they know, W for what they want to know, and L for what they learned).*
    - Before they read, the book they should write a paragraph about what they already know about attention disorders.
    - Under W, they should write a few questions about what they want to know.
    - After they read the book, have the students visit the web page, Understanding AD/HD by CHADD (Children and Adults with Attention Deficit/Hyperactivity Disorder) at http://www.chadd.org/AM/Template.cfm?Section=Understanding
    - After they examine the website, have them write a paragraph under L for what they learned about AD/HD. When they finish the KWL chart, have the students discuss some of Joey's symptoms that were exhibited in the book.

Recommended Resources

Bibliotherapy Bookshelf by the Carnegie Library at Pittsburgh: http://www.carnegielibrary.org/kids/books/bibtherapy.cfm

Bibliotherapy and Realistic Fiction—Library Booklists: http://librarybooklists.org/fiction/children/jbibliotherapy.htm#jbibbully

Bibliotherapy—Young Adult Booklists—Library Booklists: http://librarybooklists.org/fiction/ya/yageneral.htm#yabib

Children's Books about Disability – Teacher Vision: http://www.teachervision.fen.com/learning-disabilities/reading/5316.html

Children's Literature Promotes Understanding by Melissa Thibault—LEARN NC: http://www.learnnc.org/lp/pages/635

Using Literature to Help Children Cope with Problems—ERIC Digest on Bibliotherapy: http://www.ericdigests.org/2000-3/cope.htm

7.

MEDITATIVE PRACTICES FOR CHILDREN AND ADOLESCENTS

Betsy Wisner and James J. Starzec

Overview of Chapter

To set the stage for appropriate use of meditative practices with child and adolescent populations, this chapter includes the following sections:
- Meditative Practices: Definition and Foundations
- Relevant Theoretical Frameworks of Meditative Practices
- Prior Research on Treatment Efficacy of Meditative Practices
- Application of Meditative Practices with Specific Therapeutic Populations and in Various Settings
- Therapeutic Components of Meditative Practices
- Interpersonal Neurobiology, Neural Integration, and Meditative Practices for Children and Adolescents
- Ethical and Cultural Considerations of Meditative Practices for Children and Adolescents
- Case Study
- Summary
- Activities to Extend Your Learning

Meditative Practices: Definition and Foundations

Definition

Meditative practices include mindfulness meditation (MM) and mantra meditation. Yoga, Tai Chi, and Qi Gong, which involve bodily movement and concentration on the breath, are also considered meditative practices (Ospina et al., 2007). Meditative practices typically take place in a quiet location, involve use of particular postures, and require an open, nonjudgmental attitude (National Center for Complementary and Alternative Medicine, 2007).

The National Center for Complementary and Alternative Medicine (NCCAM) identifies meditation as one of the practices used within Complementary and Alternative Medicine (CAM). When meditation is used for wellness, to treat medical conditions, or to relieve stress it is considered a mind-body practice within the framework of CAM. These practices are often used along with conventional medicine.

According to Shapiro (1984), meditation involves "…a family of techniques which have in common a conscious attempt to focus attention in a nonanalytical way and an attempt not to dwell on discursive thought" (p. 6). Freeman (2004) identified three primary ways that meditation may be used. Meditation can be used for self-regulation, for example, emotional control, pain management, and stress management. Meditation may also be used to promote self-exploration and self-awareness. Finally, meditation may be used within a spiritual or religious discipline as a technique for attaining spiritual self-liberation. Meditative practices targeting self-regulation and self-awareness are most relevant to adolescents and children and will be the primary focus of this chapter.

Foundations

There have been few studies conducted with yoga, Tai Chi, and Qi Gong as the primary interventions. Other types of meditative practice, however, have been the focus of a large number of studies and we will discuss the two types of formal meditation practice most frequently used in research studies. These are concentration meditation (which includes mantra meditation) and MM.

Concentration meditation involves the repeated focusing on a particular word, phrase (e.g., a mantra), or object in an effort to quiet the mind. Among the most used concentration or mantra meditation techniques are Transcendental Meditation™ and Benson's relaxation response method. Transcendental Meditation (TM) was developed in the 1950s by Maharishi Mahesh Yogi. It involves meditation instruction from a certified teacher, the use of a personal mantra, and typically includes payment of a fee for instruction. TM practitioners usually meditate in a seated position with eyes closed and use a personal mantra during meditation. The relaxation response method is a secular mantra-based practice. The participant uses a personal mantra of their choosing. The mantra may be a word, sound, or even a short prayer. The relaxation response does not require a certified teacher and can be learned through personal guidance or the use of printed materials (Benson, 1975).

Mindfulness meditation does not involve focusing on a word, phrase, or object; rather it involves awareness of and acceptance of the present moment (NCCAM, 2007). Mindfulness meditation "…can be defined as the effort to intentionally pay attention, nonjudgmentally, to present-moment experience and sustain this attention over time. The aim is to cultivate a stable and nonreactive present moment awareness" (Miller, Fletcher, & Kabat-Zinn, 1995, p. 193) and to resist concentrating on thoughts and emotions (Brown, 1984). Mindfulness meditation is not an effortful control of thinking nor is it intended to result in the absence of thought. Relaxation may occur during MM, but relaxation training and MM are not identical (Kabat-Zinn, 2005).

Research regarding MM as an intervention component has been strongly influenced by the work of Jon Kabat-Zinn (1990) and his colleagues at the University of Massachusetts Medical Center. The Stress Reduction Clinic at the medical center offers a comprehensive program (Mindfulness Based Stress Reduction [MBSR]) that uses meditation and yoga as part of a treatment approach for patients with a wide range of medical and psychiatric diagnoses. Both MBSR and MM are frequently taught without reference to the original spiritual or religious foundation of the meditation techniques

(Kabat-Zinn, 1990). Many MM practices and interventions incorporating mindfulness are loose adaptations of MBSR (Schoeberlein & Koffler, 2005) and these practices have been adapted for use with children and adolescents (Biegel, Brown, Shapiro, & Schubert, 2009; Burke, 2009; Greco & Hayes, 2008; O'Brien, Larson, & Murrell, 2008; Semple, Reid, & Miller, 2005; Thompson & Gauntlett-Gilbert, 2008).

Relevant Theoretical Frameworks of Meditative Practices

Cognitive-Behavioral Perspectives

The cognitive-behavioral theoretical perspective elucidates the importance of behavioral aspects of human functioning while also giving equal credence to the cognitive aspects of functioning (Payne, 2005). The cognitive perspective encompasses perception and information processing, while the behavioral perspective encompasses learning theories.

Prochaska and Norcross (2007) define cognitive-behavioral therapy as the use of cognitive techniques and explanations in order to bring about behavioral change. According to Beck, Rush, Shaw, and Emery (1979), cognitive therapy involves encouraging clients to attend to the present as opposed to the past, teaching them to monitor thinking in order to identify negative thoughts and feelings or behaviors, and to alter irrational thought patterns. Initially, cognitive-behavioral techniques were developed to treat depression, but they have been adapted to deal with other problems, for example, panic and anxiety disorders, post-traumatic stress disorder, obesity, and eating disorders (Hollon & Beck, 2004).

Lantz (1996) discussed the importance of cognitive-behavioral theory in therapeutic interventions. The therapist, at times, functions as an educator who assists the client in recognizing the role played by cognition in the client's concerns. Lantz points out the importance of focusing on the "present moment" for change to be successful. In discussing the use of meditation in social work treatment, Keefe (1996) identified cognitive theoretical underpinnings of meditation. He suggested that what an individual experiences as stressful depends on how events are perceived. Through meditation, one can become aware of the internal (cognitive and emotional) stimuli that a particular situation elicits. Thus, the role of meditation as an intervention has its basis in cognition.

Cognitive-behavioral theory and therapy provide lenses through which meditative practices, comprising both cognitive and behavioral components, may be understood and implemented. This guidance provides a strong impetus for using these practices in general and in therapeutic environments where the aim is to modify some aspect of current behavioral or cognitive functioning. The application of these concepts with a high school student is explored in more detail through the case study in this chapter.

Systems Theory

The systems theoretical approach asserts that as an individual changes, the systems within which the individual operates also change (Prochaska & Norcross, 2007).

Payne (2005), in a review of systems and ecological perspectives, held that systems views are important since these views go beyond the individual and address broader social concerns. The individual is viewed as a complex system interacting with other complex systems, and it is important to consider the reciprocal interaction between systems in order to understand behavior in the context of a person's life. Thus, change in a child or adolescent might effect change in relationships with classmates, friends, teachers, parents and other family members, as well as the school classroom and the family as a whole. Change in these other systems might, in turn, affect the future behavior of the child or adolescent. Interventions, such as meditation, then, can have potentially far-reaching effects when used with child and adolescent populations. The possibilities for these types of systemic change are also further explored through the school-based case study presented in this chapter.

Prior Research on Treatment Efficacy of Meditative Practices

The use of meditation and other mind/body practices are enjoying wide acceptance by the general U.S. population and those in the helping professions (Honda & Jacobson, 2004; Russinova, Wewiorski, & Cash, 2002; Upchurch & Chyu, 2005). In fact, meditation, one of the most frequently used mind/body practices, is now considered "part of mainstream practice" (Henderson, 2000, p. 68). The literature on meditative practices, particularly mindfulness meditation, is rapidly growing.

There are now a number of review studies that assess the empirical evidence for the benefits of meditative practices. While Brown and Ryan (2003) suggest, "The study of mindfulness is very much in its infancy" (p. 844), a growing number of studies investigate the physical and emotional health benefits of mindfulness meditation. This is reflected by the recent literature reviews addressing mindfulness practices. Ott, Norris, and Bauer-Wu (2006) provide a critical review of research, published between the years 2000 and 2005, on the benefits of mindfulness meditation as an intervention for patients with cancer, primarily breast and prostate cancer. The authors conclude that benefits of mindfulness meditation for these populations include improved psychological functioning (e.g., reductions in scores on state anxiety tests), reduction in stress symptoms (e.g., improved sleep quality), and enhanced coping and well-being (e.g., improvements in health behaviors).

Baer (2003) conducted a literature review and meta-analysis specifically addressing the incorporation of mindfulness meditation in clinical interventions. While there are numerous programs that incorporate cognitive-behavioral therapy and mindfulness meditation, sometimes referred to as acceptance-based therapies, there are four main programs that have been identified in the psychotherapy literature and that have been exposed to substantiation through research (Baer, 2003; Germer, Siegel, & Fulton, 2005). These therapies are MBSR, Dialectical Behavior Therapy (DBT), Mindfulness-Based Cognitive Therapy (MBCT), and Acceptance and Commitment Therapy (ACT). As previously mentioned, MBSR combines mindfulness meditation and yoga to treat a wide range of physical illnesses, diseases, and emotional disorders (Kabat-Zinn, 1990). Dialectical Behavior Therapy uses cognitive-behavioral techniques combined with mindfulness to achieve personal goals and to improve emotional self-regulation for those with personality disorders. Mindfulness-Based Cognitive Therapy combines elements of MBSR with traditional cognitive therapy to treat depressive relapse (Segal, Williams, & Teasdale, 2002). Acceptance and Commitment Therapy incorporates the assumption that human suffering is intricately interwoven with verbal activity (in contrast to verbal content) and the therapeutic approach teaches individuals to observe their thoughts, sensations, and emotions in a way that prevents continued problematic behaviors (Hayes, Strosahl, & Wilson, 1999). This therapeutic approach has been used in stress reduction programs and to treat problems such as addiction.

Baer (2003) concluded that, although the literature is not without limitations, the current evidence suggests that interventions using mindfulness meditation may be helpful, particularly for reducing stress, and improving the ability to cope with a number of problems such as depression, anxiety, chronic pain, eating disorders, personality disorders, and substance abuse. Baer provided the posttreatment effect sizes for the studies she reviewed; the effect sizes ranged from 0.15 to 1.65 with a mean effect size of 0.59. Baer discussed the clinical significance of selected studies in the meta-analysis and concluded that those participants reporting mild to moderate psychological distress prior to the mindfulness intervention reported psychological reactions either within or close to the normal range following the intervention.

In a review of 813 studies of meditation practices for health, it was found that the literature reflects the potential for meditation practices to provide health benefits, especially for hypertension, stress reduction, and reductions in anxiety (Ospina et al., 2007). While most literature reviews have focused almost exclusively on research with adults, Burke (2009) offers a literature review specifically targeting mindfulness-based interventions for children and adolescents. Burke also recognizes the limitation of the current literature but suggests that studies with child and adolescent participants do offer some support for the efficacy of these interventions in clinical and non-clinical samples.

Application of Meditative Practices with Specific Therapeutic Populations and in Various Settings

The benefits of using meditation as complementary treatment for illnesses such as *hypertension, heart disease, cancer, epilepsy, chronic pain, HIV/AIDS,* and other health-related conditions in adults are well documented (Benson, 1975, 1984; Carmody & Baer, 2008; Freeman, 2004; Kabat-Zinn, 1990, 1994; Matchim & Armer, 2007; McBee, Westreich, & Likourezos, 2004; Ott et al., 2006; Shapiro & Walsh, 1984, 2003; Speca, Carlson, Goodey, & Angen, 2000). There are also a number of research studies that address the benefits of using meditation as a treatment for mental health concerns such as *anxiety, depression, panic disorder, and perceived level of distress* (e.g., Derezotes, 2000; Jain et al., 2007; Kabat-Zinn, 1994; Kabat-Zinn et al., 1992; Miller et al., 1995; Waelde, Thompson, & Gallagher-Thompson, 2004; Wolf & Abbell, 2003). In addition, there are studies that address the use of meditation as an intervention to help those with *chemical dependency, suicidal ideation, personality disorders, serious men-*

tal illness, eating disorders, disordered body image, learning disabilities, and Attention Deficit Hyperactivity Disorder (e.g., Beauchemin, Hutchins, & Patterson, 2008; Kissman & Maurer, 2002; Kristeller & Hallett, 1999; Niederman, 2003; Plasse, 2001; Russinova et al., 2002; Stewart, 2004; Sweet & Johnson, 1990; Williams, Duggan, Crane, & Fennell, 2006; Zylowska et al., 2008).

Thus, professionals in a variety of practice settings have incorporated meditation into the therapeutic milieu. The practice of mindfulness meditation and other meditative practices have been integrated into a wide range of settings including substance abuse and chemical dependence treatment clinics (Kissman & Maurer, 2002; Linehan et al., 1999; Niederman, 2003; Plasse, 2001), gerontology facilities (McBee et al., 2004), counseling clinics (Linehan et al., 1999; Sweet & Johnson, 1990; Williams, Duggan, Crane, & Fennell, 2006), juvenile justice facilities (Derezotes, 2000), correctional facilities (Alexander, Walton, & Goodman, 2003; Hawkins, 2003), hospice care (Bruce & Davies, 2005), hospitals (Lin, Lee, Kemper, & Berde, 2005), and schools (Barnes et al., 2001, 2003; Barnes, Davis, et al., 2004; Barnes, Treiber, et al., 2004; Beauchemin et al., 2008; Benson et al., 1994; Dixon et al., 2005; Redfering & Bowman, 1981; Rosaen & Benn, 2006; Semple et al., 2005; Warner, 2005, Wisner, 2008).

Meditative Practices with Children

While there is not a great deal of research on the effects of meditative practices with children, what research there is suggests that such practices can be effective interventions. For example, Redfering and Bowman (1981) used Benson's relaxation techniques with 8- to 11-year-olds experiencing behavioral concerns. They evaluated effects on off-task and disruptive behaviors. Compared to a 5-day baseline period, children experiencing 5 days of relaxation training showed a greater decrease in the frequency of these behaviors than children in a rest-only control group. Semple et al. (2005) demonstrated that 7- and 8-year-old children experiencing anxiety were capable of engaging in mindfulness exercises adapted to their developmental level. Semple et al. concluded that mindfulness training could be useful as part of a treatment program for children with anxiety. Napoli, Krech, and Holley (2005) had children in Grades 1–3 participate in a variety of mindfulness exercises in 12 training sessions over 24 weeks. Control group children attended group sessions but without the exercises. Pretest-posttest comparisons indicated that children who experienced the mindfulness exercises showed an *increase in selective attention, decrease in test anxiety, and were rated by teachers as exhibiting fewer problems in attention and social interactions.*

Some studies have attempted to assess effects of training in TM techniques. Dixon et al. (2005) reported the results of two longitudinal studies dealing with children. Two techniques were involved, TM and Word of Wisdom. The TM involved sitting with eyes closed for 15–20 minutes twice daily while using a mantra. This approach was used for children 10 years of age and older. The Word of Wisdom technique was used for children under 10 years of age. This approach also involved the use of a mantra and was practiced twice daily, but it was done for shorter periods of time than the TM, and with eyes open while walking. In Study 1, 4-year-olds who were taught the Word of Wisdom technique and practiced it for 6 months showed *greater ability to sustain attention* than 4-year-olds in a no-treatment control group. In Study 2, 6- to 11-year-olds were taught either the TM or the Word of Wisdom technique depending upon the child's age. After 45 weeks of practice, those using the techniques showed *better performance on measures of analytical ability and self-concept* than controls. Warner (2005) looked at the effects of TM and Word of Wisdom on behaviors of 5- to 11-year-olds. Children who attended a school using the techniques as a part of the curriculum showed *greater working memory, less impulsivity on a task, and greater flexibility on a task* than control group children attending schools not using the techniques.

Wall (2005) combined MBSR and Tai Chi exercises 1 hour per week for 5 weeks with 6th and 8th graders (11–13 years old). Children indicated that they experienced *greater feelings of calmness and peacefulness as well as increased self-awareness*. Yoga was used as an intervention with 6- to 10-year-old children with attention problems by Peck, Kehle, Bray, and Theodore (2005). Children participated in deep breathing, relaxation exercises, and yoga postures for 30 minutes per session, 2 sessions per week, over 3 weeks. The children showed *increased time-on-task behavior in their classroom.*

Overall, studies show that the benefits of meditation interventions for children include improvements in off-task and disruptive behaviors, increased attention, analytical ability, and working memory, and greater cognitive flexibility, improved self-concept, decreased general anxiety and test anxiety, less impulsivity, and experienced greater feelings of calmness, peacefulness, and self-awareness (Dixon et al. 2005; Napoli et al., 2005; Peck et al., 2005; Redfering & Bowman, 1981; Semple et al., 2005; Wall, 2005; Warner, 2005).

Meditative Practices with Adolescents

Meditation practices, including the relaxation response method of meditation, TM, and MM have been used as sole interventions and as components of successful programs to treat a variety of concerns in adolescent populations.

Meditation as a Component of a Treatment Program.   Bootzin and Stevens (2005) used MBSR as one aspect of treatment aimed at dealing with sleep disturbances for 13- to 19-year-olds who were in a treatment program for substance abuse. The treatment involved information regarding sleep, instructions to assist sleep behaviors, and cognitive restructuring as well as MBSR , over 6 weeks (90-minute weekly sessions). Those who completed the program (23 of 55) *showed reduced anxiety and improved sleep.* MBSR-based meditation was also an aspect of a school-based program to treat symptoms of Posttraumatic Stress Disorder (PTSD) in 12- to 19-year-olds from Kosovo (Gordon, Staples, Blyta, & Bytyqi, 2004). During 6 weekly 3-hour sessions, adolescents participated in exercises that included biofeedback, relaxation, guided imagery, and meditation. Pretest-posttest data showed a significant reduction in PTSD symptoms. MBSR was used by Biegel et al. (2009) as part of a treatment program for 14- to 18-year-old outpatients at a psychiatric facility. A control group received the usual treatment appropriate to their diagnosis, while an experimental group received

MBSR in addition to the usual treatment. MBSR participants attended 8 two-hour classes per week involving forms of meditation (sitting, walking), hatha yoga, informal mindfulness, and at-home practice. The MBSR group participants reported *reductions in depression and anxiety and increases in self-esteem* compared to controls.

Benson et al. (1994) studied effects of the relaxation response in high school sophomores. For one semester, students were either exposed to a health curriculum incorporating the relaxation response or not. The health classes were held three times a week and the first 15 minutes of class involved the relaxation response for those having it in the curriculum. In addition to instructions in the relaxation response, information on stress management, drug use, and nutrition was also presented. For the following semester, each group was exposed to the opposite condition. Comparisons across groups indicated that the curriculum with the relaxation response resulted in *increased self-esteem and greater internal locus of control* compared to the curriculum without the relaxation response experience.

Derezotes (2000) had 14 adolescent male sex offenders receive yoga and meditation instructions (method not specified) over a 3-month period. Interview data suggested that yoga and meditation resulted in *increased feelings of relaxation and decreased anxiety*. Participants also reported an *increased ability to control emotions and thoughts*.

Meditation as a Sole Intervention.   Barnes, Davis, et al. (2004) looked at the impact of a school-based MM program on heart rate and blood pressure in middle school students (mean age 12.3 years). Classrooms were randomly assigned to either a MM condition or a health education control condition. MM occurred over 3 months and involved two daily 10-minute meditation sessions (one during school, one at home) as well as a 20-minute instructional period once a week. Control participants experienced daily 20-minute walks and a weekly 20-minute education session dealing with physical activity, weight loss, and dietary change. Students in the MM group showed decreased resting systolic blood pressure and decreased ambulatory systolic and diastolic blood pressure both during school and after school. The MM group also showed *decreases in heart rate*.

Wisner (2008) conducted an 8-week MM group program for all students (Grades 10–12) at an alternative high school. Students and staff began with 4-minute meditation sessions that gradually increased to 10 minutes 4 days per week. Preintervention-postintervention teacher ratings suggested student *improvements in inter- and intrapersonal strengths, family involvement, school functioning, and affective strength.* Qualitative data collected from the students indicated that students found the MM to aid in *increasing self-regulation, self-calming, stress relief, relaxation, and emotional coping*. Students reported an *increase in ability to pay attention and control thinking, and also reported a more positive school atmosphere*.

A number of studies with adolescents have assessed the impact of TM. Barnes, Davis, et al. (2001) investigated effects of TM on cardiovascular reactivity. Thirty-four high school students (ages 15–18) were assigned to a TM condition or a control condition. The TM students received meditation instructions and were asked to practice twice daily over a 2-month period, with one of the 15-minute practice sessions occurring during school on school days. Control group students met for a 1 hour lifestyle education session once a week for 7 weeks. These education sessions included information regarding lowering blood pressure through managing body weight using exercise and diet. Compared to the control group, the TM group showed *less cardiovascular reactivity in response to acute stress and larger decreases in resting systolic blood pressure.* Barnes et al. (2003) measured effects of TM on a number of school-related behavioral problems. The TM group involved the same experience as the TM group had in Barnes et al. (2001) except that the meditation practice occurred over a 4-month period. Control group students spent the 15-minute daily in-school period in education. Compared to the 4 months prior to the intervention, during the 4 month TM program, the TM group had *decreases in class periods absent, rule violations, and days suspended from school* compared to the control group which showed increases in these measures.

In three studies, So and Orme-Johnson (2001) assessed effects of TM on a variety of cognitive factors in Chinese high school students. The TM practice sessions were 20 minutes twice daily for 6 months (Studies 1 and 2) or 1 year (Study 3). In all three studies, students in the TM conditions showed *increases in measures of practical intelligence and creativity, and decreases in measures of state and trait anxiety* compared to control group students. Rosaen and Benn (2006) conducted a qualitative study aimed at identifying themes that were present in interviews of 10 students (ages 12–14) who had been practicing TM for two 10-minute sessions each school day over a 1-year period. Qualitative data analyses yielded themes of *increased emotional intelligence, improved academic performance, and restful alertness.* The students indicated that they felt that the meditation aided them in achieving greater concentration, relaxation, and energy, and helped improve their self-control, particularly with regard to anger. Students also reported an increased sense of being able to adapt to different situations and increases in patience and tolerance. Finally, they perceived improvements in the area of academic performance, which they felt were due to the meditation.

Overall, studies show that the benefits of meditation interventions for adolescents include improvements in cognitive functioning (enhanced ability to pay attention, improved concentration, and academic success), increases in internal locus of control, self-esteem, frustration tolerance, and self-control, improvements in emotional self-regulation, emotional intelligence, and social skills, an increased feeling of well-being, a reduction in behavioral problems, decreases in anxiety, decreases in blood pressure and heart rate, and an improved school climate, as well as improvements in sleep behavior (e.g., Barnes et al., 2001, 2003; Barnes, Davis, et al., 2004; Barnes, Treiber, et al., 2004; Beauchemin et al., 2008; Benson et al., 1994; Bootzin & Stevens, 2005; Derezotes, 2000; Rosaen & Benn, 2006; So & Orme-Johnson, 2001; Wisner, 2008; Zylowska et al., 2007).

Limitations of Prior Research

Literature reviews mentioned previously (Baer, 2003; Burke, 2009; Ospina et al., 2007), although offering support for the efficacy of meditation practices, also evoke common concerns about research studies on meditative practices. Among these concerns are studies with methodological flaws including the lack of a control group, small sample size, and concerns about treatment fidelity.

Limitations in the literature may also include the confounding of meditation with other components of interventions and lack of a thorough description of the intervention and methodology or little discussion of the credentials of the person teaching the meditation (Wisner, 2008). In addition, the available literature on using meditation practices for adolescents and children, while growing, is often restricted to a few researchers working with small numbers of participants.

Adolescents tend to be neglected in research studies, highlighting the importance of studying meditative practices with adolescents and providing evidence that these practices are efficacious. Moreover, meditation models used with adolescents are typically based on models designed for and used almost exclusively with adults (e.g., practicing meditation for 15 to 20 minutes twice a day). There is support for the contention that modified models with briefer meditation periods are effective for children and adolescents. For example, briefer meditation periods have proven effective without compromising benefits to students (Benson et al., 1994; Barnes, Davis, et al., 2004; Rosaen & Benn, 2006; Wisner, 2008). Shorter meditation times of 10 to 12 minutes practiced once per day or several times a week may provide adolescents with the typical benefits of a meditation practice. Model programs show a level of effectiveness across a variety of settings (i.e., public middle, junior, and senior high schools, an alternative school, a private residential school, a vocational school, and schools in international settings) pointing to the utility and adaptability of a variety of meditative techniques for youth (i.e., TM, MM, the relaxation response method, yoga, and Tai Chi).

Therapeutic Components of Meditative Practices

Meditative practices offer therapeutic benefits that span the range of bio-psycho-social-spiritual functioning. We will discuss a number of these benefits in terms of potential therapeutic and educational outcomes.

Behavioral and Emotional Self-Regulation

Practicing meditation offers children and adolescents the opportunity to simply be themselves, to learn that sometimes not acting is an appropriate and advantageous response. For example, in practicing mindfulness meditation, the idea is to stay in the present moment and resist the urge to make things different than they currently are, to resist taking any action. For many of us, and particularly for youth, this is a very challenging thing to be asked to do. However, if we are successful with this, we can learn a valuable lesson. Sometimes, not taking action is the best action to take. Similarly, adolescents are often overtaken by their emotions. The ongoing practice of meditation can help to circumvent the dominance of emotions and the ruminating that often occurs with adolescents. Episodes of anger, sadness, and anxiety are not uncommon in children and adolescents, and meditation offers opportunities for coping with these feelings in a positive way. The individual learns to tolerate frustrating circumstances while increasing behavioral self-control and improving emotional regulation (Barnes et al., 2001, 2003; Barnes, Davis, et al., 2004; Barnes, Treiber, et al., 2004; Rosaen & Benn, 2006; Wisner, 2008). With extended meditation practice, we see benefits that move beyond simple emotional and behavioral regulation into heightened levels of emotional intelligence (Rosaen & Benn, 2006).

Meditation, yoga, and Tai Chi are also effective stress management practices and coping strategies. In fact, one of the main benefits of mindfulness meditation integrated into an alternative high school curriculum, as indicated by the students, was the reported stress management effect of the meditation (Wisner, 2008).

Cognitive Benefits

School-based meditation programs are shown to be valuable for the cognitive development of children and adolescents (e.g., Beauchemin et al., 2008; Rosaen & Benn, 2006; So & Orme-Johnson, 2001; Wisner, 2008). Even relatively brief meditation programs have been shown to help students improve their abilities to focus, pay attention, and concentrate on the task at hand. The importance of this for students cannot be overemphasized. If students are not able to optimize their cognitive abilities, school is an extremely frustrating place for them. Especially crucial are meditation programs targeted toward youth with challenges such as Attention Deficit Hyperactivity Disorder (ADHD). Providing these students with a behavioral option that helps them focus and concentrate on a particular task is a lesson that will serve them well, not only in school, but throughout their lives.

Developmentally, older children and young adolescents are becoming capable of abstract thinking and are moving into adolescent egocentrism. This advancement in thinking is often accompanied by perceived challenges to self-concept and self-esteem. Young people often experience self-doubt and self-conscious feelings. Meditation can provide a "safe place" for becoming comfortable with the self in the moment and for interrupting the bombardment of thoughts and the movement into the stories adolescents tell themselves about what others think of them. Adolescents have described meditation as helpful for decreasing disruptive thoughts and increasing beneficial thoughts (Wisner, 2008), thereby improving self-esteem and mood.

Psychological Benefits

Alterations in perception of self, and creating a deep sense of self-awareness, are perhaps among the most fundamental changes that occur through use of meditative practices. Not only do we see improvements in self-esteem and emotional intelligence (Benson et al., 1994; Rosaen & Benn, 2006) but there are also deeper levels of self-exploration. In other words, meditation allows the individual to come to a fuller and deeper understanding of the motivations, desires, fears, and narratives that underlie behavior and make up everyday life. These psychological factors are very much related to the components of meditation practice just discussed (self-regulation and cognition) and play a pivotal role in the success of social relationships.

Although not directly addressed in most secular settings, and not a focus of this chapter, it should be briefly noted that meditation may be used for spiritual and religious purposes. Some incorporate meditation into their lives to experience a sense of transcendence or communion. Children and adolescents, depending on their spiritual and religious affiliations, may also seek or discuss this type of experience and with parental permission this could be explored in a culturally sensitive way.

Strengthening Interpersonal Skills

Human beings find meaning in social relationships and struggle to connect with others in a positive manner while maintaining their own independence. Adolescents, in particular, place a high level of importance on peer relationships for social connections and thus may experience a certain vulnerability to or dependence on peer acceptance. The process of meditation offers a means to monitor repetitive and ruminative thinking regarding acceptance and relationships. The goal of meditation is not to control these thoughts but to become aware of them at a very deep level and to learn that not acting on these thoughts is an option. As meditation helps children and adolescents tolerate frustration and regulate their behavior (becoming more successful in the intrapersonal realm) their peer relationships are likely to improve. For example, Beauchemin et al. (2008) suggest that MM may promote social skills and academic success by decreasing anxiety and increasing the ability to control the self-focused attention previously discussed.

Group and Community Support

While meditation may be learned and applied individually, there are compelling reasons for learning meditation in a group setting. Practicing meditation in a community of learners is often a very powerful experience, offering opportunities to learn from peers, to provide support to others in the learning process, and to recognize common challenges and benefits of meditation practice. Emphasizing the experiential component of group meditation instruction is an important facet of successful group work for adolescents (Thompson & Gauntlett-Gilbert, 2008) and infusing a sense of creativity and energy into the group process is recommended (Woodberry, Roy, & Indik, 2008).

It has been suggested that meditation integrated into the school curriculum has a positive effect on school climate. Students in an alternative high school judged the systemic effects of meditation to be among the most important changes that occurred from an 8-week course of mindfulness meditation offered in the school setting. Students reported that meditation improved school climate, reduced the "drama" in the school, and seemed to make the school a calmer place (Wisner, 2008, p. 141).

Therapeutic and Instructional Support

Interactions with a knowledgeable and supportive therapist or instructor are essential in learning how to effectively meditate. The instructor models the expected behaviors and guides the learner through the challenges and benefits of the practice. Establishing an ongoing meditation practice is an important foundation of being an effective meditation teacher. Often meditation is taught in a group setting in which case the teacher needs to have group facilitation skills as well.

For those teaching children and adolescents, adapting the language and instructional strategies to match the developmental level and academic capabilities of the students or clients will provide a much richer and more accessible program. Saltzman and Goldin (2008) offer guidance for adapting mindfulness programs for children and adolescents and provide an MBSR course outline for use with children. The authors also stress that, when implementing group mindfulness training in school-based settings, teacher input and support is crucial to the success of the program (Saltzman & Goldin, 2008).

Parent/Guardian Support

Enlisting the support and help of the parent or guardian is often the first step in working toward successfully integrating meditation into a treatment plan or offering the practice in a school setting. Parental permission is important and providing parents with written information is helpful, as is offering to meet with parents to explain the meditative practice in detail. Some parents already have experience with meditation or express an interest in learning meditation with the child. Once parents see the positive changes in the child or adolescent in terms of behavioral self-regulation and other benefits the parent typically has few objections to the practice. Another approach to increase parental understanding of and support for the practices is to invite parents to participate in the meditation practices themselves (Thompson & Gauntlett-Gilbert, 2008).

Transfer of Learning

Engaging in mindfulness meditation, on a regular basis, will eventually result in mindfulness being infused throughout a person's experiences. The behavioral, cognitive, psychological, and social benefits of being mindful will filter throughout a person's life and likely bring a level of success in many areas.

A 10-year-old child who struggles with ADHD may find it difficult to pay attention in class and may feel the need to move her feet constantly to the extent that this interferes with her completing her math assignment. Meditation, practiced on a regular basis, may empower her to concentrate on her assignment and also to resist the urge to move. This would then enable her to complete her assignment, experience more academic success, and possibly improve her academic self-concept in this area.

Interpersonal Neurobiology, Neural Integration, and Meditative Practices for Children and Adolescents

Interpersonal neurobiology, as the intersection of biology, brain development, knowledge acquisition, and social interaction holds particular relevance for children and adolescents. Neural development in childhood and adolescence contains periods of rapid synaptic growth followed by episodes of neural pruning. Siegel (2007) discusses the importance of understanding the connections between interpersonal neurobiology, the developmental stages of childhood and adolescence, and the potential benefits of mindfulness and reflection for brain development. Siegel contends that helping a child become more mindful and gain skills in reflective thinking sets the stage for later neural development in adolescence that may result in more skillful social and cognitive behavior.

According to Siegel (2007), "Neural integration entails coordination and balance in the functioning of the brain" (p. 199), which, in turn, facilitates a sense of well-being and self-efficacy. Neural integration plays a significant role in interpersonal neurobiology. One way to promote neural integration is through *internal attunement*. This attunement results in a connected, engaged brain (Siegel, 2007). Thus, one way to facilitate neural integration is to engage in meditative practices. An introductory practice in many meditative approaches is awareness of the breath and Siegel frames breath awareness as a foundational practice that helps to focus attention and to encourage self-awareness and self-monitoring. Breath awareness is an example of "intrapersonal attunement" (p. 174). According to Siegel, this attunement is said to promote neural integration and support coherence of the mind and the development of empathy in relationships.

Meditative practices offer children and adolescents simple, unique, effective, and inexpensive ways to promote neural integration, internal attunement, and better interpersonal relationship skills. These skills are important for the psychosocial development of children and for the adolescent the skills may provide invaluable resources given the paramount importance of peer relationships for adolescents.

Ethical and Cultural Considerations of Meditative Practices for Children and Adolescents

It is vital, given the current global emphasis on ambition and acquisition, that we offer our children and adolescents an opportunity to welcome silence, to foster concentration and mindful awareness, to attain a level of self-acceptance, and to set the stage for successful relationships. Meditative practices provide an avenue to this end.

Routine engagement in meditation or Tai Chi practice can actually modify neural pathways. As such, these powerful practices should be taken seriously. The ethical importance of providing evidence-based practice is now well accepted. Perhaps this is especially crucial when the participants in these practices are children and adolescents. The study of meditative practices as prevention and intervention strategies for children and adolescents is relatively new and much more work in this area is needed. However, one could also argue, given the current indications of positive outcomes for children and adolescents that it is ethically imperative that these practices be provided on a much broader scale than is currently available and be the focus of more ongoing investigations. It is also important that children and adolescents are given the clear message that these meditative practices are voluntary and that participation is optional. Adults often present options for youth without giving clear permission to decline participation.

It is wise to consider the individual or group needs of the participants in meditative practices when using these interventions with children and adolescents. Meditative practices are viewed as mind/body techniques that play a complementary role in treatment of physical or emotional disorders and this may be the case in the treatment of children and adolescents. However, meditative practices are now being used in schools as stand-alone programs for the general school populations or are integrated into programs designed to facilitate social and emotional learning for non-clinical populations (Schoeberlein & Koffler, 2005).

Some additional factors to consider when integrating meditative practices into a treatment plan or a group program is to begin with very brief sessions (sometimes sessions as short as 2- to 4-minutes are recommended) as some individuals are hypersensitive to meditation or similar practices. Brief sessions followed by discussion of the experiences will provide feedback for assessing the application of a particular practice with individuals. Another concern is that children or adolescents who have experienced grief or loss may feel overwhelmed by these emotions during meditation. The short initial sessions followed by the discussion period will also facilitate identification of these potential concerns. Screening of children and adolescents is recommended since meditation should be used cautiously with those having severe psychiatric problems, for example, psychosis, depression, and anxiety (Baer, 2003; Beauchemin et al., 2008; Ospina et al., 2007; Shapiro & Walsh, 2003).

Many of the meditative practices discussed in this chapter are derived from Buddhist and Eastern philosophies. Thus, some may perceive a clash between these practices and closely held cultural beliefs. Most of these practices are actually secular in nature, but it is important to be aware of the secular or religious foundations of particular meditative practices in order to provide full explanations of these practices to participants. Once children and adolescents, and their parents, understand the foundations of the practices, they are in a better position to make an informed choice about participation in these practices. The therapist or teacher can explore, with the participants, any potential cultural mismatches that may occur. In our experience, most people who at first perceive meditation as a "new age" or Buddhist practice are open to hear more about the practices. Initial hesitation or perceived cultural clashes are often resolved after discussion of the practices. Some people report a concern that meditation conflicts with their particular faith tradition. In actuality, forms of contemplation and meditation are found in all major religious traditions. Open discussions, in the absence of pressure to try the techniques, often results in greater understanding of meditation practices. As more people become familiar with meditation perhaps these concerns will be encountered less and less often.

The following case study offers an example of the application of group meditative practice within an alternative high school setting and an analysis of the experiences of one of the group members.

Case Study

David

David was a 16-year-old, Caucasian, 10th-grade student in a public alternative high school located in a small city in the northeastern United States. All students in David's alternative high school class had experienced significant problems in their home schools. These concerns ranged from attendance and academic problems to being bullied by peers or in some cases being a bully to their peers. Students had been judged as at-risk of dropping out of high school had they remained in their home school environments. The home schools purchased a spot for the student at the alternative high school in an effort to improve academic success and to prevent the student from dropping out of school.

Many students attending the alternative school had met with limited academic and social success in school and were likely to perceive school as a difficult place for them. Moreover, students often experienced other problems as well, ranging from living in a home with no central heating, to being estranged from family members and living alone in an apartment, to encountering substance abuse or dependence.

Students were bused to the school from a number of different school districts and as a result, although ethnicity was fairly homogeneous, students attending the school were diverse in terms of urban and rural backgrounds. All students in David's grade were new to the school that year and were developing relationships with peers, their teachers, and also with the meditation instructors (a psychologist and a school social worker). David and his peers tended to be highly interactive, constantly sparring with each other verbally and physically. David had taken the role of class clown, often making fun of himself, and often the target of student teasing. David certainly took no leadership role in the class. He seemed younger than his 16 years.

David's teacher had requested that meditation be incorporated in the 10th-grade curriculum at the alternative school and showed a strong level of support for the program. The teacher, a patient and positive role model, was a full participant in the program. The alternative school philosophy, while encouraging students to capitalize on their strengths, at the same time expected students to try new and different ways of looking at themselves and of interacting with peers and adults. The students were coached to let go of old patterns and to develop new ones. Even in this context David, and a number of his peers, initially found meditation to be a practice they did not see themselves enjoying or benefitting from.

David and his classmates participated in a mindfulness meditation program incorporated into a classroom curriculum from September until March of the school year. Meditation occurred twice weekly (Tuesdays and Thursdays) at the beginning of class on the days that the class met. There were 36 days on which meditation sessions occurred. David was absent for only 2 of the days.

Initial instructions for meditation highlighted the following: (a) sitting on a cushion or meditation bench, (b) maintaining an erect posture, (c) eyes either closed or looking downwards at the floor, and (d) hands either folded in the lap or placed on the knees. The aforementioned were demonstrated to the students prior to the first meditation session. Regarding mindfulness, the students were first told to count breaths from 1 to 10, either counting each breath cycle (inhalation and exhalation) or counting each exhalation. If the count reached 10, counting was to return to 1. If one became distracted and lost count, when one became aware of this, they were to resume counting at 1. After about a month of breath counting, students were given the option of following the breath without counting, simply paying attention to the physical experience of inhalation and exhalation.

The first few meditation sessions were short (two 2-minute blocks) and over the 28 weeks of the program, the time was gradually increased by a minute or two per session until the sessions were 10 minutes in length (either one 10-minute block or two 5-minute blocks separated by either a brief rest period or short discussion).

As is typical in group process, the students, teacher, and meditation instructors struggled along for the first month or so of the meditation program, working through the process of clarifying their relationships with each other. Students overcame some initial misconceptions about meditation and worked through some common challenges of initiating a meditation practice: boredom, lack of trust, difficulty concentrating, painful sitting postures, falling asleep in the lying-down meditation, and uncomfortable feelings emerging (e.g., sadness or fear). The group worked through this together and learned from each other. Eventually the benefits of meditation began to emerge. Students began to share positive experiences about the meditation during the group discussion following each practice session. Students began to take a leadership role in the class and began to seem calmer and more relaxed.

For the first 15 weeks, all sessions were held in silence and involved meditation in a seated posture. As the group as a whole acclimated to meditating, noises produced by the students began to diminish (e.g., sounds produced by fidgeting, readjusting posture). As this occurred, the awareness of other noises (people speaking in the hallway outside of the room, noises produced in adjacent rooms, noise from the heating system, computer fans) increased. Likewise, any whispering by a student was highly noticeable. At first, it was suggested that students might make awareness of the sounds the focus of their mindfulness. The unpredictable nature of many of the sounds however, made it difficult for many students not to be distracted by the sounds. To deal with this, tapes or CDs of nature sounds were incorporated into classroom meditation sessions. The nature sounds served two functions: (a) they masked some of the distracting environmental sounds, and (b) they allowed students the option of using awareness of the sounds as an object of meditation.

On Week 21, students had the option of lying down for one of the two daily sessions. During Week 26, walking meditation in the school gym was introduced. Students practiced walking meditation in the large, dark, drafty gymnasium. It was here that David truly emerged as a leader among his peers. David led a group of about 20 people in a slow, methodical, meditative walk in a circle around the gymnasium. David placed one foot down slowly and then very slowly brought the other foot forward and took a step. Each person followed suit and stepped in unison with David's footsteps. David reported that he found this meditation to be an extremely positive experience and described a sense of calmness from the meditation. This was reflected in his outward demeanor and in his calm actions.

Most daily sets of meditation sessions were followed by a class discussion of the sessions, the meditation program in general, or emotional and behavioral issues related to students' behavior during the sessions. Throughout the academic year, students completed in-class writing assignments, called Journal Entries, in which they provided their thoughts regarding issues related to the meditation program. At the end of the program, individual structured interviews were conducted with the student participants.

At the end of the second week of the program, students wrote their first journal entry. They were asked to indicate their impression when they first heard that meditation was to be a part of their class experience. David was among the half of the class expressing a negative opinion: "I thought that it was stupid and didn't want to do it. I still don't like it because it's uncomfortable and boring sitting there quietly." Journal Entry 2, at the end of Week 3, asked students to write about how they felt doing breath counting meditation. David responded that he did not meditate and he did not like meditation because he had a difficult time "getting relaxed."

Five weeks into the program, students were asked to describe "the point" of doing the meditation. David's attitude toward meditation had apparently changed. He wrote, "It is a time where I sit and quiet down and relax. I feel less stressed about work at home, homework, and school. It seems to make my day go better." David was among five students who also mentioned that they used the meditation technique outside of the classroom setting to deal with strong emotions: "At times at home when I am upset or angry I sometimes sit on my bed and meditate until I feel relaxed. Then I go on with my day."

Students had the option of meditating with eyes open and gazing downward, or eyes closed. David used both approaches, closing his eyes when he wanted to relieve stress and keeping them open when he felt uncomfortable with eyes closed. A common theme among class members was a lack of trust in classmates; a feeling that others would look at them, touch them, or laugh at them if they closed their eyes. David indicated that regardless of whether others closed their eyes or not, meditated or not, it was important for all to maintain quiet so as not to disturb one another.

At the conclusion of Week 21, students were asked to comment on changes they had noticed since the beginning of the program. David described the class atmosphere during sessions as much quieter, with no movement or talking, adding, "I have finally taken charge as well. I have finally accepted meditation because it relaxes me from my stress." In the final written journal, David commented that as a result of taking part in the meditation program, he felt that his mood had improved as well as his self-control.

In his exit interview, David said that the meditation program had helped him relax and deal with feelings of irritation and anger that occurred from time to time in school. However, David thought that the program had a greater impact on his behavior at home. When he would feel anger towards his parents, or feel under stress due to some event at home, he would go to his room and meditate. He said that this would have the effect of reducing his feelings of stress and anger. David believed that his mother had noticed a change in his behavior. She had told him that he appeared to be more relaxed and less likely to display anger towards her. David attributed his increased self-control at home to meditation. He said, "It made me think before reacting a lot. It made me think about people and it made me think before I would stay stuff that would hurt their feelings. I used to tell my mom to shut up a lot and I found I was hurting her feelings and now that I realize it hurts her feelings I won't tell her to shut up any more." David held that his relationship with his mother had improved as a result of his self-control. Similarly, David used the same approach with friends and teachers, reflecting before he would say something.

David summarized, "I'm not angry as much. I'm happier. I always have a smile on now."

Discussion

In summary, this case study helps us to describe and analyze the outcome of a group meditation curriculum provided to high school students within an alternative educational setting. Support for this program occurred at all levels, from the school administration, to the school teacher coordinating the 10th-grade curriculum, to the meditation instructors, and, of course, to the students.

Through the lens of David's practice, we illustrate the typical experiences that may occur as someone starts a meditation program. Early experiences may include physical, cognitive, and psychological challenges that could interfere with fully embracing a meditation program. As the meditation program progresses, however, the potential benefits of the practice emerge.

David's progression through the meditation curriculum showed both the early struggles and the later benefits. As David became more proficient in his meditation practice, he showed an emerging maturity, a willingness to step forward as a leader, and an increasing level of self-control and emotional stability. He seemed more content with his academic progress, happier and more secure in himself, and more secure in his relationships with his peers (see Table 7.1 for an overview of the application of the therapeutic components of mindfulness meditation to this case study).

David's story illustrates the best-case scenario. David had a level of willingness to trust his teacher. The supports were in place. The adults helping David were available and approachable. Meditation proved to be a helpful practice for David. This will not always be the case. The individual needs of the particular child or adolescent must dictate the interventions and practices that are offered to the participant or client. Clinicians and teachers are encouraged to develop their own meditative practices and to integrate these practices into their classrooms and practices.

Summary

Meditative practices are emerging as important tools for clinicians, teachers, and health professionals and are appropriate for use with wide-ranging populations. We have introduced a number of meditation practices that are useful with children and adolescent populations. While there is much research on these practices with adult populations, the relevant literature guiding those working with children and adolescents is small but growing. The research, while establishing that meditative practices can be helpful for clinical and non-clinical populations, and in a variety of practice settings, does have limitations. More rigorous research is needed and will emerge to guide practitioners.

We used a case study in a school-based setting to illustrate some of the benefits that

Table 7.1   Application Examples of the Therapeutic Components of the Meditation Intervention

Therapeutic Components	Application Examples
Behavioral and Emotional Self-Regulation	• Breathing slows and physical relaxation occurs as meditation progresses • There is a reduction in fidgeting during meditation • Students learn to sit in meditation without readjusting posture • Verbal and physical sparring are voluntarily eliminated as the meditation sessions progress • Students seem calmer and more relaxed as the meditation program progresses • Students learn to move at a slow pace during the walking meditation • Uncomfortable feelings of boredom, painful sitting postures, and sleepiness are processed • Feelings of sadness and fear are decrease • Feelings of anger decrease • Verbal self-control increases
Cognitive Benefits	• Focusing attention on breath increases the ability to concentrate • Focusing attention on walking sensations reduces mind chatter
Psychological Benefits	• Feelings of distress are reduced • Sense of self-efficacy occurs as the task of learning meditation is mastered • Self-awareness is enhanced allowing enhanced self knowing • Students take leadership roles assisting peers with sitting and walking meditation
Strengthening Interpersonal Skills	• Helping peers with meditation instruction fosters peer relationships • Prosocial peer relationships occur in the absence of verbal or physical sparring • A deeper understanding of reciprocal relationships with peers and parents becomes apparent
Group and community support	• Students support each other in coping with the challenges of developing a meditation practice • The group worked through initial struggles together, learned from each other, and strengthened peer-group bonds • Students shared positive experiences about meditation during the group discussion following each practice session
Therapist and teacher support	• The teacher and meditation instructors empowered students to help themselves and each other • The teacher and meditation instructors offered support, guidance, and encouragement throughout the group process
Parent/guardian involvement	• The parents were given detailed information about the meditation and gave written permission for students to take part in the meditation curriculum
Transfer of learning	• David describes using meditation as a self-regulation strategy at home to cope with anger • David takes personal responsibility for his actions and emotions at home and describes improved relationships with family members
Ethical and cultural considerations	• Parental permission is provided for participation in the meditation program

children and adolescents may experience when provided with a meditative practice. An exciting development that shows promise is the connection between meditative practices and brain structure and function. The concepts of interpersonal neurobiology and neural integration have important implications for using meditative practices with children and adolescents.

As is always the case when working with children and adolescents, ethical concerns are paramount. Parental permission and full disclosure regarding meditative practices for children and adolescents is a crucial step in working with these populations.

Activities to Extend Your Learning

1. Which of the meditative practices mentioned in this chapter (mindfulness meditation, mantra meditation, yoga, Tai Chi, or Qi Gong) most appeals to you? Find practitioners or classes in your community that teach this skill and begin your own personal meditative practice.

2. YouTube searches on the topic of meditation offer many opportunities to explore meditative practices. Visit the YouTube link (http://www.youtube.com/watch?v=3nwwKbM_vJc) that shows Jon Kabat-Zinn guiding a meditation for Google employees. You can actually follow Kabat-Zinn's instructions and do the meditation along with the video.

3. Practice your mindfulness and meditation skills in the classroom. Invite a professor, student, or community member who is willing to guide meditation activities such as mindful eating, walking meditation, tai chi. Discuss your experiences and ways that these practices may be helpful with children and adolescents.

4. This may be done individually or as a group activity.
   - Choose a concern that is common among children or adolescents.
   - Examples are: athletic performance, academic issues, anxiety or depression, bullying, eating concerns, peer relationships, self-control, family relationships, etc.
   - Discuss how meditative practices might be used to help children or adolescents cope with the challenges confronting them.

Recommended Resources

Websites

Center for Mindfulness in Medicine, Health Care, and Society: http://www.umassmed.edu/Content.aspx?id=41252
Committee for Stress-Free Schools: http://www.tmeducation.org/
The Garrison Institute: http://www.garrisoninstitute.org/
Mindful Awareness Research Center: http://marc.ucla.edu/
Mindfulness in Education Network: http://www.mindfuled.org/
National Center for Complementary and Alternative Medicine: http://nccam.nih.gov/health/

Readings

Baer, R. A. (2003). Mindfulness training as a clinical intervention: A conceptual and empirical review. *Clinical Psychology: Science and Practice, 10*, 125–143.
Germer, C. K., Siegel, R. D., & Fulton, P. R. (2005). *Mindfulness and psychotherapy.* New York: Guilford.
Greco, L. A., & Hayes, S. C. (2008). *Acceptance and mindfulness treatments for children and adolescents: A practitioner's guide.* Oakland, CA: Context Press/New Harbinger.
Kabat-Zinn, J. (1994). *Wherever you go, there you are: Mindfulness meditation in everyday life* New York: Hyperion.
Kabat-Zinn, J. (2005). *Coming to our senses: Healing ourselves and the world through mindfulness.* New York: Hyperion.
Keefe, T. (1996). Meditation and social work treatment. In F. J. Turner (Ed.), *Social work treatment: Interlocking theoretical approaches* (2nd ed., pp. 434–460). New York: The Free Press.

Epilogue
THE THREE As

Christine Lynn Norton

Introduction

Working in the field of child and adolescent mental health is a complex, interdisciplinary endeavor. The mental health needs of children and adolescents are intricate, and there are various key players involved in decision making on behalf of the young person. Hopefully, *young people themselves* are involved in the process of deciding what types of interventions will work well for them, but certainly families, schools, mental health professionals, child welfare, and even the courts get involved in these decisions. As Seligman and Reichenberg (2007) wrote, "Children experience at least two systems—the family and the school—that affect their behaviors and emotional well-being … Treatment of the child will usually require contact and cooperation with all the agencies and professionals concerned" (p. 57).

It can be very easy to apply cookie cutter approaches when referring young people for various types of services, but it is essential to remember that not every approach is appropriate for every child or adolescent. Likewise, multiple approaches may be necessary. According to Seligman and Reichenberg (2007), "Interventions that take into account the child's stage of development, level and stage of change, demographic factors (for example, race, ethnicity, and socioeconomic status), and such personality traits as impulsivity and coping skills have been found to improve treatment outcomes and reduce dropout rates" (p. 57).

Finally, all approaches should be asset-building experiences, and should include other "non-intervention" opportunities in the community that promote positive youth development, social justice and youth empowerment. After all, it is not enough to provide treatment to young people, but rather we must help to foster an ongoing sense of wellness and creativity that allows them to contribute to society in meaningful ways. These important areas to consider can be categorized through *The Three As*:

- Assessment
- Adjunctive Approaches
- Assets

Assessment

Assessment is the process of gathering information about a client in order to select the most appropriate intervention strategies. A thorough assessment considers various client characteristics such as genetic and other predisposing factors, demographics, source of referral and client's motivation for treatment, treatment history, personality profile, and the client's developmental history (Seligman & Reichenberg, 2007). Together, all of these factors can help the mental health professional decide what interventions may fit the client best.

This book has presented various innovative interventions that can be used with distinctive child and adolescent populations; however, it is important to consider how to best match these interventions with a client. According to Seligman and Reichenberg, "Matching therapy to specific disorders would seem to be the answer to improving effectiveness. Yet research has not fully supported this method, which suggests that effective therapy is more complicated and involves a host of variables that have more of a synergistic relationship than simply matching people with appropriate treatment" (p. 4). With some of the interventions presented in this book, the use of specific interventions with particular treatment issues is supported with research. We have seen, for example, that bibliotherapy has been shown to be an excellent intervention in the treatment of ADHD. Likewise, animal-assisted therapy can be highly effective in treating trauma. These are only a few research-based examples presented in this book.

During the assessment process, we should also rule out various interventions because of the safety needs or physical or developmental limitations of the client, as in the case of wilderness therapy. We might rule out using animal-assisted therapy depending on the child's prior history with animals. What is most important, however, when considering the innovative interventions in this book for child and adolescent clients is for clinicians to *engage in a holistic assessment process in which multiple factors are considered in order to select the best "fit" between the client and the intervention*. While this book does not offer a formula for doing so, this epilogue seeks to provide a general map for mental health professionals to follow.

Seligman also encourages therapists to consider the client's readiness for change, based on Prochaska and Norcross's (2006) stages of change model, which include: precontemplation, contemplation, preparation, action and maintenance. These stages are not linear, but are more like a spiral in which people visit and revisit the various stages. Table E.1 highlights the specific aspects of the stages of change.

The stages of change model can be applied to children and adolescents as well and is an excellent assessment tool that can help clinicians reframe what may be thought of as resistance or disinterest. The stages of change model can also help other people in the client system, such as family members or teachers, understand the stage a child or adolescent is in, and to find ways of helping the client move forward. An example of a wilderness therapy client helps clarify this point:

Clara, a 17-year-old Latina female, had been expelled from her high school for drug use, disrespect, truancy and academic reasons. Her parents decided her only option was for her to attend an alternative school for her senior year. First, however, they decided to send her to a wilderness therapy program because her attitude was so defiant. As an incentive for participating in this program, they told her they would give her a week to see her friends back home before sending her to this new school. Clara was angry and did not feel

Table E.1   Stages of Change Model (adapted from Prochaska & Norcross, 2006)

Stage of Change	Characteristics of the Stage	Tasks Necessary for Moving on to the Next Stage
Precontemplation	People in this stage have no intention of changing. They are unwilling to do anything that might lead to change, and have often not even considered changing. They are often stuck in destructive patterns of behavior for years.	The person must recognize and admit there is a problem.
Contemplation	In this stage, the person is able to admit they need to change and that they want to change, but they are still just thinking about change and have not begun to take an action steps.	The person must begin to take action—even small steps—towards changing their behavior.
Preparation	In this stage, behavior and intentions are aligned. The person is ready to set goals and make positive changes.	The person must make an action plan in preparation for moving on, complete with specific, measurable, achievable, realist, and timely goals (SMART).
Action	In this stage, people spend time and energy towards changing their behavior and achieving their goals. This stage may last for a varied amount of time, from one day to six months.	The person must acquire strategies and coping skills to prevent relapse.
Maintenance	After six months, the person works on maintaining the positive changes they have made.	The person must continue to use the strategies and skills they have developed and build a solid support system to help them maintain change.

this was a good incentive, but she agreed to attend the wilderness therapy program just to get away from home. Clara still did not see the impact of her actions on her family and blamed them for wanting to send her away. Clearly, she was in the stage of *precontemplation*. After spending a month at the wilderness therapy program, however, Clara had a lot of time to think, literally, to contemplate her actions and what she wanted out of her life. She moved from precontemplation to *contemplation* and then, with the help of the wilderness therapy instructors began making an action plan and setting goals for her life. She entered the *preparation* stage with hope; however, as one of her goals, Clara wanted to approach her high school one more time to see if they would give her another chance. Clara completed the wilderness therapy program successfully, putting into *action* some of the new skills and strategies she had learned. When she got back home, with her parents' permission, Clara made an appointment with her former principal. She talked with him about the changes she was making as a result of her participation in the wilderness therapy program. The principal was rightfully skeptical, however, and called the wilderness therapy instructors directly, to get their input. They advocated on Clara's behalf. The principal said, "Why should I believe that after one month, she is a different kid?" The wilderness therapy instructor replied, "She is not a different kid. She is the same kid, but now she is *ready to change her behavior*." Based on this feedback, the principal gave Clara one more chance, and she went on to remain at home with her family and graduate from her home high school, demonstrating that she was in the *maintenance* stage of change.

This readiness to change is a critical factor is assessing what interventions will work best with various children and adolescents. Many of the innovative interventions in this book work well with the stages of change model, because they are interventions that *promote client engagement in the process* and may more naturally help clients move forward through these stages of change simply *by actively involving them in novel experiences and connections with others.*

Adjunctive Approaches

As was mentioned in first chapter, all of the innovative interventions presented in this volume are meant to be used as a part of the larger system of care. This means that they should not be used in isolation, but as a part of the systems in which clients exist, such as the family, the community, etc. Likewise, *many of these interventions work best as adjunct approaches to more traditional forms of therapy* such as individual, family and group treatment. Some of the interventions in this book can also work well together. Art therapy and wilderness therapy can be combined by encouraging young people to make art out of nature, such as famed naturalist artist Andrew Goldsworthy might do. The act of self-expression in the natural world can be a powerful combination. Music therapy and meditation may also be combined by having clients meditate to the rhythm of a drum.

Most importantly, however, is that the use of innovative interventions as adjunctive modalities is *intentionally aligned with the client's overall treatment plan.* These interventions are not meant to be used haphazardly, but with the same therapeutic intent as any other intervention strategy. Say, for example, that an adolescent client is being seen for aggression and mistreatment of his/her siblings. This client may have treatment goals of increasing impulse control and empathy. While this client may benefit greatly from family therapy, based on the research, he/she may also be a good candidate for an animal-assisted intervention. If a client is lacking in coping skills, and his/her treatment goal is to increase the client's sense of self-efficacy, then a wilderness therapy program may be a perfect complement to his/her overall treatment plan.

When considering adjunctive approaches to working with children and youth, however, it is also important to consider what additional sources of support, education, and training, clients and others in the client system might need (Seligman & Reichenberg, 2007). For example, parenting skills training can be an important adjunct to treatment of children and adolescents with specific mental health concerns such as conduct disorder, and can help to reinforce what the child is learning in therapy (Seligman, 2007). Support groups may also be helpful for clients battling addiction or the addiction of a loved one or those who are experiencing grief and loss. Likewise, multi-family support groups can be helpful for parents experiencing the mental health and substance abuse problems of their children. Clients may also need social services to address basic needs that if unmet will only exacerbate any existing mental health concerns. It is important to thing broadly and holistically when working with children and adolescents, but to never lose sight of their original treatment goals. According to Seligman, *"All adjunct services should reinforce the goals the client is working on.* Whether it is an exercise program, volunteer activities to improve socialization, bibliotherapy, or biofeedback to help people recognize bodily sensations, the types of services suggested should reinforce progress that a client is making in individual therapy" (p. 46).

Assets: Positive Youth Development

Developmental assets is a term that is quite in vogue right now. Current theory on positive youth development touts the need for fostering and promoting internal and external assets that can become the building blocks for healthy psychosocial development of children and youth. Since its creation in 1990, the Search Institute's framework of Developmental Assets has become the most widely used approach to positive youth development in the United States. According to the Search Institute (2010):

> Grounded in extensive research in youth development, resiliency, and prevention, the Developmental Assets represent the relationships, opportunities, and personal qualities that young people need to avoid risks and to thrive. Studies of more than 2.2 million young people in the United States consistently show that the more assets young people have, the less likely they are to engage in a wide range of high-risk behaviors and the more likely they are to thrive. Assets have power for all young people, regardless of their gender, economic status, family, or race/ethnicity. Furthermore, levels of assets are better predictors of high-risk involvement and thriving than poverty or being from a single-parent family. However, the average young person experiences fewer than half of the 40 assets. (¶1–4)

For a complete list of all of the Search Institute's developmental assets by age go to http://www.search-institute.org/developmental-assets/lists.

While this book is about the use of innovative interventions in child and adolescent mental health and not positive youth development per se, the authors want to make it clear that the two should not be mutually exclusive. As a matter of fact, we believe that effective *interventions in child and adolescent mental health should be asset-building experiences* that contribute both to the reduction of mental health problems, and to the overall wellness and positive development of the young person. Currently, there is not much research in this area, and more research is needed that considers the asset-building impact of mental health interventions on children and adolescents, especially given the powerful data presented that shows the more assets a young person has, the less at risk they are of a host of problems, such as dropping out of school substance abuse, etc. Dababnah and Cooper (2006) reinforce this belief by encouraging the promotion of mental wellness and positive social and behavioral competencies *by engaging children and youth in interesting and appropriate activities*. Certainly, the innovative interventions presented in this book provide those types of opportunities and can address mental health and positive youth development concurrently.

The Need for Enriched Environments: Social Justice and Youth Empowerment

In the Surgeon General's (1999) report on the mental health needs of children and adolescents, strong recommendations were included that focused not only on mental health treatment but about *the need to improve the environments of children and youth at risk*. The socioeconomic and environmental stressors that many youth face in the United States in particular create developmental vulnerabilities than can contribute to the onset of mental health problems. Poverty, abuse and neglect, and multi-generational problems impact the developmental and neurobiological trajectory of children and adolescents.

What is needed most for optimal development are enriched environments that promote positive psychosocial and neurobiological development. These types of environments are safe environments in which children's basic needs are met, but where they also have access to positive relationships and opportunities for growth. According to Lehrer (2006), Elizabeth Gould's neurological research at Princeton University supports the reality that "the structure of our brain, from the details of our dendrites to the density of our hippocampus, is incredibly influenced by our surroundings" (¶1). Enriched environments foster healthy brain development and give children a head start. Unfortunately, the converse is true. When children and youth are marginalized because of race, ethnicity, or socioeconomic status and denied access to quality housing, education and health care, they are further at risk of experiencing multiple problems, and the lack of enriched environments can cause neurological deficits, causing these children to be further behind from the start. As Lehrer said, "The social implications of this research are staggering. If boring environments, stressful noises, and the primate's particular slot in the dominance hierarchy all shape the architecture of the brain—and Gould's team has shown that they do—then the playing field isn't level. Poverty and stress aren't just an idea: they are an anatomy. Some brains never even have a chance" (2006, ¶1).

For this reason, the authors of this book want to remind readers to consider *the ecological approach* when intervening in child and adolescent mental health, which considers the "person-in-environment" and the interplay between the two (Jack, 2005). By integrating a systemic mindset, we can more adeptly focus on social justice, youth and community empowerment, which will make our job as mental health practitioners easier. As we advocate for change in the environments in which our children and adolescents live, while concurrently applying innovative interventions to child and adolescent mental health problems, we may ensure the lasting impact of our work.

Social Justice

According to the National Association of Social Workers (2010), a social justice perspective encompasses the view "that everyone deserves equal economic, political and social rights and opportunities" (¶ 2). Practitioners in child and adolescent mental health should advocate for socially-just responses to structural problems that face their clients, and "armed with the long-term goal of empowering their clients, they [*should*] use knowledge of existing legal principles and organizational structure to suggest changes to protect their clients, who are often powerless and underserved" (NASW, 2010, ¶ 4).

Social justice has a two-fold importance in child and adolescent mental health. First, a focus on social justice will foster a culture of advocacy and macro-level change in which mental health practitioners take an active role in advocating for economic, political, and social rights, and opportunities for their clients. This can lead to the promotion of enriched environments in which children and adolescents can grow and develop in a healthy way. Second, a social justice approach to child and adolescent mental health can continue to advocate against the stigma of mental illness that so many children and adolescents face. According to Johnstone (2008), people suffering from mental illness and other mental health problems are among the most stigmatized, discriminated against, marginalized, disadvantaged, and vulnerable members of society. For these reasons, child and adolescent mental health professionals are encouraged to be both practitioners and advocates for social change.

Youth Empowerment

Several of the innovative interventions in this book encourage self-expression through a variety of creative means. This need for self-expression, especially in adolescence, can be understood as the need to have a voice, to influence one's world, and to be active in shaping one's own life. Often, treatment in child and adolescent mental health is treatment "done to" the client, rather than being a co-created process in which the mental health practitioner and the client journey towards change together. While the interventions in this book seek to empower young people, it is also important that we begin to create a larger environment in which the voices of children and adolescents are heard and respected.

The youth empowerment movement is an attempt to "foster, develop and support youth initiative, and a strong representational youth voice in the service and decision-making life of our community, and to engage youth as resources on a county, state-wide, national and international basis" (Youth Empowerment Project, 2003, ¶1). Youth empowerment projects include community service, leadership opportunities for youth, youth media, peer juries, restorative justice, etc. Youth empowerment is an asset-building endeavor in which young people develop a greater sense of self-efficacy, civic engagement, and sense of purpose. The youth empowerment movement engages young people to help in the process of creating enriched environments that will aid in the healthy growth and development of young people. Part of working in child and adolescent mental health is to connect our clients to youth empowerment opportunities in which they can have a voice, express themselves, and become part of larger solutions in society.

This can be a highly therapeutic process for young people who have experienced trauma or loss or for young people suffering from mental health problems. Examples of this can be seen in young people who lose a parent to gun violence and become active in the gun-control movement, or in youth who lose a parent to cancer and mobilize their classmates to raise money for cancer research, or in youth who are raped and become active in teaching self-defense classes to young women. All of these responses to loss are based on the principles of youth empowerment and should be incorporated into our work in child and adolescent mental health. A poignant story illustrates this:

> As a high school social worker, I had a 16-year-old male client who lost his best friend
> to suicide. This client had already been struggling with depression of his own as well as

substance abuse and self-injurious behavior. When his friend died, he fell apart and his own thoughts of suicide flourished. However, with the help and encouragement of his friends (several of whom had also lost loved ones to suicide), he eventually became active in a movement to raise awareness at his school to the problems of depression and youth suicide. He spoke to several student groups, and as he shared his story, other students came out of the woodwork. They created a large mural together, and handed out yellow ribbon cards and pins, monikers of hope in their anti-suicide campaign.

This act of youth empowerment did not make my client's own depression and substance abuse magically disappear, but it helped him to not feel alone, and gave him a sense of purpose that carried him through the pain of his own transformation.

Summary

When utilizing innovative interventions in child and adolescent mental health, it is important to remember *The three As:* assessment, adjunctive approaches, and assets. A thorough assessment of client characteristics can help us select the most appropriate intervention strategies that can help our clients effectively address their treatment goals. Innovative interventions can and should be used as adjunctive approaches to traditional means of therapy, and clients and others in the client system should have access to other adjunctive services and supports during the treatment process. Interventions in child and adolescent mental health should also be asset-building interventions that help create the building blocks necessary for positive youth development. Finally, child and adolescent mental health treatment cannot and should not occur in isolation. There is a need to not only consider but improve the environments in which our children and adolescents live through *advocacy, social justice, and youth empowerment.*

Activities to Extend Your Learning

- Follow Seligman and Reichenberg's (2007) assessment guidelines and do a client map treatment plan including one or more of the innovative interventions presented in this book.
- Select one innovative intervention from this book to apply to a client or client system with which you are working or have worked. Select several adjunctive services or approaches to go along with the intervention. Explain why you selected these adjunctive approaches based on a review of the current literature.
- Go the Search Institute website: http://www.search-institute.org/developmental-assets/lists and do a self-assessment of the developmental assets in your own life. Consider the life experiences and relationships that helped develop these assets.
- Write down your own personal definition of *social justice*. Compare this with another person whose background is different from your own. Discuss aspects of privilege and oppression each of you have experienced.
- Consider what it means to have a voice. Think of times in your life where you felt empowered. Give an example of a time in which an empowerment approach could have helped you cope more effectively.

Recommended Resources

Websites

The Free Child Project: Youth Led Social Activism: http://www.freechild.org/youth_activism_2.htm
National Alliance on Mental Illness Child and Adolescent Action Center: http://www.nami.org/template.
    cfm?section=Child_and_Teen_Support
The Search Institute: http://www.search-institute.org/
Youth Empowerment Project: http://www.youthempowerment.com/

Readings

Claus, J., & Ogden, C. (Eds.) (2001). *Service learning for youth empowerment and social change*. New York: Peter Lang.
Felix, A. (October). Making youth voice a community principle. *Youth Service Journal, 1*(1), 1–10. Youth Serve America: Washington, DC. Retrieved March 23, 2010, from http://tools.ysa.org/downloads/tipsheets/youthvoice/MakingYouthVoiceACommunityPrinciple.pdf
Seligman, L., & Reichenberg, L. W. (2007). *Selecting effective treatments: A comprehensive, systematic guide to treating mental disorders*. San Francisco: Wiley.

REFERENCES

Chapter 1

American Psychiatric Association. (2002). *Childhood disorders*. Retrieved June 2002, from http://www.psych. org/public_info/childr~1.cfm

Arbuckle, M., & Herrick, C. (2006). *Child & adolescent mental health: Interdisciplinary systems of care*. Sudburry, MA: Jones and Bartlett.

Bandura, A. (1977). Self-efficacy: Toward a unifying theory of behavioral change. *Psychological Review, 84*(2), 191–215.

Bandura, A. (1993). Perceived self-efficacy in cognitive development and functioning. *Educational Psychologist, 28*(2), 117–148.

Bandura, A. (1997). *Self-efficacy: The exercise of control*. New York: Worth.

Barber, B. L., & Crockett, L. J. (1993). Preventive interventions in early adolescence: Developmental and contextual challenges. In R. M. Lerner (Ed.), *Adolescence: Perspectives on research, policy, and intervention* (pp. 311–314). Hillsdale, NJ: Erlbaum.

Child Development Institute. (2009). *Development*. Retrieved November 15, 2009, from http://www.childdevelopmentinfo.com

Cole, M., & Cole, S. R. (1996). *The development of children*. New York: W.H. Freeman.

Council on Social Work Education (CSWE). (2008). *Educational policies and standards*. Retrieved December 10, 2009, from http://www.cswe.org/File.aspx?id=13780

Cozolino, L. (2002). *The neuroscience of psychotherapy*. New York: W.W. Norton.

Crosby, A. (1995). A critical look: The philosophical foundations of experiential education. In K. Warren, M. Sakofs, J. S. Hunt, Jr. (Eds.), *The theory of experiential education* (pp. 3–13). Dubuque, IA: Kendall-Hunt.

Dababnah, S., & Cooper, J. (2006). *Challenges and opportunities in children's mental health: A view from families and youth*. New York: National Center for Children in Poverty.

Deutsch, H. (1960). *The psychology of women, a psychoanalytic interpretation*. New York: Greene and Stratton.

Dewey, J. (1965). *The philosophy of John Dewey*. New York: Macmillian. (Reprinted from *Experience and education, pp. 511–523*, by J. J. McDermott (Ed.), 1981. Chicago: University of Chicago Press.)

Fonagy, P. (2000). *Evidence based child mental health: The findings of a comprehensive review*. Paper presented to Child mental health interventions: What works for whom? New York: Center for Child and Adolescent Psychiatry.

Frankl, V. E. (1959). *Man's search for meaning*. New York: Simon & Schuster.

Frost, J. L. (1998, June). *Neuroscience, play and child development*. Paper presented at the IPA/USA Triennial National Conference. Longmont, CO.

Healy, J. M. (2004). *Your child's growing mind*. New York: Broadway Books.

Highland, A. C. (1979). Depression in adolescents: A developmental view. *Child Welfare, 58*(9), 577–585.

InCrisis. (2005). *The prevalence of mental health and addictive disorders*. Retrieved December 2007, from http://www.incrisis.org/Articles/PrevalenceMHProblems.htm

Koplewicz, H. (2002). *More than moody*. New York: G.P. Putnam.

Luna, B., Thulborn, K. R., Munoz, D. P., Merriam, E. P., Garver, K. E., Minshew, et al. (2001). Maturation of widely distributed brain function subserves cognitive development. *NeuroImage, 13*, 786–793.

Malchiodi, K., & Perry, B. D. (2008). *Creative interventions with traumatized children*. New York: Guilford.

Mental Health: A Report of the Surgeon General (1999). Retrieved December 7, 2009, from http://www.surgeongeneral.gov/library/mentalhealth/home.html

National Institute of Mental Health. (2001). *Blueprint for change: Research on child and adolescent mental health*. Report of the National Advisory Mental Health Council's workgroup on child and adolescent mental health intervention. Washington, DC: NIMH.

National Institute of Mental Health. (2005) *Mental illness exacts heavy toll, beginning in youth*. Retrieved December 11, 2009, from http://www.nimh.nih.gov/science-news/2005/mental-illness-exacts-heavy-toll-beginning-in-youth.shtml

New Freedom Commission on Mental Health. (2003). *Achieving the promise: Transforming mental health care in America*. Retrieved December 11, 2010, from http://www.mentalhealthcommission.gov/reports/Final-Report/toc.html

Nock, M., Goldman, J., Wang, Y., & Albano, A. (2004). From science to practice: The flexible use of evidence-based treatments in clinical settings. *Journal of the American Academy of Child & Adolescent Psychiatry, 43*(6), 777–780.

Norton, C. (2010). *Exploring the wilderness experience as a bridge between identity Complexity and the development of youth purpose*. Unpublished manuscript.

Orlinsky, D. E., & Howard, K. J. (1986). Process and outcome in psychotherapy. In S. L. Garfield & A. E. Bergin (Eds.), *Handbook of psychotherapy and behavior change* (pp. 311–381). New York: Wiley.

Perls, F., Hefferline, R., & Goodman, P. (1951). *Gestalt therapy: Excitement and growth in human personality*. New York: Dell.

Pink, D. (2006). *A whole new mind: Why right-brainers will rule the future*. New York: Penguin Group.

Play for Peace. (2009). *Play for peace*. Retrieved December 17, 2009, from http://www.playforpeace.org

Radkowsky, M., & Siegel, L. J. (1997). The gay adolescent: Stressors, adaptations, and psychosocial interventions. *Clinical Psychology Review, 17*(2), 191–216.

Resnick, M. (2000). *Protective factors, resiliency and healthy youth development*. Minneapolis, MN: Division of General Pediatrics and Adolescent Health, University of Minnesota. Retrieved December 16, 2009, from http://vcuwomenshealth.officebusinesses.com/education/wh_2006/Articles/Resnick_ProtectiveFactors.pdf

Rogers, C. (1942). *Counseling and psychotherapy*. Boston: Houghton Mifflin.

Saari, C. (1991). *The creation of meaning in clinical social work*. New York: Guilford.

Schmidt, N. (1997). *The mystery field trip: Focusing on spiritual development in experiential Education* (Unpublished master's thesis). The University of Minnesota-Duluth.

Seligman, L., & Reichenberg, L. W. (2007). *Selecting effective treatments: A comprehensive, systematic guide to treating mental disorders*. San Francisco, CA: Wiley.

Sproul, B. A. (2006). Foreword. In M. Arbuckle & C. A. Herrick (Eds.), *Child & adolescent mental health: Interdisciplinary systems of care* (pp. xi–xxi). Sudbury, MA: Jones and Bartlett.

Sylwester, R. (2007). *The adolescent brain: Reaching for autonomy*. Thousand Oaks, CA: Corwin Press.

U.S. Department of Health and Human Services. (1999). *Mental health: A report of the surgeon general*. Rockville, MD: U.S. Government Printing Office.

U.S. Department of Health and Human Services. (2001). *Report of the surgeon general's conference on children's mental health: A national action agenda*. Washington, DC: U.S. Government Printing Office.

Woodruff, D., Osher, D., Hoffman, C., Gruner, A., King, M., Snow, S., et al. (1999). *The role of education in a system of care: Effectively serving children with emotional or behavioral disorders. In Systems of care: Promising practices in children's mental health, 1998 series, volume III*. Washington, DC: Center for Effective Collaboration and Practice, American Institutes for Research.

Chapter 2

American Art Therapy Association. (2009). American Art Therapy Association. Retrieved December 10, 2009, from http://www.arttherapy.org/aata-aboutus.html

Appleton, V. (2001). Avenues of hope: Art therapy and the resolution of trauma. *Art Therapy: Journal of the American Art Therapy Association, 18*(1), 6–13.

Belkofer, C. & Konopka, L. (2008). Conducting art therapy research using quantitative EEG measures. *Art Therapy: Journal of the American Art Therapy Association, 25*(2), 56–63.

Block, D., Harris, T., & Laing, S. (2005). Open studio process as a model of social action: A program for at risk youth. *Art Therapy: Journal of the American Art Therapy Association, 22*(1), 32–38.

Chapman, L., Morabito, D., Ladakakos, C., Schrieer, H., & Knudson, M. (2001). The effectiveness of art therapy interventions in reducing post traumatic stress disorder symptoms in pediatric trauma patients. *Art Therapy: Journal of the American Art Therapy Association, 18*(2), 100–104.

Chilcote, R. (2007). Art therapy with child tsunami survivors in Sri Lanka. *Art Therapy: Journal of the American Art Therapy Association, 24*(4), 156–162.

Eaton, L., Doherty, K., & Widrick, R. (2007). A review of research and methods used to establish art therapy as an effective treatment for traumatized children. *The Arts in Psychotherapy, 34*, 256–262.

Frank, K. (2003). *The handbook for helping kids with anxiety & stress.* Chapin, SC: Youth Light.

Friedberg, R., & McClure, J. (2002). *Clinical practice of cognitive therapy with children and adolescents: The nuts and bolts.* New York: Guilford.

Goodman, R., Chapman, L., & Gantt, L. (2008). Creative arts therapies for children. In E. Foa, T. Keanne, & M. Friedman (Eds.), *Effective treatment for PTSD: Practice guidelines from the international society of traumatic stress studies* (pp. 491–507). New York: Guilford.

Horovitz, E., & Eksten, S. (Eds.). (2009). *The art therapists' primer: A clinical guide to writing assessments, diagnosis, and treatment.* Springfield, IL: Charles C. Thomas.

Hoshino, J. (2008). The development of family therapy and family art therapy. In C. Kerr, J. Hoshino, J. Sutherland, S. Parashak, & L. McCarley (Eds.), *Family art therapy: Foundations of theory and practice* (pp. 25–63). New York: Taylor & Francis.

Huebner, D. (2006). *What to do when you worry too much: A kid's guide to overcoming anxiety.* Washington DC: Magination Press

Kalmanowitz, D., & Lloyd, B. (2005). Art therapy and political violence. In D. Kalmanowitz & B. Lloyd (Eds.), *Art therapy and political violence: With art, without illusion* (pp. 14–34). New York: Routledge.

Kerr, C., Hoshino, J., Sutherland, J., Parashak, S., & McCarley, L. (2008). *Family art therapy: Foundations of theory and practice.* New York: Taylor & Francis.

Klingman, A., Shalev, R., & Pearlman, A. (2000). Graffiti: A creative means of youth coping with collective trauma. *The Arts in Psychotherapy, 27*(5), 299–307.

Klorer, P. G. (2000). *Expressive therapy with troubled children.* Northvale, NJ: Jason Aronson.

Kramer, E. (1958). *Art therapy in a children's community.* Springfield, IL: Charles C. Thomas.

Kramer, E. (1971). *Art as therapy with children.* New York: Schocken Books.

Levick, M. (1998). *See what I'm saying: What children tell us through their art.* Dubuque, IA: Islewest Publishing.

Levick, M. (2009). *Levick emotional and cognitive art therapy assessment: A normative study.* Bloomington, IN: Authorhouse.

Lusebrink, V. (1995). *Imagery and visual expression in therapy.* New York: Plenum Press.

Malchiodi, C. (2005). The impact of culture on art therapy with children. In E. Giil & A. Drewes (Eds.), *Cultural issues in play therapy* (pp. 96–111). New York: Guilford.

March, J., & Mulle, K. (1998). *OCD in children and adolescents: A cognitive-behavioral treatment manual.* New York: Guilford.

McCann, M. (2003). *Health hazards: Manual for artists* (5th Ed.). Guilford, CT: Lyons.

Moon, B. (1994). *Introduction to art therapy: Faith in the product.* Springfield, IL: Charles C. Thomas.

Moon, B. (1999). The tears make me paint: The role of responsive artmaking in adolescent art therapy. *Art Therapy: The Journal of the American Art Therapy Association, 16*(2), 78–82.

Moon, B. (2000). *Ethical issues in art therapy.* Springfield, IL: Charles C. Thomas.

Naumburg, M. (1973). *An introduction to art therapy: Studies of the "free" art expression of behavior problem children as a means of diagnosis and therapy.* New York: Teachers College Press.

Noble, J. (2001). Art as an instrument for creating social reciprocity: Social skills group for children with autism. In S. Riley, *Group process made visible: Group art therapy* (pp. 82–114). Philadelphia: Taylor & Francis.

Orr, P. (2007). Art therapy with children after a disaster: A content analysis. *The Arts in Psychotherapy, 34*, 350–361.

Perry, B., Pollard, R., Blakely, T., Baker, W., & Vigilante, D. (1995). Childhood trauma, the neurobiology of adaptation, and "use-dependent" development of the brain: How states become traits. *Infant Mental Health Journal, 16*, 271–291.

Plasq Inc. (2009). *Comic-life 1.5.* [Software]. Retrieved September 1, 2009, from http://plasq.com

Riley, S. (1999). Brief therapy: An adolescent intervention. *Art Therapy: Journal of the American Art Therapy Association, 16*(2), 83–86.

Riley, S. (2001). *Group process made visible: Group art therapy.* Philadelphia: Taylor & Francis.

Rode, D. (1995). Building bridges within the culture of pediatric medicine: The interface of art therapy and child life programming. *Art Therapy: Journal of the American Art Therapy Association, 12*(2), 104–110.

Rubin, J. (1978). *Child art therapy: Understanding and helping children to grow.* New York: Van Nostrand Reinhold.

Rubin, J. (2001). *Approaches to art therapy: Theory and technique* (2nd ed.). New York: Routledge.

Safran, D. (2002). *Art therapy and AD/HD: Diagnostic and therapeutic approaches.* London: Jessica Kingsley.

Seiden, D. (2001). *Mind over matter: The uses of materials in art, education and therapy.* Chicago: Magnolia Street Publishers.

Silver, R. (2007). *The silver drawing test and draw a story: Assessing depression, aggression, and cognitive skills.* New York: Routledge.

Spring, D. (2004). Thirty-year study links neuroscience, specific trauma, PTSD, image conversion and language translation. *Art Therapy: Journal of the American Art Therapy Association, 21*(4), 200–209.

Stein, M. (2001). The use of family drawings by children in pediatric practice. *Pediatrics, 107*(4), 855–860.

Tripp, T. (2007). A short term therapy approach to processing trauma: Art therapy and bilateral stimulation. *Art Therapy: Journal of the American Art Therapy Association, 24*(4), 176–183.

Virshup, E. (1993). *California art therapy trends.* Chicago: Magnolia Street Publishers.

Wadeson, H. (1980). *Art psychotherapy.* New York: Wiley.

Wadeson, H. (2002). Confronting polarization in art therapy. *Art Therapy: Journal of the American Art Therapy Association, 19*(2), 77–84.

Wise, S. (2005). A time for healing: Art therapy for children, post September 11, New York. In D. Kamanowitz, & B. Lloyd, (Eds.), *Art therapy and political violence: With art, without illusion* (pp. 142–153). New York: Routledge.

Wix, L. (2009). Aesthetic empathy in teaching art to children: The work of Friedl Dicker-Brandeis in Terizin. *Art Therapy: Journal of the American Art Therapy Association, 26*(4), 152–158.

Chapter 3

Allen, M., & Edwards, D. M. (2003). *Wilderness treatment: A Journey of discovery.* Retrieved from http://home.earthlink.net/~durangodave/html/writing/Wilderness.htm

Alvarez, A., & Welsh, J. J. (1990). Adventure: A model of experiential learning. *Social Work in Education, 13*(1), 49–57.

Asher, S. J., Huffaker, G. Q., & McNally, M. (1994). Therapeutic considerations of wilderness experiences for incest and rape survivors. *Women & Therapy, 15,* 161–174.

Association for Experiential Education (AEE). (2002). What is the definition of experiential education? Boulder, CO: Author.

Bandoroff, S., & Scherer, D. G. (1994). Wilderness family therapy: An innovative treatment approach for problem youth. *Journal of Child and Family Studies, 3* (2), 175–191.

Bandura, A. (1971) Social *learning theory.* Morristown, NJ: General Learning Press.

Berman, D. S., & Davis-Berman, J. (1989). Wilderness therapy: A therapeutic adventure for adolescents. *Journal of Independent Social Work, 3*(3), 65–77.

Berman, D. S., & Davis-Berman, J. (1994). *Wilderness therapy: Foundations, theory and research.* Dubuque, IA: Kendall/Hunt.

Berman, D., & Davis-Berman, J. (1995). Adventure as psychotherapy: A mental health perspective. *Journal of Leisurability, 22*(2), ¶ 1–9. Retrieved March 23, 2010, from http://lin.ca/resource-details/2774

Bernal, J., & Hollins, S. (1995). Psychiatric illness and learning disability: A dual diagnosis. *Advances in Psychiatric Treatment, 1,* 138–145.

Blatt, S. J., Quinlan, D. M., Chevron, E. S., & Zuroff, D. (1982). Dependency and self criticism: Psychological dimensions of depression. *Journal of Consulting and Clinical Psychology, 50*(1), 113–124.

Brower, A. M. (1989). Group development as constructed social reality: A social cognitive understanding of group formation. *Social Work with Groups, 12,* 23–41.

Campis, L., Lyman, R. D., & Prentice-Dunn, S. (1986). The parental locus of control scale: Development and validation. *Journal of Clinical Child Psychology, 15*(3), 260–268.

Carson, D., & Gillis, H. L. (1994) A meta-analysis of outdoor adventure programming with adolescents. *The Journal of Experiential Education, 17*(1), 40–47.

Catherine Freer Wilderness Therapy Programs. (2009). Outcome research. Retrieved on December 5, 2009, from http://www.cfreer.com/outcome-research/

Clark, J. R., Marmol, L. M., Cooley, R., & Gathercoal, K. (2004). The effects of wilderness therapy on the clinical concerns (on Axes I, II, and IV) of troubled adolescents. *Journal of Experiential Education, 27*(2), 213–232.

Cohen, J. (1988). *Statistical power analysis for the behavioral sciences* (2nd ed.). New York: Academic Press.

Cohen, B. D., & Schermer, V. L. (2002). On scapegoating in therapy groups: A social constructivist and intersubjective outlook. *International Journal of Group Psychotherapy, 52*(1), 89–109.

Connor, M. (2007). Wilderness therapy programs: A powerful intervention for adolescents. *The National Psychologist: The Independent Newspaper for Practitioners, 16*(1). Retrieved January 15, 2010, from http://www.nationalpsychologist.com/articles/art_v16n1_3.htm

Cozolino, L. (2002). *The neuroscience of psychotherapy: Building and rebuilding the human brain.* New York: W.W. Norton.

Crisp, S., & O'Donnell, M. (1998). Wilderness adventure therapy in adolescent psychiatry. In C. Itin (Ed.), Exploring *the boundaries of adventure therapy: International perspectives*. Boulder, CO: Association for Experiential Education.

Deutsch, H. (1945). *The psychology of women* (Vol. I & II). New York: Grune & Stratton.

Dewey, J. (1938). *Experience and education*. New York: Macmillan.

Erikson, E. (1968). *Identity: Youth and Crisis*. New York: W.W. Norton.

Friese, G. T., Hendee, J. C., & Kinziger, M. (1998). *Studies of the use of wilderness experience programs for personal growth, therapy, education, and leadership development: An annotation and evaluation*. Moscow, ID: Wilderness Research Center.

Garland, J. A., Jones, H. E., & Kolodny, R. L. (1973). A model for stages of development in social work groups. In S. Bernstein (Ed.), *Explorations in group work* (pp. 17–71). Boston, MA: Milford House.

Gass, M. A. (1985). Programming the transfer of learning in adventure education. *Journal of Experiential Education, 8*(3), 24–32.

Gass, M. A. (1993). Foundations of adventure therapy. In M. Gass (Ed.), *Adventure Therapy: Therapeutic Applications of Adventure Programming*. Dubuque, IA: Kendall/Hunt.

Gilligan, C. (1982). *In a different voice: Psychological theory and women's development*. Cambridge, MA: Harvard University Press.

Gillis, H. L. (1992) *Therapeutic uses of adventure-challenge-outdoor-wilderness: Theory and research*. Paper presented at the Coalition of Reeducation in the Outdoors Symposium Bradford Woods Indiana University, Martinsville, IN. Retrieved from http://fdsa.gcsu.edu:6060/lgillis/AT

Goldenberg, I., & Goldenberg, H. (1985). *Family therapy: An overview*. Pacific Grove, CA: Brooks/Cole.

Hait, M.D., E. (2002, May 24). *Medline editorial: Adolescent depression*. Cleveland, OH: Department of Pediatrics, Rainbow Babies and Children's Hospital, Case Western Reserve University. Retrieved December 10, 2009, from http://www.nlm.nih.gov/medlineplus/ency/article/001518.htm

Han, T. (1997). A meta-analytic review of the effects of adventure programming on locus of control (Unpublished master's thesis), Georgia State College, Midgeville, GA.

Handley, R. (1998). Provoking thought, evoking meaning. Giving explanation to adventure therapy. In C. Itin (Ed.), *Exploring the boundaries of adventure therapy: international perspectives* (pp. 37–45). Boulder, CO: Association for Experiential Education.

Harper, N. J., Russell, K. C., Cooley, R., & Cupples, J. (2007). Catherine Freer wilderness therapy expeditions: An exploratory case study of adolescent wilderness therapy, family functioning, and the maintenance of change. *Child and Youth Care Forum, 36*(2), 111–129.

Harper, N. J., & Russell, K. C. (2008). Family involvement and outcome in adolescent wilderness treatment: A mixed-methods evaluation. *International Journal of Child & Family Welfare 1*, 19–36.

Hattie, J., Marsh, H. W., Neill, J. T., & Richards, G. E. (1997). Adventure education and Outward Bound: Out of class experiences that make a lasting difference. *Review of Educational Research, 67*(1), 48–87.

Hawley, G. A. (2005). *Measures of psychosocial development*. Lutz, FL: Psychological Assessment Resources.

Hoyer, S. (2004). Effective wilderness therapy: Theory informed practice. In S. Bandoroff & S. Newes (Eds.), *Coming of age: The evolving field of adventure therapy* (pp. 56–72). Boulder, CO: Association for Experiential Education.

Huntington, D. D., & Bender, W. N. (1993). Adolescents with learning disabilities at risk? *Journal of Learning Disabilities, 26*(3), 159–166.

Hutton, C. (1988). *The effects of wilderness and follow-up advocacy programming on the behavior of juvenile delinquents* (Unpublished master's thesis). Southern Illinois University, Carbondale, IL.

Itin, C. M. (1999, Fall). Reasserting the philosophy of experiential education as a vehicle for change in the 21st century. *Journal of Experiential Education, 22*(2), 91–98.

Kaplan, L. (1979). Outward Bound: A treatment modality unexplored by the social work profession. *Child Welfare, LVIII*(1), 37–47.

Kaplan, R., & Kaplan, S. (1989). *The experience of nature: A psychological perspective*. Cambridge, UK: Cambridge University.

Kaplan, S., & Talbot, J. F. (1983). Psychological benefits of a wilderness experience. In I. Altman & J. F. Wohlwill (Eds.), *Behavior and the natural environment* (pp. 163–203). New York: Plenum Press.

Kendall, P. C. (2005). *Child and adolescent therapy: Cognitive-behavioral procedures* (3rd ed.). New York: Guilford.

Kiewa, J. (1994). Self-control: The key to adventure? Towards a model of the adventure experience. In E. Cole, E. Erdman, & E. D. Rothblum (Eds.), *Wilderness therapy for women: The power of adventure*. New York: Haworth Press.

Kimball, R. O., & Bacon, S. B. (1993). The wilderness challenge model. In M. Gass (Ed.), *Adventure Therapy: Therapeutic Applications of Adventure Programming* (pp. 11–41). Dubuque, IA: Kendall/Hunt Publishing.

Knapp, C. (1988). *Creating humane climates outdoors: A people skills primer.* Washington, DC: Office of Educational Research and Improvement. (ERIC Document Reproduction Service No. 294706).

Knapp, C. (2005). *Exploring the power of solo, silence, and solitude.* Boulder, CO: Association for Experiential Education.

Kohlberg, L. (1974). *Moral development.* Austin, TX: Holt, Rinehart & Winston.

Levine, D. (1994). Breaking through barriers: Wilderness therapy for sexual assault survivors. In E. Cole, E. Erdman, & E. D. Rothblum (Eds.), *Wilderness therapy for women: The power of adventure.* New York: Haworth Press.

Lightfoot, C. (1997). *The culture of adolescent risk-taking.* New York: Guilford.

Liu, X., Kurita, H., Uchiyama, M., Okawa, M., Liu, L., & Ma, D. (2000). Life events, locus of control, and behavior problems among Chinese adolescents. *Journal of Clinical Psychology, 56,* 1565–1577.

Loughmiller, C. (1965). *Wilderness road.* Austin, TX: The Hogg Foundation for Mental Health.

Louv, R. (2005). *Last child in the woods: Saving our children from nature deficit disorder.* Chapel Hill, NC: Algonquin Books.

Mahler, M. (1968). *On human symbiosis and the vicissitudes of individuation.* New York: International Universities Press.

Marsh, H. W., Richards, G. E., & Barnes, J. (1986). Multidimensional self concepts: A long-term follow-up of the effects of participation in an Outward Bound program. *Personality and Social Psychology Bulletin, 12,* 475–492.

Maslow, A. (1962). *Toward a psychology of being.* New York: The Free Press.

McPhee, P., & Gass, M. (1987). A group development model for adventure therapy programs. *Journal of Experiential Education, 10*(3), 39–46.

Miles, J. (1987). Wilderness as a healing place. *Journal of Experiential Education, 10*(3), 4–10.

Mitten, D. (1994). Ethical considerations in adventure therapy: A feminist critique. *Women and Therapy, 15,* 55–84.

Neil, J. (2006). Meta-analysis research methodology. Retrieved January 7, 2010, from http://wilderdom.com/research/meta-analysis.html

Norton, C. (2009). Into the wilderness—A case study: The psychodynamics of adolescent depression and the need for a holistic intervention. *Clinical Social Work Journal* Retrieved on November 15, 2009, from http://www.springerlink.com/content/u724456544683314/fulltext.pdf

Norton, C. (in press). Understanding the impact of wilderness therapy on adolescent depression and psychosocial development. *Illinois Child Welfare Journal.*

Nortrom, A. (2004). *The efficacy of wilderness therapy in the treatment of adolescent depression* (master's thesis), Prescott College, Prescott, AZ.

OMNI Youth Services. (2009). *Journey: Skills for life.* Retrieved December 17, 2009, from http://www.omni-youth.org/content/adventure-therapy-services_2.aspx

Outward Bound. (2009). *Intercept—A special program for at-risk youth.* Retrieved December 17, 2009, from http://www.outwardbound.org/index.cfm/do/are.program_intercept

Paxton, T., & McAvoy, L. (1998). *Self-efficacy and adventure programs: Transferring outcomes to everyday life.* Bradford Woods, IN: Coalition for Education in the Outdoors Research Symposium Proceedings.

Peterson, M. (2009). *Cognitive therapy for troubled teens.* Retrieved December 17, 2009, from http://www.articlesbase.com/parenting-articles/cognitive-therapy-for-troubled-teens-689168.htmlhref="http://www.articlesbase.com/parenting-articles/cognitive-therapy-for-troubled-teens-689168.html" title="Cognitive Therapy for Troubled Teens">Cognitive Therapy for Troubled Teens</a></p>

Prochaska, J. O., & Norcross, J. C. (2006). *Systems of psychotherapy.* Florence, KY: Wadsworth/Cengage Publishing.

Reynolds W. M. (2002). *Reynolds adolescent depression scale.* Odessa, Fla.: Psychological Assessment Resources,

Roszak, T., Gomes, M. E., & Kanner, A. D. (1995). *Ecopsychology.* San Francisco: Sierra Club Books.

Russell, K. C. (1999) *The theoretical basis, process, and reported outcomes of wilderness therapy as an intervention and treatment for problem behavior in adolescents* (Unpublished doctoral dissertation), College of Natural Resources, Moscow, ID.

Russell, K. C. (2001). What is Wilderness Therapy? *Journal of Experiential Education, 24*(2), 70–84.

Russell, K. C. (2002). *A longitudinal assessment of treatment outcomes in outdoor behavioral healthcare.* Technical Report 28, Idaho Forest, Wildlife, and Range Experiment Station. Moscow ID: University of Idaho-Wilderness Research Center.

Russell, K. C. (2003). Assessing treatment outcomes in outdoor behavioral healthcare using the Youth Outcome Questionnaire. *Child and Youth Care Forum, 32*(6), 355–381.

Russell, K C. (2004) Research directions in wilderness therapy. In S. Bandoroff & S. Newes (Eds.), *Coming of age: The evolving field of adventure therapy* (pp. 137–155). Boulder, CO: Association for Experiential Education.

Russell, K. C. (2006). *Examining substance abuse frequency and depressive symptom outcome in a sample of outdoor behavioral healthcare participants.* A report published by the Outdoor Behavioral Healthcare Research Cooperative. Bellingham: Western Washington University.

Russell, K. C. (2008). Adolescent substance-use treatment: Service delivery, research on effectiveness, and emerging treatment alternatives. *Journal of Groups in Addiction & Recovery, 2*(2), 68–96.

Saari, C. (1991). *The creation of meaning in clinical social work.* New York: Guilford.

Schiller, L. Y. (1997). Rethinking stages of development in women's groups: Implications for practice. *Social Work with Groups, 20*(3), 3–19.

Schoel, J., Prouty, D., & Radcliffe, P. (1988). *Islands of healing: A guide to adventure based counseling.* Hamilton, MA: Project Adventure.

Schwartz, W. (1960). Camping. In *Social work year book, 1960* (pp. 112–117). New York: National Association of Social Workers.

Seligman, M. E. (1975). *Helplessness: On depression, development and death.* San Francisco: W. H. Freeman.

Stich, T. F. (1983). Experiential therapy. *Journal of Experiential Education, 5*(3), 24.

Stoltz, P. (1998). Stories of change. In C. Itin (Ed.), *Exploring the boundaries of adventure therapy: International perspectives* (pp. 149–152).. Boulder, CO: Association for Experiential Education.

Tippet, S. (1993). Therapeutic wilderness programming for borderline adolescents. In M. Gass (Ed.), *Adventure therapy: Therapeutic applications for adventure programming* (pp. 83–94). Dubuque, IA: Kendall-Hunt.

U.S. Department of Health and Human Services. (2008). Results from the 2008 National Survey on Drug Use and Health: National Findings. Retrieved January 14, 2009, from http://www.oas.samhsa.gov/nsduh/2k8nsduh/2k8Results.cfm

Wall, S. (1992). *The effects of a wilderness survival school on adolescent depression scores.* Unpublished manuscript.

Weisz, J. R., Donenberg, G. R., Han, S. S., & Kauneckis, D. (1995). Child and adolescent psychotherapy outcomes in experiments versus clinics: Why the disparity? *Journal of Abnormal Child Psychology, 23*(1), 83–106.

Will, O. (1959). Human relatedness and the schizophrenic reaction. *Psychiatry, 22*(3), 205–223.

Wilson, S. J., & Lipsey, M. W. (2000). Wilderness challenge programs for delinquent youth: A meta-analysis of outcome evaluations. *Evaluation and Program Planning, 23* (1), 1–12.

Winnicott, D. W. (1965). *The maturational processes and the facilitating environment: Studies in the theory of emotional development.* New York: International Universities Press.

Chapter 4

Ahmadi, F. (2009). Hard and heavy music: Can it make a difference in the young cancer patients' life? Voices: A World Forum for Music Therapy. Retrieved December 18, 2009, from http://www.voices.no/mainissues/mi40009000302.ph

Ansdell, G. (1995) *Music for life: Aspects of creative music therapy with adult clients.* London: Jessica Kingsley.

Ansdell, G. (2002). Community music therapy and the winds of change. *Voices: A World Forum for Music Therapy, 2.* Retrieved June 4, 2002, from http://www.voices.no/mainissues/Voices2(2)ansdell.html

Bonny, H. (1990). Music and change. *Journal of the New Zealand Society for Music Therapy 12*(3), 5–10.

Bonny, H. L. (2002). *Music and consciousness: The evolution of guided imagery and music* (L. Summer, Ed.). Gilsum, NH: Barcelona.

Boyle, J. D. (1988). *Psychological foundations of musical behavior* (2nd ed.). Springfield, IL: Charles C. Thomas.

Brown, J. (2002). Towards a culturally centered music therapy practice. *Voices: A World Forum for Music Therapy.* Retrieved December 18, 2009, from http://www.voices.no/mainissues/Voices2 (1) brown.html

Bruscia, K. E. (1998). *The dynamics of music psychotherapy.* Gilsum NH: Barcelona.

Camilleri, V. (2002). Community building through drumming. *The Arts in Psychotherapy, 29*, 261–264.

Christenson, P. G., DeBenedittis, P., & Lindlof, T. R. (1985). Children's use of audio media. *Communication Research, 12*(3), 327–343.

Christenson, P. G., & Roberts, D. F. (1998). *It's not only rock & roll: Popular music in the lives of adolescents.* Cresskill, NJ: Hampton Press.

Cohen, J. M. (1987). Music therapy with the overcontrolled offender: Theory and practice. *The Arts in Psychotherapy, 14*, 215–221.

Cook, N. (1998) *Music: A very short introduction.* Oxford, UK: Oxford University Press.

De Nora, T. (2000). *Music in everyday life.* Cambridge, UK: Cambridge University Press.

De Nora, T. (2003). *After Adorno: Rethinking music sociology*. Cambridge, UK: Cambridge University Press.

Derrington, P. (2005). Teenagers and songwriting: Supporting students in a mainstream secondary school. In F. Baker & T. Wigram (Eds.), *Songwriting: Methods, techniques and clinical applications for music therapy clinicians, educators and students* (pp. 68–81). Philadelphia: Jessica Kingsley.

Dissel, A. (1997). Alternative sentencing in South Africa. *Reconciliation International, 41.* Retrieved from http://www.csvr.org.za/articles/artdiss2.htm

Fouche, S., Torrance, K. (2005). Lose yourself in the music, the moment, yo! Music therapy with an adolescent group involved in gangsterism. *Voices: A world forum for music therapy.* Retrieved January 16, 2010, from http://www.voices.no/mainissues/mi40005000190.html

Gardner, K. (1990). *Sounding the inner landscape: Music as medicine*. Rockport, MA: Element.

Gardstrom, S. C. (1996). Music therapy for juvenile offenders in a residential treatment setting. In B. L. Wilson (Ed.), *Models of music therapy interventions in school settings: From institution to inclusion* (pp. 127–141). Silverspring, MD: National Association for Music Therapy.

Gouk, P. (Ed.). (2000). *Music healing in cultural contexts*. Aldershot,UK: Ashgate.

Hoskyns, S. (1988). Studying group music therapy with adult offenders: Research in progress. *Psychology of Music, 16,* 25–41.

Laiho, S. (2004). The psychological functions of music in adolescence. *Nordic Journal of Music Therapy, 13*(1), 47–63.

Loeber, R., & Dishion, T. (1983). Early predictors of male delinquency: A review. *Psychological Bulletin, 94,* 68–99.

Loth, H. (1996). Music therapy. In C. Cordess & M. Cox (Eds.), *Forensic psychotherapy: Crime, psychodynamics, and the offender patient: vol. 2. Mainly practice* (pp. 561–566). Bristol, PA: Jessica Kingsley.

MacDonald, R., Hargreaves, D., & Miell, D. (Eds.). (2002). *Musical identities*. Oxford, UK: Oxford University Press.

Martin, P. (1995). *Sounds and society: Themes in the sociology of music*. Manchester, UK: Manchester University Press.

Mendel, R. A. (1996). What Works in the prevention of youth crime? *Child and Youth Care, 14*(10), 4–6.

Moffitt, T. E. (1993). Adolescence-limited and life-course-persistent antisocial behaviour: A developmental taxonomy. *Psychological Review, 100,* 674–701.

North, A. C., Hargreaves, D. J., & O'Neill, S. A. (2000). The importance of music to Aaolescents. *British Journal of Education Psychology, 70,* 255–272.

Patterson, G. R., DeBaryshe, B., & Ramsey, E. (1997). A developmental perspective on antisocial behaviour. In M. Gauvain & M. Cole (Eds.), *Readings on the development of children* (pp. 263–272). New York: W. H. Freeman.

Pavlicevic, M. (1997). *Music therapy in context: Music, meaning and relationship*. London: Jessica Kingsley.

Pavlicevic, M. (2003). *Groups in music: Strategies from music therapy*. London: Jessica Kingsley.

Pavlicevic, M., & Ansdell, G. (2004). *Community music therapy*. London: Jessica Kingsley.

Pinnock, D. (1998). Rites of passage: Creating alternative rituals for gang members. *Track Two, 2*(3), 18–20.

Priestly, M. (1994). *Essays on analytical music therapy*. Phoenixville, NH: Barcelona.

Rio, R. E., & Tenney, K. S. (2002). Music therapy for juvenile offenders in residential treatment. *Music Therapy Perspectives, 20,* 89–97.

Roscoe, B., & Peterson, K. L. (1984). Older adolescents: A self-report of engagement in developmental tasks. *Adolescence, 74,* 391–396.

Rutter, M., Giller, H., & Hagell, A. (1998). *Antisocial behaviour by young people*. Cambridge, UK: Cambridge University Press.

Ruud, E. (1998). *Music therapy: Improvisation, communication and culture*. Saint Louis, MO: MMB Music.

Ryan, T. (1997). *Drugs, violence and governability in the future SA: draft*. Retrieved October 9, 2007, from http://www.iss.co.za/Pubs/PAPERS/22/Paper22.html

Skaggs, R. C. (1997). Music-centered creative arts in a sex offender treatment program for male juveniles. *Music Therapy Perspectives, 15*(2), 73–78.

Small, C. (1998). *Musicking*. Hanover NH: Wesleyan University Press.

Steyn, F. (2005). *Review of South African innovations in diversion and reintegration of youth at risk*. Newlands: Open Society Foundation for South Africa.

Stige, B (2002). *Culture-centered music therapy*. Gilsum, NH: Barcelona.

Tajfel, H. (1981). *Human groups and social categories*. Cambridge, UK: Cambridge University Press.

Tarrant, M., North, A. C., & Hargreaves, D. J. (2002). Youth identity and music. In R. MacDonald, D., Hargreaves, & D. Miell (Eds.), *Musical identities* (pp. 134–150). Oxford, UK: Oxford University Press.

Tervo, J. (2005). Music therapy with adolescents. *Voices: A world forum for music therapy.* Retrieved April 4, 2010, from http://www.voices.no/mainissues/mi40005000169.html

That, M. H. (1987). A new challenge for music therapy: The correctional setting. *Music Therapy Perspectives*, 4(1), 44–50.

Tumbleson, H. (2001). A better definition of "at-risk" youths. *International Child and Youth Care Network, Today*. Retrieved from http://www.cyc-net.org/today/today010824.html

Turry, A. (2005). Music psychotherapy and community music therapy: Questions and considerations. *Voices: A World Forum for Music Therapy*. Retrieved December 18, 2009, from http://www.voices.no/mainissues?mi40005000171.html

Watson, D. M. (2002). Drumming and improvisation with adult male sexual offenders. *Music Therapy Perspectives*, 20(2), 105–111.

Wigram, T., Pedersen, I. N., & Bonde, L. O. (2002). *A comprehensive guide to music therapy: Theory, clinical practice, research and training.* Philadelphia: Jessica Kingsley.

Wyatt, J. G. (2002). From the field: Clinical resources for music therapy with juvenile offenders. *Music Therapy Perspectives, 20,* 80–88.

Zimpfer, D. G. (1992). Group work with juvenile delinquents. *Journal for Specialists in Group Work, 17*(2), 116–126.

Chapter 5

Ascione, F. R. (1997). Humane education research; evaluating efforts to encourage children's kindness and caring toward animals. *Genetic, Social and General Psychology Monographs, 123*(1), 57–77.

Ascione, F. R. (2005). *Children and animals: Exploring the roots of kindness and cruelty.* West Lafayette, IN: Purdue University Press.

Ascione, F. R. (Ed.). (2008). *International handbook of animal abuse and cruelty: Theory, research, and application.* West Lafayette, IN: Purdue University Press.

Ascione, F. R. (2009). Examining children's exposure to violence in the context of animal abuse: A review of recent research. In A. Linsey (Ed.). *The link between animal abuse and human violence* (pp. 106–115). East Sussex, UK: Sussex Academic Press.

Ascione, F. R., Kaufmann, M. E., Brooks, S. M. (2006). Animal abuse and developmental psychopathology: Recent research, programmatic and therapeutic Issues and challenges for the future. In A. H. Fine (Ed.,) *Handbook on animal assisted therapy: Theoretical foundation and guidelines for practice* (2nd ed., pp. 355–388). San Diego, CA: Academic Press.

Ascione, F. R., & Maruyama, M. (in press). Animal abuse and developmental psychopathology. In P. McCardle, S. McCune, J. Griffin, & V. Maholmes (Eds.), *Human-animal interaction: Child development, health, and therapeutic interventions.* Washington, DC: American Psychological Association.

Ascione, F. R., & Shapiro, K. J. (2009). People and animals, kindness and cruelty: Research directions and policy implications. *Journal of Social Issues, 65,* 569–587.

Banman, J. K. (1995). Animal-assisted therapy with adolescents in a psychiatric facility. *Journal of Pastoral Care, 49*(3) 274–278.

Baun, M., Bergstrom, N., Langston, N., & Thoma, L. (1984). Physiological effects of companion animal dogs: Influences of attachment. In R. K. Anderson, B. L. Hart, & L. A. Hart (Eds.), *The companion animal connection* (pp. 162–170). Minneapolis: University of Minnesota Press.

Beck, A. M., Seraydarian, L., & Hunter, G. F. (1986). Use of animals in the rehabilitation of psychiatric inpatients. *Psychological Reports, 58,* 63–66.

Beck, J. S. (1995). *Cognitive therapy: Basics and beyond.* New York: Guilford.

Benda, W., & Lightmark, R. (2004, June-August). People whisperers: Integral health and healing. *Shift: At the Frontiers of Consciousness,* 30–33.

Benda, W., McGibbon, N. H., & Grant, K. L (2003). Improvements in muscle symmetry in children with cerebral palsy after equine assisted therapy (hippotherapy). *The Journal of Alternative and Complementary Medicine, 9*(6), 817–825.

Boat, B. W., Loar, L., & Phillips, A. (2008). Collaborating to assess, intervene, and prosecute animal abuse: A continuum of protection for children and animals. In F. R. Ascione (Ed.), *International handbook of animal abuse and cruelty: Theory, research, and application* (pp. 393–422). West Lafayette, IN: Purdue University Press.

Bowlby, J. (1958). The nature of the child's tie to his mother. *International Journal of Psycho-Analysis, 39,* 350–373.

Bowlby, J. (1988). *A secure base.* New York: Basic Books.

Bowlby, R. (2007). Babies and toddlers in non-parental daycare can avoid stress and anxiety if they develop a lasting secondary attachment bond with one career who is consistently accessible to them. *Attachment & Human Development, 9*(4), 307–319.

Brickel, C. M. (1982). Companion animal facilitated psychotherapy: A theoretical explanation via attention shifts. *Psychological Reports, 50*, 71–74

Bustad, L. K. (1979). How animals make people human and humane. *Modern Veterinary Medicine Practice, 60*, 707–710.

Camp, J. (2008). *The soul of a horse: Life lessons from the herd.* New York: Crown.

Chandler, C. K. (2005). *Animal assisted therapy in counseling.* New York: Routledge Taylor and Francis Group.

Cooper, T., & Jobe, T. (2007). Equine encounters. *Reclaiming Children and Youth, 16*(1), 40–44.

Corson, S. A., Corson, E. O'L., & Gwynne, P. H. (1975). Pet-facilitated psychotherapy. In R. S. Anderson (Ed.), *Pet animals and society* (pp. 19–36). Baltimore, MD: Williams and Wilkins.

Covert, A. M., Whirren, A. P., Keith, J., & Nelson, C. (1985). Pets, early adolescents and families. *Marriage Family Review, 8*, 95–108.

Crawford, E. K., Worsham, N. L., & Swinehart, E. R. (2006). Benefits derived from companion animals and the use of the term "attachment." *Anthrozoös, 19*(2), 98–112.

Dadds, M. R. (2008). Conduct problems and cruelty to animals in children: What is the link? In F. R. Ascione (Ed.), *The international handbook of animal abuse and cruelty: Theory, research, and application* (pp. 111–131). West Lafayette, IN: Purdue University Press.

Delta Society. (1996). *Animal assisted therapy: Standards of practice.* Author.

Delta Society. (n.d.). *What are animal assisted activities/therapy?* Retrieved December 1, 2009, from http://www.deltasociety.org/Document.Doc?id=10

Equine Assisted Growth and Learning Association (EAGALA). (2006). *Fundamentals of EAGALA model: Practice untraining manual* (5th ed.). Author.

Equine Facilitated Mental Health Association (EFMHA). (2010). What is equine facilitated psychotherapy (EFP)? Retrieved December 1, 2009, from http://www.narha.org/SecEFMHA/WhatIsEFMHA.asp

Esterling, B. A., Kiccolt-Glaser, J., Bodnar, J. C., & Glaser, R. (1994). Chronic stress, social support and persistent alternations in the natural killer cell response to cytokines in older adults. *Health Psychology, 13*, 291–328.

Ewing, C. A., MacDonald, P. M., Taylor, M., & Bowers, M. J. (2007). Equine-facilitated learning for youths with severe emotional disorders: A quantitative and qualitative study. *Child Youth Care Forum, 36*, 59–72.

Fine, A. H. (2006). *Handbook on animal assisted therapy: Theoretical foundations and guidelines for practice* (2nd ed.). San Diego, CA: Academic Press.

Frame, D. (2006). Practices of therapists using equine facilitated/assisted psychotherapy in the treatment of adolescents diagnosed with depression: A qualitative study (Unpublished master's thesis). New York University School of Social Work.

Friedmann, E., Katcher, A. H., Lynch, J., & Thomas, S. (1980). Animal companions and one-year survival of patients after discharge from a coronary care unit. *Public Health Reports, 95*, 307–312.

Friedman, E., & Thomas, S.A. (1995). Pet ownership ownership, social support and one-year survival after acute myocardial infarction in the Cardiac Arrhythmia Suppression Trial (CAST). *American Journal of Cardiology, 76*(17), 1213–1217.

Garcia, J. A., & Weisz, J. R. (2002). When youth mental health care stops: Therapeutic relationship problems and other reasons for ending youth outpatient treatment. *Journal of Consulting and Clinical Psychology, 70*, 439–443.

Green Chimneys. (2009). Retrieved November 29, 2009, from http://www.greenchimneys.org/index.php?option=com_content&view=frontpage&Itemid=1

Hawke, J.M., Jainchill, N., & De Leon, G. (2000). The prevalence of sexual abuse and its impact on the onset of drug use among adolescents in therapeutic community drug treatment. *Journal of Child and Adolescent Substance Abuse, 9*(3), 35–49.

Horses in the Hood. (2009). Retrieved November 29, 2009, from http://horsesinthehood.org/index.html

Iannone, V. N. (2003). *Evaluation of a vocational and therapeutic riding program for severely emotionally disturbed adolescents* (Unpublished thesis). The Catholic University of America, Washington, DC.

Isaacs, S. (1930). *Intellectual growth in young children.* London: Routledge Kegan Paul.

Katcher, A. H., Friedman, E., Beck, A. M., & Lynch, J.J. (1983). Looking, talking and blood pressure: The physiological consequences of interaction with the living environment. In A. H. Katcher & A. M. Beck (Eds.), *New perspectives on our lives with companion animals* (pp. 351–359). Philadelphia: University of Pennsylvania Press.

Kidd, A. H., & Kidd, R. M. (1987). Reactions of infants and toddlers to live and toy animals. *Psychological Reports, 61*, 455–464.

Kovacs, Z., Kis, R., Rozsa, S., Rozsa, L. (2004). Animal-assisted therapy for middle-aged schizophrenia patients living in a social institution: A pilot study. *Clinical Rehabilitation 18*, 483–486.

Kruger K. A., Trachtenburg, S. W., & Serpell, J. A. (2004). *Can animals help humans heal? Animal assisted interventions in adolescent mental health.* Philadelphia: Center for the Interaction of Animals in Society, University of Pennsylvania School of Veterinary Medicine.

Kumar, G., Steer, R. A., & Deblinger, E. (1996). Problems in differentiating sexually from non-sexually abused adolescent psychiatric inpatients by self-reported anxiety, depression, internalization, and externalization. *Child Abuse and Neglect, 20,* 1079–1086.

Lefkowitz, C., Paharia, I., Prout, M., Debiak, D., & Bleiberg, J. (2005). Animal-assisted prolonged exposure: A treatment for survivors of sexual assault suffering posttraumatic stress disorder. *Society and Animals, 13*(4), 275–295.

Levinson, B. M. (1964) Companion animals: A special technique in child psychotherapy. *Mental Hygiene, 48,* 243–248.

Levinson, B., & Mallon, G. P. (1997). *Pet oriented child psychotherapy.* Springfield, IL: Charles C Thomas.

Mandrell, P. J. (2006). *Introduction to equine-assisted psychotherapy: A comprehensive overview.* Author.

Melson, G. (2003). Child development and the human-companion animal bond. *Animal Behavior Specialist, 47*(1), 31–39.

Melson, G. F., & Schwartz, R. (1994). *Pets as social supports for families with young children.* Paper presented to the annual meeting of the Delta Society, New York City.

Mental Health Center of Denver. (2009). *Animal assisted therapy.* Retrieved November 29, 2009, from: http://www.mhcd.org/Services/animal_assisted_therapy.html

Moses, T. (2000). Attachment theory and residential treatment: A study of staff-client relationships. *American Journal of Orthopsychiatry, 70*(4), 474–490.

Nichols, M. P. (2009). *Essentials of family therapy* (4th ed.). Boston: Pearson Education.

North American Riding for the Handicapped Association (2010). About NARHA. Retrieved December 1, 2009, from: http://www.narha.org/WhoIsNARHA/About.asp

Phillips, A., & McQuarrie, D. (2009). *Therapy animals supporting kids (TASK) program manual.* Englewood, CO: American Humane.

Pichot, T., & Coulter, D. (2006). *Animal-assisted brief therapy: A solution-focused approach.* New York: Hawthorne Press.

Preush, P. C. (1997). *Therapeutic riding and self-esteem* (Unpublished master's thesis). D'Youville College. Buffalo, NY.

Randour, M. L., & Davidson, H. (2008). *A common bond: Maltreated children and animals in the home.* Englewood, CO: American Humane.

Ricard, M., & Allard, L. (1992). The reaction of 9- to 10-month-old infants to an unfamiliar animal. *Journal of Genetic Psychology, 154,* 14.

Risley-Curtiss, C., Holley, L. C., & Wolf, S. (2006). The animal-human bond and ethnic diversity. *Social Work, 51*(3), 257–268.

Salotto, P. (2001). *Companion animal assisted therapy: a loving intervention and an emerging profession: Leading to a friendlier, healthier, and more peaceful world.* Norton, MA: D.J. Publications.

Sherbourne, C. D., Meredith, L. S., Rogers, W., & Ware, J. E. (1992). Social support and stressful life events: Age differences in the effects of health-related quality of life among the chronically ill. *Quality of Life Research, 1,* 235–246.

Shultz, B. N. (2005). The effects of equine assisted psychotherapy on at risk adolescents, ages 12–18 (Unpublished master's thesis). Denver Seminary, Denver, Colorado.

Siegel, J. (1995). Pet ownership and the importance of pets among adolescents. *Anthrozoos 8*(4), 217–273.

Souter, M. A., & Miller, M. D. (2007). Do animal assisted activities effectively treat depression: A meta-analysis. *Anthrozoos, 20*(2), 167–180.

Swarthout, G. (1995). *Bless the beasts and children.* New York: Pocket Books.

Trotter, K.S. (2006). *The efficacy of equine assisted group counseling with at-risk children and adolescents* (Unpublished master's thesis). University of North Texas, Denton, Texas.

Vila, C., Savolainen, P., Maldonado, J. E., Amorim, I. R., Rice, J. E., Honeycutt, R. L., et al. (1997). Multiple and ancient origins of the domestic dog. *Science, 236*(5319), 1687–1689.

Wesley, M. C., Minatrea, N. B., & Watson, J. C. (2009). Animal-assisted therapy in the treatment of substance dependence. *Anthrozoos, 22*(2), 137–148.

Whealin, J. (2009). *Child sexual abuse.* US Dept. of Veterans Affairs. National Center for PTSD. Retrieved December 1, 2009, from http://www.ptsd.va.gov/public/pages/child-sexual-abuse.asp

Wilbanks, B. J. (1989). Effects of the presence of a pet in counselor's office on institutionalized and non-institutionalized adolescents' perception of counselor credibility. (Unpublished master's thesis). Texas Tech University, Lubbock, Texas.

Chapter 6

Ackerson, J., Scogin, F., McKendree-Smith, N., & Lyman, R. (1998). Cognitive bibliotherapy for mild and moderate adolescent depressive symptomatology. *Journal of Consulting and Clinical Psychology, 66*(4), 685–690.

Afolayan, J. A. (1992). Documentary perspective of bibliotherapy in education. *Reading Horizons, 33,* 137–148.

Aiex, N. K. (1993). Bibliotherapy (Report NO.EDO-C3-93-05). Bloomington, IN: Indiana University, Office of Educational Research and Improvement. (ERIC Document Reproduction Service No. ED 357 333)

Allan, J. (2002). *Using literature to help troubled teenagers cope with end-of-life issues.* Westport, CT: Greenwood Press.

Alvermann, D. E. (1987). Using discussion to promote reading comprehension. Newark, DE: International Reading Association. (ERIC Document Reproduction Service No. ED287160)

Bakhtin, M. M. (1986). *Speech genres and other late essays.* Austin, TX: University of Texas Press.

Bang, M. (1999). *When Sophie gets angry – really, really angry.* New York: Blue Sky Press.

Borders, S., & Paisley, P. O. (1992). Children's literature as a resource for classroom guidance. *Elementary School Guidance and Counseling, 27*(2), 131–140.

Carroll, P. S. (1999). *Using literature to help troubled teenagers cope with societal issues.* Westport, CT: Greenwood Press.

Conly, J. L. (1993). *Crazy lady!* New York: HarperCollins.

Corr, C. A. (2004). Bereavement, grief, and mourning in death-related literature for children. *OMEGA, 48,* 337–363.

Daniels, H., & Steineke, N. (2004). *Mini-lessons for literature circles.* Portsmouth, NH: Heinemann.

Doll, B., & Doll, C. (1997). *Bibliotherapy with young people: Librarians and mental health professionals working together.* Englewood, CO: Libraries Unlimited.

Duimestra, L. (2003). Teaching and name-calling: Using books to help students cope. *Teacher Librarian, 31*(2), 8–11.

Faust, M., Cockrill, J., Hancock, C., & Isserstedt, H. (2005). *Student book clubs: Improving literature instruction for middle and high school.* Norwood, MA: Christopher-Gordon.

Forgan, J. (2002). Using bibliotherapy to teach problem solving. *Intervention in School and Clinic, 38*(2), 75–82.

Gantos, J. (1998). *Joey Pigza swallows the key.* New York: Farrar, Straus, and Giroux.

Gladding, S. T., & Gladding, C. (1991). The ABCs of bibliotherapy and school counselors. *Elementary School Counselor, 39*(1), 7–12.

Gregory, K., & Vessey, J. (2004). Bibliotherapy: A strategy to help students with bullying. *The Journal of School Nursing, 20*(3), 127–133.

Guthrie, J. T. (2008). *Engaging adolescents in reading.* Thousand Oaks, CA: Corwin Press.

Herbert, T. P., & Kent, R. (2000). Nurturing social and emotional development in gifted teenagers through young adult literature. *Roeper Review, 22*(3), 167–172.

Hynes, A., & Hynes-Berry, M. (1986). *Bibliotherapy: The interactive process.* Boulder, CO: Westview Press.

Iaquinta, A., & Hipsky, S. (2006). Practical bibliotherapy strategies for the inclusive elementary classroom. *Early Childhood Education Journal, 34*(3) 209–213.

Kadahota, C. (2004). *Kira Kira.* New York: Atheneum.

Kaplan, J. S. (1999). *Using literature to help troubled teenagers cope with identity issues.* Westport, CT: Greenwood Press.

Kaywell, J. F. (1999). *Using literature to help troubled teenagers cope with family issues.* Westport, CT: Greenwood Press.

Kramar, P. A., & Smith, G. G. (1998). Easing the pain of divorce through children's literature. *Early Childhood Education Journal, 26*(2), 89–94.

Kurtts, S. A., & Gavigan, K. (2008). Understanding (dis)abilities through children's literature. *Education Libraries, 31*(1), 23–31.

Lack, C. R. (1985, Spring). Can bibliotherapy go public? *Collection Building, 27–32.*

Lenkowsky, R.S. (1987).Bibliotherapy: A review and analysis of the literature. *The Journal of Special Education, 21,* 123–132.

Manifold, M. C. (2007). The healing picture book: An Aesthetic of sorrow. *Teacher Librarian, 34*(3), 20-26.

McCarty, H., & Chalmers, L. (1997). Bibliotherapy: Intervention and prevention. *Teaching Exceptional Children, 29*(6) 12–13.

Morawski, C. M. (1997). A role for bibliotherapy in teacher education. *Reading Horizons, 37,* 243–259.

O' Neill, A., & Huliska-Beith, L. (2002). *The recess queen.* New York: Scholastic.

Pardeck, J. T. (1994). Using literature to help adolescents cope with problems. *Adolescence, 70*(114), 421–428.

Penn, A. (2003). *A.D.D. not B.A.D.* Terre Haute, IN: Tanglewood Press.

Prater, M. A., & Dyches, T. T. (2008). *Teaching about disabilities through children's literature.* Westport, CT: Libraries Unlimited.

Prater, M. A., Johnstun, M. L., Dyches, T. T., & Johnstun, M. R. (2006, Summer). Using children's books as bibliotherapy for at-risk students: A guide for teachers. *Preventing School Failure,* 5–13.

Raphael, T. E., Florio Ruane, S., & George, M. (2001). Book club plus: A conceptual framework to organize literacy instruction. *Language Arts, 79*(2), 159–169.

Regan, K., & Page, P. (2008). "Character" building: Using literature to connect with youth. *Reclaiming Children and Youth, 16*(4), 37–43.

Rosenblatt, L. (1978). *The reader, the text, the poem: The transactional theory of the literary work.* Carbondale, IL: Southern Illinois University Press.

Rudman, M. K., Gagne, K. D., & Bernstein, J. E. (1993). *Books to help children cope with separation and loss: An annotated bibliography.* New Providence, NJ: R.R. Bowker.

Schlicter, C., & Burke, M. (1994). Using books to nurture the social and emotional development of gifted students. *Roeper Review, 16*(4), 280–283.

Schreur, G. (2006). Using bibliotherapy with suspended students. *Reclaiming Children and Youth, 15*(2), 106–111.

Sridhar, D., & Vaughn, S. (2000). Bibliotherapy for all: Enhancing reading comprehension, self-concept, and behavior. *The Council for Exceptional Children, 33*(2), 74–82.

Stringer, S., Reynolds, G., & Simpson, M. (2003). Collaboration between classroom teachers and a school counselor through literature circles: Building self-esteem. *Journal of Instructional Psychology, 30*(1), 69–76.

Vare, J. W., & Norton, T. L. (2004). Bibliotherapy for gay and lesbian youth: Overcoming the structure of silence. *The Clearing House, 77*(5), 190–194.

Vygotsky, L. S. (1978). *Mind in society: The development of higher mental psychological processes.* Cambridge, MA: Harvard University Press.

Warner, L. (1980). The myth of bibliotherapy. *School Library Journal, 27,* 107–111.

Warner, L. (1989). Bibliotherapy: Two sides to the coin. *School Library Media Activities Monthly, 6,* 34–36.

Chapter 7

Alexander, C. N., Walton, K. G., & Goodman, R. S. (2003). Walpole study of the transcendental meditation program in maximum security prisoners 1: Crosssectional differences in development and psychopathology. *Journal of Offender Rehabilitation, 36,* 97–125.

Baer, R. A. (2003). Mindfulness training as a clinical intervention: A conceptual and empirical review. *Clinical Psychology: Science and Practice, 10,* 125–143.

Barnes, V. A., Bauza, L. B., & Treiber, F. A. (2003). Impact of stress reduction on negative school behavior in adolescents. *Health and Quality of Life Outcome.* Retrieved November 3, 2006, from http//www.hqlo.com/content/1/1/10

Barnes, V. A., Davis, H. C., Murzynowski, J. B., & Treiber, F. A. (2004). Impact of meditation on resting and ambulatory blood pressure and heart rate in youth. *Psychosomatic Medicine, 66,* 909–914.

Barnes, V. A., Treiber, F. A., & Davis, H. C. (2001). Impact of Transcendental Meditation on cardiovascular function at rest and during acute stress in adolescents with normal blood pressure. *Journal of Psychosomatic Research, 51,* 597–605.

Barnes, V. A., Treiber, F. A., & Johnson, M. H. (2004). Impact of Transcendental Meditation on ambulatory blood pressure in African American adolescents. *American Journal of Hypertension, 17,* 366–369.

Beauchemin, J., Hutchins, T. L., & Patterson, F. (2008). Mindfulness meditation may lessen anxiety, promote social skills, and improve academic performance among adolescents with learning disabilities. *Complementary Health Practice Review, 13,* 34–45. Retrieved June 22, 2009, from http://chp.sagepub.com/cgi/content/abstract/13/1/34

Beck, A. T., Rush, A. J., Shaw, B. F., & Emery, G. (1979). *Cognitive therapy of depression.* New York: Guilford.

Benson, H. (1975). *The relaxation response.* New York: Avon.

Benson, H. (1984). *Beyond the relaxation response.* New York: Times Books.

Benson, H., Kornhaber, A., Kornhaber, C., LeChanu, M. N., Zuttermeister, P. C., Myers, P., et al. (1994). Increases in positive psychological characteristics with a new relaxation-response curriculum in high school students. *The Journal of Research and Development in Education, 27*(4), 226–231.

Biegel, G. M., Brown, K. W., Shapiro, S. L., & Schubert, C. M. (2009). Mindfulness-based Stress reduction for the treatment of adolescent psychiatric outpatients: A randomized clinical trial. *Journal of Consulting and Clinical Psychology, 77,* 855–866.

Bootzin, R. R., & Stevens, S. J. (2005). Adolescents, substance abuse, and the treatment of insomnia and daytime sleepiness. *Clinical Psychology Review, 25*(5), 629–644.

Brown, D. P. (1984). A model for the levels of concentrative meditation. In D. H. Shapiro & R. N. Walsh (Eds.), *Meditation: Classic and contemporary perspectives* (pp. 281–316). Hawthorne, NY: Aldine.

Brown K. W., & Ryan, R. M. (2003). The benefits of being present: Mindfulness and its role in psychological well-being. *Journal of Personality and Social Psychology, 84,* 822–848.

Bruce, A., & Davies, B. (2005). Mindfulness in hospice care: Practicing meditation in action. *Qualitative Health Research, 15,* 1329–1344.

Burke, C. A. (2009). Mindfulness-based approaches with children and adolescents: A preliminary review of current research in an emergent field. *Journal of Child and Family Studies.* doi: 10.1007/s10826-009-9282-x

Carmody, J., & Baer, R. A. (2008). Relationships between mindfulness practice and levels of mindfulness, medical and psychological symptoms and well-being in a mindfulness-based stress reduction program. *Journal of Behavioral Medicine, 31,* 223–233.

Derezotes, D. (2000). Evaluation of yoga and meditation training with adolescent sex offenders. *Child and Adolescent Social Work Journal, 17*(2), 97–113.

Dixon, C. A., Dillbeck, M. C., Travis, F., Msemaje, H. I., Clayborne, B. M., Dillbeck, S. L., et al. (2005). Accelerating cognitive and self-development: Longitudinal studies with preschool and elementary school children. *Journal of Social Behavior and Personality, 17,* 65–91.

Freeman, L. W. (2004). *Mosby's complementary & alternative medicine: A research-based approach.* St. Louis, MO: Mosby.

Germer, C. K., Siegel, R. D., & Fulton, P. R. (2005). *Mindfulness and psychotherapy.* New York: Guilford.

Gordon, J. S., Staples, J. K., Blyta, A., & Bytyqi, M. (2004). Treatment of Posttraumatic Stress Disorder in post-war Kosovo high school students using mind-body skills groups: A pilot study. *Journal of Traumatic Stress, 17*(2), 143–147.

Greco, L. A., & Hayes, S. C. (2008). *Acceptance and mindfulness treatments for children and adolescents: A practitioner's guide.* Oakland, CA: Context Press/New Harbinger.

Hawkins, M. A. (2003). Effectiveness of the transcendental meditation program in criminal rehabilitation and substance abuse recovery: A review of the research. *Journal of Offender Rehabilitation, 36,* 47–65.

Hayes, S. C., Strosahl, K. D., & Wilson, K. G. (1999). *Acceptance and commitment therapy: An experiential approach to behavior change.* New York: Guilford.

Henderson, L. (2000). The knowledge and use of alternative therapeutic techniques by social work practitioners: A descriptive study. *Social Work in Health Care, 30*(3), 55–71.

Hollon, S. D., & Beck, A. T. (2004). Cognitive and cognitive-behavioral therapies. In M. J. Lambert (Ed.), *Bergin and Garfield's handbook of psychotherapy and behavior change* (5th ed., pp. 447–492). New York: Wiley.

Honda, K., & Jacobson, J. S. (2004). Use of complementary and alternative medicine among United States adults: The influences of personality, coping strategies, and social support. *Preventive Medicine, 40*(1), 46–53.

Jain, S., Shapiro, S. L., Swanick, S., Roesch, S. C., Mills, P. J., Bell, I., et al., (2007). A randomized controlled trial of mindfulness meditation versus relaxation training: Effects on distress, positive states of mind, rumination, and distraction. *Annals of Behavioral Medicine, 33*(1), 11–21.

Kabat-Zinn, J. (1990). *Full catastrophe living: Using the wisdom of your body and mind to face stress, pain, and illness.* New York: Delacorte.

Kabat-Zinn, J. (1994). *Wherever you go, there you are: Mindfulness meditation in everyday life.* New York: Hyperion.

Kabat-Zinn, J. (2005). *Coming to our senses: Healing ourselves and the world through mindfulness.* New York: Hyperion.

Kabat-Zinn, J., Massion, A. O., Kristeller, J. Peterson, L. G., Fletcher, K. E., Pbert, L., et al. (1992). Effectiveness of a meditation-based stress reduction program in the treatment of anxiety disorders. *American Journal of Psychiatry, 149,* 936–943.

Keefe, T. (1996). Meditation and social work treatment. In F. J. Turner (Ed.), *Social work treatment: Interlocking theoretical approaches* (2nd ed., pp. 434–460). New York: The Free Press.

Kissman, K., & Maurer, L. (2002). East meets west: Therapeutic aspects of spirituality in health, mental health and addiction recovery. *International Journal of Social Work, 45*(1), 35–43.

Kristeller, J. L., & Hallett, C. B. (1999). An exploratory study of a meditation-based intervention for eating disorder. *Journal of Health Psychology, 4,* 357–363.

Lantz, J. (1996). Cognitive theory and social work treatment. In F. J. Turner (Ed.), *Social work treatment: Interlocking theoretical approaches* (pp. 94–115). New York: The Free Press.

Lin, Y. C., Lee, A. C., Kemper, K. J., & Berde, C. B. (2005). Use of complementary and alternative medicine in pediatric pain management service: a survey. *Pain Medicine, 6,* 452–458.

Linehan, M. M., Schmidt, H., Dimeff, L. A., Craft, J. C., Kanter, J., & Comtois, K. A. (1999). Dialectical behavior therapy for patients with borderline personality disorder and drug-dependence. *The American Journal on Addictions, 8,* 279–292.

Matchim, Y., & Armer, J. M. (2007). Measuring the psychological impact of mindfulness meditation on health among patients with cancer: A literature review. *Oncology Nursing Forum, 34*(5), 1059–1066.

McBee, L., Westreich, L., & Likourezos, A. (2004). A psychoeducational relaxation group for pain and stress management in the nursing home. *Journal of Social Work in Long-Term Care, 3*(1), 15–28.

Miller, J., Fletcher, K., & Kabat-Zinn, J. (1995). Three-year follow-up and clinical implications of a mindfulness meditation-based stress reduction intervention in the treatment of anxiety disorders. *General Hospital Psychiatry, 17,* 192–200.

Napoli, M., Krech, P. R., & Holley, L. C. (2005). Mindfulness training for elementary school students: The attention academy. *Journal of Applied School Psychology, 21*(1), 99–125.

National Center for Complementary and Alternative Medicine (NCCAM). (2007, October). Meditation for Health Purposes. Retrieved March 30, 2007, from http://nccam.nih.gov/health/meditation/overview.htm

Niederman, R. (2003). The effects of chi-kung on spirituality and alcohol/other drug dependency recovery. *Alcoholism Treatment Quarterly, 21*(1), 79–87.

O'Brien, K. M., Larson, C. M., & Murrell, A. R. (2008). Third-Wave behavior therapies for children and adolescents: Progress, challenges and future directions. In L. A. Greco & S. C. Hayes (Eds.), *Acceptance and mindfulness treatments for children & adolescents: A practitioner's guide* (pp. 15–35). Oakland, CA: New Harbinger.

Ospina, M. B., Bond, K. B., Karkhaneh, M., Tjosvold, L., Vandemeer, B., Liang, Y., et al. (2007). *Meditation practices for health: State of the research.* Evidence Report/Technology Assessment No. 155. (Prepared by the University of Alberta Evidence-based Practice Center). AHRQ Publication No. 07-E010. Rockville, MD: Agency for Healthcare Research and Quality. Retrieved December 8, 2007, from http//nccam.nih.gov/health/meditation/ overview.htm

Ott, M. J., Norris, R. L., & Bauer-Wu, S. M. (2006). Mindfulness meditation for oncology patients: A discussion and critical review. *Integrative Cancer Therapies, 5*(2), 98–108.

Payne, M. (2005). *Modern social work theory* (3rd ed.). Chicago: Lyceum Books.

Peck, H. L., Kehle, T. J., Bray, M. A., & Theodore, L. (2005). Yoga as an intervention for children with attention problems. *School Psychology Review, 34,* 415–424.

Plasse, B. R. (2001). A stress reduction and self-care group for homeless and addicted women: Meditation, relaxation and cognitive methods. *Social Work with Groups, 24*(3/4), 117–133.

Prochaska, J. O., & Norcross, J. C. (2007). *Systems of psychotherapy: A transtheoretical analysis* (6th ed.). Belmont, CA: Thomson Brooks/Cole.

Redfering, D. L., & Bowman, M. J. (1981 Summer). Effects of a meditative-relaxation exercise on non-attending behaviors of behaviorally disturbed children. *Journal of Clinical Child Psychology,* 126–127.

Rosaen, C., & Benn, R. (2006). The experience of Transcendental Meditation in middle school students: A qualitative report. *Explore, 2,* 422–425.

Russinova, Z., Wewiorski, N. J., & Cash, D. (2002). Use of alternative health care practices by persons with serious mental illness: Perceived benefits [Electronic version]. *American Journal of Public Health, 9*(10). Retrieved October 22, 2006, from http//vnweb.hwwilsonweb.comhww/results_single_fulltext.jhtml;jsessionid=1I1Z

Saltzman, A., & Goldin, P. (2008). Mindfulness-based stress reduction for school-age children. In L. A. Greco & S. C. Hayes (Eds.) *Acceptance and mindfulness treatments for children and adolescents: A practitioner's guide* (pp. 139–161). Oakland, CA: Context Press/New Harbinger.

Schoeberlein, D., & Koffler, T. (2005). Garrison Institute report: Contemplation and education: A survey of programs using contemplative techniques in K–12 educational settings: A mapping report. New York: Garrison Institute. Retrieved July 8, 2008, from http://www.garrisoninstitute.org/programs/Mapping_Report.pdf

Segal, Z., V., Williams, J. M., & Teasdale, J. D. (2002). *Mindfulness-based cognitive therapy for depression: A new approach to relapse.* New York: Guilford.

Semple, R. J., Reid, E. F. G., & Miller, L. (2005). Treating anxiety with mindfulness: An open trial of mindfulness training for anxious children. *Journal of Cognitive Psychotherapy: An International Quarterly, 19,* 379–392.

Shapiro, D. H. (1984). Overview: Clinical and physiological comparison of meditation with other self-control strategies. In D. H. Shapiro & R. N. Walsh (Eds.), *Meditation: Classic and contemporary perspective* (pp. 5–12). New York: Aldine.

Shapiro, D., & Walsh, R. (Eds.). (1984). *Meditation: Classic and contemporary perspectives.* New York: Aldine.

Shapiro, S. L., & Walsh, R. (2003, Spring/Summer). An analysis of recent meditation research and suggestions for future directions, *The Humanistic Psychologist, 31,* 86–114.

Siegel, D. J. (2007). *The mindful brain*. New York: W.W. Norton.

So, K., & Orme-Johnson, D. (2001). Three randomized experiments on the longitudinal effects of the transcendental meditation technique on cognition. *Intelligence, 29*, 419–440.

Speca, M., Carlson, L., Goodey, E., & Angen, M. (2000). A randomized, wait-list 204 controlled clinical trial: The effect of a mindfulness-based stress reduction program on mood and symptoms of stress in cancer outpatients. *Psychosomatic Medicine, 64*, 613–622.

Stewart, T. M. (2004). Light on body image treatment: Acceptance through mindfulness. *Behavior Modification, 28*, 783–811.

Sweet, M. J., & Johnson, C. G. (1990). Enhancing empathy: The interpersonal implications of a Buddhist meditation technique. *Psychotherapy, 27*, 19–29.

Thompson, M., & Gauntlett-Gilbert, J. (2008). Mindfulness with children and adolescents: Effective clinical application. *Clinical Child Psychology and Psychiatry, 13*, 395–407. Retrieved July 8, 2009, from http://ccp. sagepub.com/cgi/content/abstract/13/3/395

Upchurch, D. M., & Chyu, L. (2005). Use of complementary and alternative medicine among American women. *Women's Health Issues, 15*(1), 5–13.

Waelde, L. C., Thompson, L., & Gallagher-Thompson, D. (2004). A pilot study of a yoga and meditation intervention for dementia caregiver stress. *Journal of Clinical Psychology, 60*(6), 677–687.

Wall, R. B. (2005). Tai Chi and mindfulness-based stress reduction in a Boston public middle school. *Journal of Pediatric Health Care, 19*(4), 230–237.

Warner, T. Q. (2005). Awareness and cognition: The role of awareness training in child development. *Journal of Social Behavior and Personality, 17*, 47–64.

Williams, J. M., Duggan, D. S., Crane, C., & Fennell, M. J. (2006). Mindfulness-based cognitive therapy for prevention of recurrence of suicidal behavior. *Journal of Clinical Psychology, 62*(2), 201–210.

Wisner, B. L. (2008). *The impact of meditation as a cognitive-behavioral practice for alternative high school students* (Unpublished doctoral dissertation). The University of Texas at Austin.

Woodberry, K. A, Roy, R., & Indik, J. (2008). Dialectical behavior therapy for adolescents with borderline features. In L. A. Greco & S. C. Hayes (Eds.), *Acceptance and mindfulness treatments for children and adolescents: A practitioner's guide* (pp. 115–138). Oakland, CA: Context Press/New Harbinger.

Wolf, D., & Abbell, N. (2003). Examining the effects of meditation techniques on psychosocial functioning. *Research on Social Work Practice, 13*(1), 27–42.

Zylowska, L., Ackerman, D. L., Yang, M. H., Futrell, J. L., Horton, N. L., Hale, S. T., et al. (2008). Mindfulness meditation training in adults and adolescents with ADHD: A feasibility study. *Journal of Attention Disorders, 11*, 737–746.

Epilogue

Dababnah, S., & Cooper, J. L. (2006). *Challenges and opportunities in children's mental health: A view from families and youth.* New York: National Center for Children in Poverty, Columbia University Mailman School of Public Health.

Jack, G. (2005). An ecological approach to social work with children and families. In N. Frost (Ed.), *Child welfare: Issues in child welfare* (pp. 299–319). New York: Routledge.

Johnstone, M. (2008). Stigma, social justice and the rights of the mentally ill: Challenging the status quo. *Australian and New Zealand Journal of Mental Health Nursing, 10*(4), 200–209.

Lehrer, J. (2006, February-March). A mind-altering idea reveals how life affects the brain. *Seed Magazine,* ¶ 1–10.. Retrieved January 17, 2010, from http://seedmagazine.com/content/article/the_reinvention_of_the_self/

National Association of Social Workers (NASW). (2010). *Social justice*. Retrieved January 17, 2010, from http://www.socialworkers.org/pressroom/features/issue/peace.asp

Prochaska, J. O., & Norcross, J. C. (2006) *Systems of psychotherapy*. Florence, KY: Wadsworth/Cengage Publishing.

U.S. Department of Health and Human Services. (1999). *Mental health: A report of the Surgeon General*. Rockville, MD: U.S. Government Printing Office.

Search Institute. (2010). *What are developmental assets?* Retrieved January 17, 2010, from http://www.search-institute.org/content/what-are-developmental-assets

Seligman, L., & Reichenberg, L. W. (2007). *Selecting effective treatments: A comprehensive, systematic guide to treating mental disorders*. San Francisco: Wiley.

Youth Empowerment Project. (2003). *Youth Empowerment Project mission*. Retrieved January 15, 2010 from http://www.youthempowerment.com/

CREDIT LINES

CONTRIBUTORS

Frank Ascione, PhD, is the American Humane Society Endowed Chair and Executive Director of the Institute for Human Animal Connection at the University of Denver Graduate School of Social Work. His recent research examines the common roots of violence toward people and animals and is directed at identifying an early indicator of at-risk status in children. He has collaborated with human services, social work, and child development staff working with abused children, with youth corrections personnel, and with state shelters for women who are battered. His recent work has been supported by the American Humane Association, the Kenneth A. Scott Charitable Trust, and the Geraldine R. Dodge Foundation. Dr. Ascione is a member of the American Psychological Association, the International Society for the Prevention of Child Abuse and Neglect, the American Professional Society on the Abuse of Children, the International Society on Anthrozoology, and the Society for Research on Child Development. Dr. Ascione serves on the Child and Animal Abuse Prevention Advisory Council of the Latham Foundation. He is past president of the Southwestern Society for Research in Human Development and has been a member of the cadre of experts for The American Psychological Association's Presidential Task Force on Violence and the Family.

Jennifer Boggs, MSW, is a graduate of the University of Denver Graduate School of Social work with a certificate in Animal Assisted Social Work. She has worked with adolescents at several equine assisted learning facilities, including equine assisted psychotherapy and therapeutic riding organizations around the country as a facilitator, volunteer, instructor, and therapist. She holds a dual certification from the Equine Assisted Growth and Learning Organization as an equine specialist and mental health specialist. Jennifer earned the OMNI Research Award for demonstrating outstanding knowledge of and commitment to social work research for her Master's Thesis. Prior to her work in the animal assisted field, Jennifer managed a psychology research lab for the Indiana University School of Medicine where she worked with inpatient adults with mental illness. Jennifer currently works for the Kaiser Permanente Institute for Health Research as a Senior Research Assistant. Jennifer is also a student therapist at the Denver Family Institute, a systems-based family and couples therapy training organization.

Karen Gavigan, PhD, is an Assistant Professor in the School of Library and Information Science at the University of South Carolina. She was the former Director of the Teaching Resources Center at the University of North Carolina at Greensboro (UNCG), and is a recent graduate of the doctoral program in the Department of Teacher Education and Development at UNCG. Her research interests include examining the ways in which male adolescents respond to graphic novels, school library media issues, and bibliotherapy.

Stephanie Kurtts, PhD, is an associate professor in the Department of Specialized Education Services at the University of North Carolina Greensboro. Her teaching and research interests include teacher preparation for inclusive education for children with disabilities and the role of service-learning in the development of collaborative practices for teachers and community agency professionals working with children with disabilities and their families.

Carol Lotter, Music Therapist and graduate from the University of Pretoria, South Africa, currently co-ordinates the Music Therapy Training Programme at the University of Pretoria. Her experience prior to this was 15 years in youth and pastoral work. Lotter also runs a small private music therapy practice, works in a private psychiatric clinic, and is involved in community work at an institution for mentally and physically challenged adults.

Megan Mimms is a doctoral student in the Department of Specialized Education Services at the University of North Carolina at Greensboro. Her research interests include special education administration and the evaluation of special education teachers using 21s^t century professional teaching standards.

Christine Lynn Norton, PhD, LCSW, Assistant Professor of Social Work at Texas State University-San Marcos, earned her PhD in Clinical Social Work from Loyola University Chicago in 2007. She has over 15 years experience working with high-risk youth in a variety of settings including therapeutic wilderness programs, juvenile justice, schools and mentoring organizations, and she is passionate about researching and utilizing innovative interventions with children and adolescents in order to promote healthy psychosocial and neurological functioning.

Barbara Parker-Bell, PsyD, ATR-BC, LPC graduated with a Doctorate in Psychology from the Philadelphia College of Osteopathic Medicine. She is now the Director of the Graduate Art Therapy Program at Marywood University, Scranton, Pennsylvania, and is an Assistant Professor of Art. She has served as the Coordinator of the Undergraduate Art Therapy Program at Marywood University, and is an Elected Member of the American Art Therapy Association (AATA) Board of Directors.

James J. Starzec, PhD, Professor Emeritus of Psychology, State University of New York College at Cortland, is a developmental psychologist, and earned bachelor's, master's, and doctoral degrees in psychology from Northern Illinois University. During his academic career he taught graduate and undergraduate courses in Experimental Psychology, Sensory and Perceptual Processes, Child Psychology, Adolescent Psychology, Developmental Psychology, and Senior Seminar. His current research interests include meditation as a coping strategy for adolescents. Results of his earlier research funded by the American Heart Association, the Heart Association of Upstate New York, and the National Institute of Neurological, Communicative Disorders, and Stroke were published in professional journals.

Phil Tedeschi, LCSW, coordinates GSSW's Animal-Assisted Social Work Certificate program and teaches forensic social work and experiential therapy approaches. A certified Master Therapeutic Riding Instructor and former course director/instructor with Outward Bound, he has many years of experience in non-traditional therapeutic approaches with children, adults and families, as well as in interpersonal violence including animal abuse and sexually abusive youth and adults. An appointed member of the Colorado Sexual Offender Management Board, he also evaluates and treats sexual offenders. He is a founder and clinical administrator of Hand Up Homes for Youth Inc. and founder of Sexual Offense Resource Services.

Betsy Wisner, PhD, LMSW, Assistant Professor of Social Work at Texas State University-San Marcos, holds master's degrees in psychology and social work and earned her doctoral degree in social work from The University of Texas at Austin. Dr. Wisner worked for many years as a clinical social worker helping children and adolescents and their families and she has also worked as a school social worker. Her personal practice of meditation and Tai Chi, combined with her expertise in family mental health, lead her to conduct research on the use of meditation as a coping strategy for adolescents. Dr. Wisner has taught graduate and undergraduate psychology courses such as Child Psychology, Adolescent Psychology, and Developmental Psychology. She currently teaches social work research, practice, and human behavior courses at Texas State University-San Marcos where she integrates meditative practices into her classes.

INDEX